Behind the Scenes

Elizabeth Hobbs Keckley

Courtesy The Lincoln Museum,
Fort Wayne, Indiana

BEHIND THE SCENES

Elizabeth Keckley

Formerly a Slave, but More Recently Modiste,
and Friend to Mrs. Lincoln
or,
Thirty Years a Slave,
and Four Years in the White House

Edited by Frances Smith Foster

UNIVERSITY OF ILLINOIS PRESS
Urbana, Chicago, and Springfield

First Illinois paperback, 2001

Reprinted by arrangement with R. R. Donnelly & Sons Company

Manufactured in the United States of America

∞ This book is printed on acid-free paper.

Library of Congress Cataloging-in-Publication Data

Keckley, Elizabeth, ca. 1818–1907.
Behind the scenes; or, Thirty years a slave and four years in the White House / Elizabeth Keckley ; edited by Frances Smith Foster.
p. cm.
Originally published: New York : G. W. Carleton, 1868; this edition originally published: Chicago : R. R. Donnelly, 1998.
Includes bibliographical references and index.
ISBN 978-0-252-07020-4 (pbk. : alk. paper)
1. Lincoln, Abraham, 1809–1865. 2. Lincoln, Mary Todd, 1818–1882. 3. Keckley, Elizabeth, ca. 1818–1907. 4. African American women—United States—Biography. 5. Women slaves—United States—Biography. 6. Slaves—United States—Biography.
7. Lincoln, Mary Todd, 1818–1882—Friends and associates.
I. Title: Behind the scenes; or, Thirty years a slave and four years in the White House. II. Title: Thirty years a slave and four years in the White House. III. Foster, Frances Smith. IV. Title
E457.15.K26 2001
973.7'092'2—dc21 2001044276
[B]

CONTENTS

LIST OF ILLUSTRATIONS AND MAP

HISTORICAL INTRODUCTION

My life, so full of romance, may sound like a dream to the matter-of-fact reader; nevertheless, everything I have written is strictly true; much has been omitted, but nothing has been exaggerated.

BEHIND THE SCENES is an extraordinary book for the facts that it reveals about nineteenth-century America and one extraordinary woman who participated in the drama of some of our country's most profound events. It is important, also, for its innovative literary form and the function it serves in uncovering the effects readers, especially reviewers and scholars, can have upon a book's fate.

Written in a conversational, first-person narrative style, *Behind the Scenes* portrays people, places, and events familiar to every school girl or boy from perspectives few have ever been privileged to view. Though it might read more "like a romance" than an actual autobiography, Elizabeth Keckley's story is true. As the personal testimony of a woman who went from being the legal property of a slaveholder to being a proprietor with more than twenty employees of her own, it delights and motivates. Its descriptions of Keckley's travels and of her friends provide intriguing glimpses of nineteenth-century interracial relationships and of details about the free black middle class whose very existence was generally as veiled and invisible to her nineteenth-century readers as it is to many of us today.

As a literary genre, *Behind the Scenes* defies simple categorization. It is a page-turner memoir. Keckley's account of the offstage demeanors of Jefferson Davis, Abraham Lincoln, Frederick Douglass, Charles Sumner, and other leading men of the Civil War era reveals soft, even spiritual, moments; strong dark forebodings; and startling instances of jealousy, intrigue, and misguided motivations. It is not the first of the "backstairs stories and insights" by African Americans who served White House residents. Isaac's *Memoirs of a Monticello Slave,* though not published until 1951, had been dictated to Charles Campbell in 1840. Paul Jennings's *A Colored Man's Reminiscences of James Madison* had been published in 1865, three years before Elizabeth Keckley's book. But it is Keckley's focus upon both national and personal events, her detailed information about women's lives, and her pictures of family life that are more the model for twentieth-century memoirs such as Lillian Parks's *My Thirty Years Backstairs at the White House* (1961) and *The Roosevelts: A Family in Turmoil* (1981).

Behind the Scenes definitely fits the classic American-Dream generic conventions. As a rags-to-riches success story enabled by self-reliance, discipline, industry, and a serious attention to establishing a good name, it outdoes the fictitious Horatio Alger, the mythic Benjamin Franklin, and even the iconic Abraham Lincoln, whose presence permeates its pages. These narratives feature characters on the low rungs of obscurity, poor but honest and ambitious boys who climb the social ladder to prominence, power, or wealth. Keckley was by race, class, and gender not supposed to be on a rung at all.

Many readers will readily recognize this book's resemblance to the American slave narrative genre. These first-person accounts of life in slavery and the narrator's ultimate escape were a popular nineteenth-century autobiographical form, which is currently enjoying a resurgence of popularity among scholars as well as the general reading public. In its accounts of suffering, resisting, enduring, and transcending savage and capricious punishments, inhumane living conditions, and tremendous psychological abuse, Keckley's book, like other slave narratives, allows us the catharsis of weeping over her trials and cheering her triumphs. However, *Behind the Scenes* differs significantly from the narratives of fugitive slaves that dominate our thinking about that genre. These were generally antebellum texts, written to arouse antislavery indignation and to enlist readers into the army of active crusaders for social reform. Keckley's narrative includes scenes of suffering and abuse and leaves no doubt that slavery was an abomination against God and against the principles of liberty and justice from which our nation was conceived. But she absolves readers of any anxieties of responsibility or lingering guilt. Writing after legal slavery is history, she reassures us that the blame for that "cruel custom" lies with "the God of nature and the fathers who framed the Constitution." More so than most antebellum slave narrators, Elizabeth Keckley employs rhetoric and conventions of sentimental fiction in a rendition of life in the "prison house of bondage" to carefully balance the "dark side of slavery" with what this former slave assures us was its "bright side."

Behind the Scenes is more accurately read as an early experiment in an autobiographical form that superseded the better-known antebellum fugitive slave narratives. Changing the metaphor from "prison house" to "crucible," this narrative emphasizes the lessons learned, the character developed, the progress achieved from the purifying fires of slavery. The *Thirty Years a Slave* section is less than 25 percent of the entire text. The price she paid for freedom, the privileges and responsibilities the reconstructed nation promises all its citizens are her central concern. In this, Keckley's book presages later autobiographical writings such as Frederick Douglass's *Life and Times of Frederick Douglass* (1881), Amanda Berry Smith's *An Autobiography: The Story of the Lord's Dealings with Mrs. Amanda Smith, the Colored Evangelist* (1893), John Mercer Langston's *From the Virginia Plantation to the National Capitol* (1894), and Booker T. Washington's *Up From Slavery* (1901).

In writing what she did in the manner that she did, Elizabeth Keckley expected her work to invite some criticism. The year 1868 was a tumultuous time, and her book offered strong opinions and disconcerting evidence on many controversial topics. The politics of Reconstruction made the "truth about slavery" an impolite subject even as it informed the negotiations between those who had supported the Blue and those who had rallied behind the Gray over the proper places of blacks. The mass media, which had contested Abraham Lincoln's actions and origins while he lived, had united in its official recording of his personal legacy but were certainly raging fierce battle over the propriety of his politics and were virtually as one in their dismay over the behavior of his widow. Women's voices, like their bodies, were expected to be confined to the hearth and home. Mary Todd Lincoln had consistently transgressed these boundaries. As the president's wife, she had come under considerable attack for her public displays of temper, extravagance, and independence. Now, Elizabeth Keckley, who by race and class was enjoined to silence, was publicly refuting the whispered campaigns of Mary Todd Lincoln's female foes and challenging the statements of prominent editors, lawyers, and statesmen. She, and most likely her publisher, G.W. Carleton, believed her book would help set the record straight while selling sufficient copies to relieve the financial distress of her friend and confidante, Mary Todd Lincoln. Publishing during the Reconstruction era, when the rights and potential of African Americans as citizens of the newly reunited states were issues of grave concern, Keckley intended that her story of how she became "worth [her] salt" would inspire and reassure the nation.

Fate decided otherwise. Despite its resemblance to other very popular literary genres, despite its emphasis upon her successful four years in the White House and its refusal to blame anyone for the misery of her thirty years in slavery, the book was not well received. Newspapers condemned it as "indecent literature," as "trash and scandal." Mary Todd Lincoln, who had continually addressed Keckley as "my dear Lizzie" and had confided to Abraham that "if it had not been for Lizzie Keckley, I do not know what I should have *done,*" refused to speak to Keckley, disparaged her as "the *colored* historian" (emphasis hers), and even denied ever having met her. No positive proof has been offered to support the rumors that Robert Lincoln pressured the publishers to withdraw the book and that "friends of Mr. Lincoln" purchased all remaining copies. But, within a few months of its publication, few "matter-of-fact" readers had perused its pages and the most persistent would-be voyeurs found it nearly impossible to procure a copy.

Behind the Scenes was reprinted in 1931, at the height of the New Negro Movement. It was a time of elaborate interest in African American art and politics, the period sometimes referred to as The Harlem Renaissance, a moment in U.S. American history when, as participant Langston Hughes declared, "The Negro was in Vogue." But this remarkable book attracted almost no attention until four years later when David Barbee, a student of the Lincoln period, declared in a Washington *Star* article that Elizabeth Keckley was a fictitious character and that white reformer and journalist Jane Swisshelm had written *Behind the Scenes.* Again, *Behind the Scenes* was controversial. This time, it was neither the authenticity nor the politics of her book, it was Keckley's very existence that excited debate. Several prominent public figures and scholars, including Professor Carter G. Woodson, founder of the National Association for the Study of Negro Life and History, and the Reverend Dr. Francis Grimke, the minister who had preached at Keckley's funeral, rallied to her defense. The controversy continued in newspapers from Washington, D.C., to St. Cloud in Minnesota and was fueled by the more polite pages of the academic and historical societies such as *The Minnesota Quarterly* and the *Journal of Negro History.*

Thus, *Behind the Scenes* is an extraordinary book for several reasons. It is an inspirational life story of an unusual and admirable woman whose observations and orchestrations augment our fact file on U.S. American history. It is an exciting mix of literary genres, combining sentimental rhetoric with incisive social commentary, employing elements of several kinds of autobiographical writing, and constructing a model that has been emulated by many writers since. It functions as an example of the power of the press to create, subvert, and challenge ways of reading, writing, and thinking. It reveals another way of calculating the price of owning oneself. It is an example of the pain and rewards individuals can experience when they set out, as did Elizabeth Keckley, to bring "a solemn truth to the surface, *as a truth.*"

To understand just who this woman was, how her words came to excite such attention, and why *Behind the Scenes* today is both a story of success and of failure, of battles lost and of a war not yet won, we need to begin at the beginning, with the contradictions of Elizabeth Keckley's birth.

* * * *

My life has been an eventful one.

By all accounts, the mid-nineteenth century was a time of changes engendering unprecedented confusion and conflict, challenges and choices. In 1840, the "frontier" was Missouri, Illinois, and Ohio. But the Mexican War, the discovery of gold and silver, and the forced removal of Native Americans to Oklahoma and other territories were redefining that term as the United States spread from sea to shining sea. The primarily British, French, and Spanish pilgrims, explorers, and entrepreneurs were being joined by hoards of refugees from European cultures whose religions and customs threatened and contradicted many of the rituals and practices established earlier. Men such as Leland Stanford and Collis Potter Huntington were developing transportation and business opportunities previously undreamed of, even as they were acquiring fantastic personal fortunes by highly questionable means. Power was being assumed by political upstarts like Abraham Lincoln and military men such as Ulysses S. Grant. Women were agitating for more rights, abolitionists were gaining in numbers, temperance reformers were becoming more brazen.

In 1840, Emerson wrote to Carlyle that people in the United States "are all a little wild here with numberless projects of social reform. Not a reading man but has a draft of a new community in his waistcoat pocket." The place of African Americans in these new communities was highly contested and by no means defined.

Elizabeth Keckley's life demonstrates this. She was an African American woman born into slavery in Virginia. She moved from one of the original colonies to St. Louis, Missouri, a rough-and-ready new settlement touted as the gateway to the West. She began life in the household of Southern slaveholders, but she joined the domestic circle of the Great Emancipator. Keckley embodied most of what defined the United States in the nineteenth century. But in color and in contour, she did not resemble most people's ideas of an all-American. Thus the difficult choices that most autobiographers have to make about what to omit and what to detail were more complicated for her. Keckley chose to omit many "strange passages" of her personal history and instead to concentrate upon "the most important incidents" that "influenced the moulding of

[her] character." Among the missing elements are some surprising details, such as her family history, her date of birth, her physical appearance, and her education. Generally, whether the autobiographer is a prominent figure or not, readers who really want to know more can consult public records for details of birth, graduation, marriage, deaths, and other vital statistics. Most American autobiographers, however, were not enslaved black women for whom such details were rarely recorded.

Most of what we know about Keckley comes from her autobiography. Historical records validate her statements but provide little that is new. She was born in the vicinity of Dinwiddie Court House, Virginia, but the date upon which her mother, Agnes, increased Colonel Armistead Burwell's fortune by one more slave is in dispute. Adele Logan Alexander, Rayford W. Logan, and Becky Rutberg, exemplary researchers, give 1818 as her birth date. Others, including Francis Grimke and Hallie Q. Brown, who knew her personally, cite 1820, 1824, 1825, and even 1840. Such ambiguity is not uncommon for people born before the Civil War, especially those born as slaves. Birth certificates were not routinely issued nor securely preserved, and babies born to slave mothers were more apt to be listed on tax records and estate inventories as a number or a single name. In the first chapter of her book, which was published in 1868, Keckley writes "I am now on the shady side of forty." *Behind the Scenes* is subtitled *Thirty Years a Slave and Four Years in the White House.* While her emancipation papers, which were issued in 1855, state that she was at that time "about 37 years of age, by trade a dress-maker and called by those who know her Garland's Lizzie," the subtitle and other internal evidence in the text suggest Keckley was born about 1824, or at least wanted us to believe that.

Details of her family history are also ambiguous. She mentions an uncle who had been so savagely beaten that he committed suicide. Her references to "Aunt Bella" may indicate a blood relative, a member of her extended family, or may simply be part of the Southern custom, especially among African Americans, of respecting one's elders by addressing them as "aunt" or "uncle." Finally, the only actual family members we have been able to identify are Keckley's son George and her mother Agnes, a slave woman owned by Armistead Burwell. Agnes, was "married" to a slave known as "George Pleasant, Hobbs a servant of Grum," and Keckley refers to her mother as Agnes Hobbs. But by law, slaves were chattel defined for purposes of taxation as three-fifths human. As such, Agnes and George could not enter into any legal contract, including marriage. However, both Burwell and Grum acknowledged their relationship and allowed George, who lived on a neighboring farm, to visit his wife and daughter twice a year. Until she was about eight years old, "darling Little Lizzie," as George called her, was the center of their parental love and devotion. When Grum fractured the Hobbs family by taking George to

Tennessee, husband, wife, and child kept in touch through letters.

In these and other circumstances Elizabeth Hobbs, though a slave, enjoyed a fairly privileged childhood. She was required to work earlier and probably harder than most children in the nineteenth-century United States. She was brutally beaten for accidents and attitudes that irked her owners. But, generally, Elizabeth grew up learning of the same responsibilities of most nineteenth-century women. She tended children, cleaned, cooked, laundered, and sewed. Literacy was forbidden most slaves by law or circumstance, but Elizabeth Hobbs learned to read and to write. Ambitious and self-reliant, Elizabeth took pride in her industry and her accomplishments. She was unusually intelligent, talented, and attractive. Presaging her career as a fashion designer and her later status as a community leader, Elizabeth, like most teenagers, liked to dress well and to socialize. Her early letters are replete with descriptions of clothes, requests for new dresses, and acknowledgements of gifts that she wore to various weddings and celebrations.

A fairly privileged childhood, especially for a slave, was certainly not without its sorrows. While they corresponded for some years, eventually his letters stopped coming, and Elizabeth and Agnes never saw George Pleasant Hobbs again. Keckley writes of seeing a playmate, Little Joe, sold. She was not sold outside the Burwell family, but she was loaned or leased to various people at the whim of her owner. When she was fourteen, Burwell sent her to work in the household of his son, Robert, a minister who had recently married a white woman who was unable to manage their household alone. Then, physical suffering was exacerbated by more emotional tribulation when they moved to Hillsborough, North Carolina, separating the teenager from her mother and her friends. While living with the minister and his family, Elizabeth writes that she was so severely beaten by the local schoolmaster and by the Burwells that the villagers were scandalized.

In one of her letters to her mother, Keckley confided that "I could fill ten pages with my griefs and misfortunes," but chose not to dwell upon them. One of those griefs was named Alexander Kirkland, a neighbor and friend of Burwell's who "had base designs" and "persecuted" her for four years.

In her application for a Civil War survivor's pension, Keckley wrote she was married to Kirkland. According to the biographer John E. Washington, her owner gave Elizabeth to Alexander Kirkland as a concubine. Given the language and tone of her narrative, this was more likely the case. Whatever the legality of the relationship, the young slave woman bore a son who, despite his "white" appearance and his free father, was classified as an African American slave. She named him George after her lost father. Ironically, Elizabeth, who like her mother was very light skinned with long straight dark hair, reportedly learned much later, as her mother lay dying, that her biological father was not George Pleasant Hobbs but her mother's master, Armistead Burwell.

Kirkland died when his son was eighteen months old. The slave mother and her slave child were sent to live with Burwell's daughter Anne and her husband, Hugh A. Garland. Garland, a lawyer and merchant, ran into financial difficulties and, seeking his fortune, he moved his growing family and dependents to the western frontier town of St. Louis, Missouri. Elizabeth's happiness over being reunited with her mother was dashed when Garland, desperate for money, decided to rent Agnes Hobbs's services to whomever had the cash to purchase them. Keckley dramatically records her reactions:

> My mother, my poor aged mother, go among strangers to toil for a living! No, a thousand times no! I would rather work my fingers to the bone, bend over my sewing till the film of blindness gathered in my eyes; nay, even beg from street to street. I told Mr. Garland so, and he gave me permission to see what I could do.

What she could do was become a successful modiste. While those years in St. Louis were clearly years of toil and trial, Keckley's creativity in designing fashionable wearing apparel and her sewing skills created an intensely loyal and generous clientele.

Soon, she was able to "keep bread in the mouths of seventeen persons for two years and five months," while Hugh Garland worked to establish himself socially and professionally. Small wonder that she began to believe that she could earn enough extra income to purchase freedom for herself and her child. As one might well suspect, Garland was not enthusiastic about such a plan, but she persisted in her efforts to have him agree to sell them to themselves.

The story of how she bought her freedom is as fantastic a feat as those by Hercules, Jason, and other heroes of classical myth. But as an autobiography, it is problematic for those who believe that freedom should be seized by any means necessary. Keckley's story runs counter to those of celebrated fugitive slaves whose narratives tell of *Running a Thousand Miles for Freedom*, as did Ellen and William Craft, or hiding in a garret for six years and eleven months, as did Harriet Jacobs. In striking contrast to her friend Frederick Douglass (and others), who made strong principled arguments against paying one cent for the freedom to which they knew themselves entitled by God's law, the Declaration of Independence, and the United States Constitution, Elizabeth insisted upon buying her freedom legally. When her owner offered her a quarter for the ferry ticket that could take her across the river into Illinois where slavery was illegal, she was insulted. Her indignant reply that "By the laws of the land I am your slave—you are my master, and I will only be free by such means as the laws of the country provide" may make our heroine appear overly dramatic and either excessively noble or incredibly naïve unless we understand what lay behind this scene.

Elizabeth's duties regularly required her to travel

between her home in St. Louis, Missouri, a slave-trading center, and the towns of neighboring Illinois, a free state. But both Hugh Garland and the woman he claimed as his property knew that living freely was more complicated than simply living where slavery was illegal. When his "slave" asked Garland, "What price must I pay for myself?" Garland knew precisely what she meant. His manner was, she said, "petulant," and his offering her the quarter for the ferry was emblematic of his own personal insecurities and of his public power. Doubtless, Garland was embarrassed that his own social and economic success had come through her efforts. His gesture showed that regardless of his indebtedness to her income, Elizabeth's freedom could come only by his generosity.

Moving to Illinois, they both knew, would make Keckley a fugitive, a criminal whose freedom existed only by luck and his good graces. Even before the Compromise of 1850 had codified the Fugitive Slave Law, freedom for any African American was perilous at best. Upon the demand of any person who asked, African Americans had to prove not only that they were not slaves but that they were entitled to be in the area. As Keckley shows when she moved to Washington, D.C., even on "free soil," African Americans often were allowed to stay only by obtaining a license. Such licenses were generally available only with the recommendation of a respected white person and upon the payment of exorbitant fees, and it was not uncommon, especially in border states, that these valuable papers were confiscated and the hapless soul jailed, or even worse, kidnapped and sold into slavery.

The actual date of this particular conversation between Elizabeth and her owner is unclear, but it certainly was around the time that the federal government superseded various local laws with the combination of legislation jointly known as the Fugitive Slave Law. Among its provisions were that any slave holder or his agent (or anyone posing as such) could claim any African American as a fugitive slave by presenting an affidavit of ownership that a justice of the peace recognized as valid. While this might seem on the surface to be a reasonable compromise between the rights of owners whose property was inclined to wander away and those individuals who recognized those new arrivals as human beings who had chosen to pursue happiness in more hospitable locations, a few particular quirks in this law made most judicial decisions favor the plaintiff. The justices of the peace authorized to enforce the Fugitive Slave Law were not local appointees. Their jobs were given by the federal government, which also mandated their compensation for rendering decisions. Accepting the slaveholder's claim earned them ten dollars. Denying that application allowed them to charge only five.

As if the perilous freedom a fugitive Keckley would share with African Americans throughout the United States were not disincentive enough, another, far more specific reason existed for this confrontation.

Dred and Harriet Scott, two other slaves in St. Louis, had asked their mistress for permission to buy their freedom. She had refused, and they had sued her. The Scotts had lived in a free state and, by legal precedent that predated the founding of the United States, enslaved individuals who moved to places where slavery was illegal were declared free. Theirs had seemed an open-and-shut case. While not easily executed, the procedure for making such claims had been codified in Missouri law. But, the Scotts' case was not proceeding according to precedent. The local court had found in their favor, but the case was being appealed.

Elizabeth's owner, Hugh Garland, was the attorney for the defendant, and it was Garland who, in 1852, won the decision by which the Scotts' petition was denied. It was Garland, in fact, who introduced a new approach to the court case by arguing that because the Scotts were slaves of African descent, they were not United States citizens and not entitled to bring suit in its courts. *Scott v. Sanford* went on to the Supreme Court, which years later agreed with Garland's analysis. Hugh Garland, however, thought better of his stance, at least toward his slave Elizabeth Keckley. He eventually promised that she could buy herself and her son for twelve hundred dollars.

Shortly thereafter Hugh Garland died, but his heirs honored the contract. Some of her sympathetic women clients loaned her the money that enabled Elizabeth to pay cash for her son and herself, to marry

Dred Scott and his wife, Harriet Scott, primary figures in Scott v. Sanford

From Frank Leslie's Illustrated Newspaper, *27 February 1857;*
courtesy University of Chicago Library

Elizabeth Keckley, frontispiece from the first edition of Behind the Scenes

Hugh A. Garland, Keckley's owner through his wife, Anne Burwell

Courtesy Missouri Historical Society

James Keckley, and to begin her successful career as an independent businesswoman.

Elizabeth Keckley was legally free, but her struggle was far from over. Elizabeth Keckley soon discovered that the truth about James Keckley was much different than it had first appeared to be. He was not a free African American as he had presented himself, and, as she says, he "proved dissipated and a burden instead of a helpmate." Keckley lived with him for eight years before reluctantly separating from the unfortunate man. During that trying time, her business flourished, and she managed to repay the women who had invested in her freedom. Here again, understanding the actions described in the published narrative is enhanced by knowing what lay behind them. Elizabeth Keckley was an active member of the First African Baptist Church, which operated a secret school for African Americans. There "under the guise of a sewing class," she taught reading and writing. Among the student body was probably her son George, for about 1859, he was admitted to Wilberforce University in Xenia, Ohio.

By 1860, Elizabeth Keckley was a local legend but a lonely one. Garland's widow had taken her slave Agnes Hobbs with her to Vicksburg, Mississippi. Keckley's husband, son, and mother were gone. This perhaps is why Elizabeth gave up her thriving business in St. Louis and moved to Baltimore, Maryland. There she tried to start a sewing school featuring her personal system of dress design and construction.

Perhaps it was that antebellum Baltimore did not have enough free African American women who could afford to enroll in such a school; perhaps it was something else. The record is not clear. But within a few months, Keckley had moved to Washington, D.C., where her skill and perspicacity won her patronage among the wives, daughters, and sisters of the capital elite. Keckley discriminated among her potential clients not by politics but by class, and she took pride in working for the families of Confederate General Lee and Union General Sumner. She gave particular attention to the patronage of Varina Davis, devoting nearly half of her personal time to her needs and developing a friendship so sincere that she seriously considered Mrs. Davis's offer to return to her home in the South with her and the soon-to-be president of the Confederacy. But, after careful thought, she chose to "cast my lot among the people of the North," and, soon thereafter, became Mary Lincoln's seamstress, nurse, spiritual advisor, and friend.

Behind the Scenes is filled with disclosures about the private thoughts and deeds of many who were principal actors on the Washington, D.C., stage. It describes costumes Keckley designed, and it details scripts she helped perform. The narrative often includes Keckley's role in public performances and her decided opinions of them. For example, we know that when the Lincoln entourage toured the captured Confederate capital, Keckley sat in the chairs formerly occupied by President Davis and Vice President

Alexander H. Stephens and that she found a copy of a resolution forbidding free African Americans from entering Virginia. The book is more vague, however, about the roles Keckley played outside the White House. Except for brief references to her roles in founding the Contraband Relief Association and her efforts to help raise money to support the president's widow, we know little of her activities or colleagues outside the White House.

Some information can be pieced together from fragments of several sources. *Behind the Scenes* mentions that her son died shortly before Willie Lincoln and that, with Mary Todd Lincoln's help, she later received a pension as a widow whose only son was killed in the Civil War. Documents of the application process tell us the slave child known as "Garland's George" had assumed his father's name. Although he attended an African American college, when he then joined the Union Army, he did so as a "white" man. George W.D. Kirkland was killed during the Battle of Wilson's Creek in Missouri on 10 August 1861, only a few months after he had enlisted.

Following up on casual comments in the book, we can discern that Elizabeth Keckley was a member of what W.E.B. DuBois would later identify as "the talented tenth." From the letters included in the text, we realize she was a friend of nationally prominent African American leaders, such as Frederick Douglass and Henry Highland Garnet. Because she was president of the Contraband Relief Association from its inception until the time of her writing, we realize Keckley had significant leadership credentials of her own. Her mention of the Fifteenth Street Presbyterian Church, her residency with the Walker Lewises, and the addresses where she resided in New York City are further clues to her life. Keckley belonged to a church renowned as the birthplace of many important institutions, including the first public schools for African American children. Another of its members was William Slade, White House steward. She enjoyed a close friendship with Slade and his wife and children, and, while in New York, she often stayed with their relatives. In Washington, D.C., according to the historian Benjamin Quarles, Keckley lived at "the boarding house which was patronized by the most distinguished leaders of colored people then in Washington," the home of the Walker Lewises. She was godmother to their daughter, Alberta Elizabeth Lewis-Savoy. Madame Keckley's dressmaking establishment adjoined that of "Madam Estern, colored, a fashionable hairdresser," who also "served the very best people of the city and vicinity." In the preface to her book, Elizabeth Keckley locates herself at "14 Carroll Place," the home of Amelia Lancaster, beautician to many of New York City's socialites, who also had "taught many young ladies the trade of hair dressing." In the nineteenth century, African American barbers and beauticians, dressmakers, caterers, nurses, and valets were professionals who by virtue of their salaries and their access

Elizabeth Keckley, ca. 1890

Courtesy Black Fashion Museum, Washington, D.C.

The Reverend
Francis Grimke

The Reverend
Henry Highland Garnet

Courtesy Moorland-Spingarn Research Center,
Howard University

Fifteenth Street Presbyterian Church in Washington, D.C., where Keckley worshipped

Courtesy Library of Congress

Bishop Daniel A. Payne

Courtesy Wilberforce University

Wilberforce University, in the late 1850s, when Keckley's son attended

Courtesy Wilberforce University

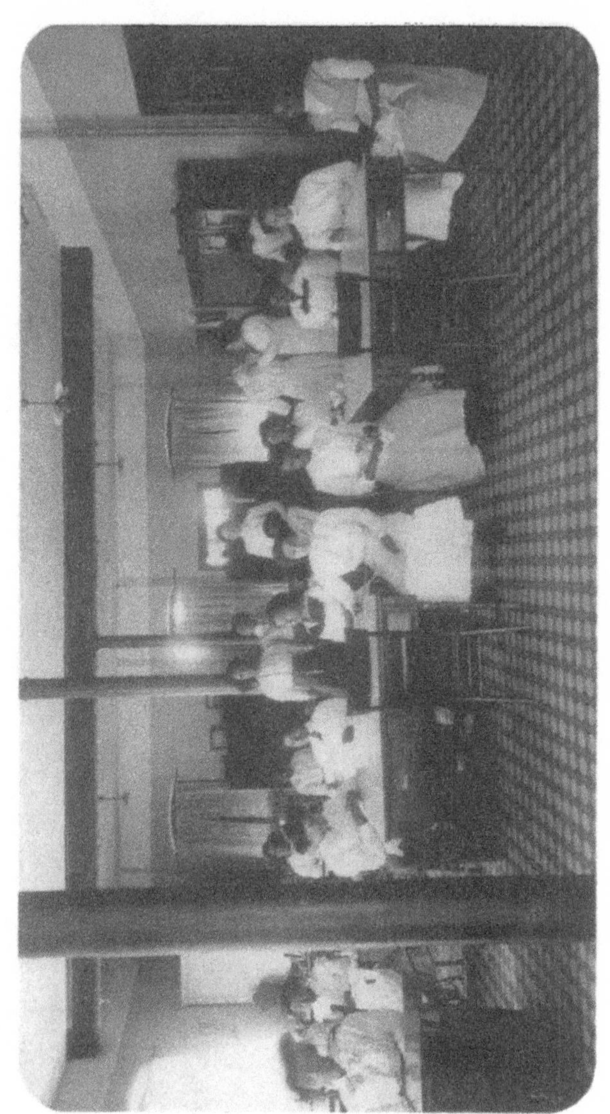

Domestic science class at Wilberforce University, where Keckley taught

Courtesy Wilberforce University

to the rich, the famous, and the powerful, held social status equal with if not exceeding those of teachers, preachers, lawyers, and politicians. Elizabeth Keckley, the slave girl whose mistress had predicted she would "never be worth her salt," had become the cream of free African American society.

After her book was published in 1868, the details of her life are even more elusive because she avoided publicity and her public life was quite circumspect. We know that she returned to the District of Columbia and tried to revive her business, but the "Old Clothes Scandal" and the brouhaha over her book severely restricted her popularity as a society woman's modiste. A recent exhibition of quilts by African Americans includes one made in 1870 by Keckley, allegedly from scraps of dresses she had designed for Mary Todd Lincoln. In 1880, the Washington, D.C., *People's Advocate* carries her advertisement for "Three Apprentices to learn Dressmaking for Six Months." Social columnists reporting on the wedding of Mr. and Mrs. Estern, which brought out "the best society of the district," notes that "Madame Keckley" had presented the couple with "ear rings worn by Mrs. President Lincoln." She continued her membership at the Fifteenth Street Presbyterian Church, where she had a reputation as a woman of impeccable taste and high moral standards. The Reverend Dr. Francis Grimke declared that little girls came to his church "just for the purpose of getting a glimpse of her as she would come in. Her fine figure, her graceful movements, everything about her seemed perfect."

In 1892, at the urging of Bishop Daniel Payne, the former president and then trustee of Wilberforce University, Keckley accepted a position as head of its Domestic Science department and moved to Xenia, Ohio. She was probably part of the Wilberforce entourage that went to Chicago in 1893, because she was responsible for creating the Wilberforce exhibit at the Chicago World's Fair. This exhibit included clothing made by her students and a pin cushion made by Keckley. Sources differ on how long she lived in Ohio. Some say she was there until 1898. Others suggest she had been there less than two years, when she suffered a mild stroke, which ended her teaching career.

The final years of her life are as shrouded in mystery as its beginnings. At some point, Elizabeth Keckley, modiste and White House intimate, became an inmate at the Home for Destitute Women and Children, an institution that she had played a role in founding. She lived very modestly, rarely appearing in public except for a weekly carriage ride and church services, causing speculation that she lived on the monthly twelve dollars of her Civil War survivor's pension. Elizabeth Keckley died in her sleep 26 May 1907. She was buried in the Harmony Cemetery in Washington, D.C.

Anna Eliza Williams, an employee at the Home for Destitute Women and Children, wrote that she once asked Keckley "about the book she had written on Mrs. Lincoln and if she would let me see a copy."

Home for Destitute Women and Children, Washington, D.C.

Courtesy Historical Society of Washington, D.C.

Keckley's reply was to sigh and become "depressed—saying her copy has been misplaced, that the book had been suppressed. . . the book caused her much sorrow and loss of friends." In an interview published in the 6 July 1901 *Minneapolis Register,* Keckley is quoted as saying "I have been honest and not avaricious. . . . I never betrayed a secret in the days when secrets were worth gold, and gold was scarce." She had been, however, betrayed herself. When she decided to publish *Behind the Scenes,* "two newspaper men" helped her. "They printed many things which ought not to have been printed; many things which caused heartaches, because they were untrue."

* * * *

In writing as I have done, I am well aware that I have invited criticism, but before the critic judges harshly, let my explanation be carefully read and weighed.

ELIZABETH KECKLEY, 1868

I never received a dollar from the publication of that book. . . . It made some enemies for me who should have always been my friends.

ELIZABETH KECKLEY, 1901

The catalyst for *Behind the Scenes* was the public outrage over Mary Todd Lincoln's attempts to raise money by selling her jewels, furs, and gowns. It was a dubious project begun in secrecy and had become "the grand exposition of Lincoln dresses," raising a cacophony of criticism that ranged from disapproval of the surreptitious manner in which the affair had begun, to the high prices assigned to a "castoff wardrobe," to the immodesty that the low-necked gowns implied. Mary Lincoln's predilection for extravagant and showy gowns, furs, and jewelry had long fueled rumors that she was pretentious, extravagant, or prone to accept valuable gifts for political favors. Newspapers that had published excerpts of her letters to the firm handling the clothing sale made her motives seem both shamelessly mercenary and political.

The *Columbus* [Georgia] *Sun* for example excoriated Mrs. Lincoln as a "mercenary prostitute" and declared that "If Mrs. Lincoln had studied her true mission as a mother and wife, she could not have discredited her sex and injured the name and fame of her country and husband."

Elizabeth Keckley had been "intimately associated" with Mary Todd Lincoln during "the most eventful periods of her life." She knew Mary Lincoln had made debts she could not pay. She knew that she was stubborn, impulsive, ambitious, and insecure. But Keckley had witnessed also her private grief and anxiety, her quiet acts of charity, and her passionately protective love for family and friends. While she was reluctant to violate the widow's confidences, Keckley believed that if the public knew some of the motivations behind

Lincoln's often bizarre and puzzling public displays, it would judge her more charitably.

Though she sincerely loved her friend and revered the president "who had freed her people," Keckley's interests were not entirely altruistic. Elizabeth Keckley's predilection for collecting historical memorabilia, her interest in politics and in social reform, and her obvious pride in her own achievements suggest that sooner or later she would have acceded to the requests of her friends and written her autobiography and, no doubt, her personality and her principles would probably have occasioned some murmurs about arrogance and elitism, if nothing else. But, in 1867, she had been publicly identified and privately condemned for abetting Lincoln in this latest episode. Some members of the African American community were particularly critical because Keckley continued to support Lincoln after she "had declined to receive aid from colored people." Madame Keckley, who had been celebrated as a living example to the postbellum United States that she, and her race, could be productive citizens, now looked a bit like Judas Iscariot. "To defend myself I must defend the lady that I have served," she rightfully concluded. When Keckley formed her plan to draw aside the veil and expose "the naked fact[s]," she had motives as good as if not better than most slave narrators, women writers, and memoirists. In 1868, she also had many successful precedents for each aspect of her project.

The antebellum narratives of former slaves, such

as Frederick Douglass, Harriet Jacobs, William Wells Brown, William and Ellen Craft, and Josiah Henson, who told of their lives in bondage and their heroically won freedom, had been so popular that one disgusted reviewer referred to them as "black tadpoles of the press." True, some disgruntled readers had attacked their authors as frauds, criminals, and liars, but, generally, slave narratives were accepted as the "insider's view of slavery," and if they told "truth stranger than fiction," it was further proof that the cloak of secrecy needed to be ripped from slavery. Slave narratives were extremely effective for the abolitionist cause. The more popular ones had also proven very effective in advancing their writers' personal progress. Douglass became a government official and diplomat. William and Ellen Craft toured Europe and taught at Mary Shelley's school in England. Josiah Henson, who Harriet Beecher Stowe noted was a model for the slave who resided in her fictitious cabin, gained fame (but not fortune) as the "original Uncle Tom."

Keckley undoubtedly knew that some readers would find her depictions of slavery problematic. Some would accuse her of being too forgiving, of writing too kindly of that institution and of those who had enslaved her. Others would judge her as impolite or impolitic for writing about the sordid past when the nation needed a clean slate upon which to compose its future. Regardless of the anticipated criticism her *Thirty Years a Slave* might engender, Keckley knew that as a slave narrator, she was in good company.

To some extent gender was a complicating factor. As articulate women who voiced decided opinions about public issues, both Mary Todd Lincoln and Elizabeth Keckley belonged to a small, valiant, and often excoriated sisterhood. But in deciding to write publicly of her perspectives on political and social issues, Keckley had plenty of examples to encourage her efforts. EuroAmerican women such as Jane Grey Swisshelm, Lydia Maria Child, Harriet Beecher Stowe, and Fanny Fern (Sarah Parton Willis) were famous for the controversial essays and stories that served to promote their causes while increasing their sales. African American women, too, while not commanding the same breadth of attention nor the same size royalties, certainly showed Elizabeth Keckley that her aspirations for *Behind the Scenes* were feasible. In 1861, Harriet Jacobs's *Linda; or Incidents in the Life of a Slave Girl* had changed the minds of a multitude of women towards their enslaved "sisters." Frances E.W. Harper's journalism, her poems, and her short stories inspired thousands to reconsider the potential roles of women and of African American men in temperance, education, and suffrage movements. As a leader in the African American community, as an individual interested in history and literature, and as confidante to women who were either themselves movers and shakers or the wives and daughters of men who were, Elizabeth Keckley knew the words and deeds of many "scribbling women." African American activists such as Harriet Jacobs and Frances E.W.

Harper worked in the same organizations and were, at least, friends of friends. Journalists, such as Jane Swisshelm, regularly visited the Lincoln White House. If Keckley had not seen Fanny Fern in Mary Lincoln's Blue Room salons, she certainly knew Fern's brother, Nathaniel P. Willis. Willis, whom Keckley quotes at length in *Behind the Scenes,* was one of Mary Todd Lincoln's favorite visitors.

Approbation was not inevitable simply because she would reveal a few confidential tidbits. In the decades before and just after the Civil War, exposés had become standard fare in newspapers, journals, and bookstores. As literary historian James D. Hart reminds us, the reading public could not get enough of "novels about soldier life, autobiographies of Army nurses and others with unusual war experiences, biographies of military officers and heroes, journalistic narratives." Memoirs that revealed the personal and idiosyncratic sides of other classes were especially popular with the growing middle class who sought vicarious thrills by learning the secret lifestyles of the rich and the poor.

White House memoirs were particularly popular. Just a year earlier, Francis B. Carpenter's *The Inner Life of Abraham Lincoln: Six Months in the White House* (1866) had been warmly welcomed by readers. Carpenter had not been writing in the wake of recent scandal, but he was trying to do for Abraham what Keckley wanted to do for Mary. Carpenter wrote his book, he said in the preface, as "a simple matter-of-fact record of daily experience and observation, fragmentary, but *true,* in all essential particulars. . . . My aim has been throughout these pages to portray *the man* as he was revealed to me."

While Elizabeth Keckley may have expected some criticism for her frankness, she believed she was compelled to enter the discourse created by people such as Abraham Lincoln's former law partner, William H. Herndon, who, despite declaring his unmitigated affection for Abraham Lincoln, insisted that truth must prevail. Herndon had started writing his own account of "Honest Abe" when he began giving a series of lectures both to enlighten and to advertise his coming book. One of these lectures, "A. Lincoln—Miss Ann Rutledge, New Salem—Pioneering, and THE poem called 'Immortality'—or 'Oh, Why Should the Spirit of Mortal Be Proud,' " shocked the public by announcing that Lincoln was not a Christian and that his first and only true love had been Ann Rutledge, the daughter of his landlord and the fiancée of Lincoln's close friend, John McNamar. Herndon then published that speech as a pamphlet. Such behavior was characterized as a gratuitous assault upon Lincoln's character and a cruel and vicious attack upon his widow and children. But many people believed him nonetheless. In Chapter XIII, "The Origin of the Rivalry Between Mr. Douglas and Mr. Lincoln," Elizabeth Keckley directly refutes many of Herndon's charges.

Critics apparently ignored Keckley's "explanation," nor did they read and weigh carefully all that she wrote. The first and most persistent tactic, one that Keckley probably did not anticipate, was to ignore her as the central character in the book and in its publication. Nineteenth-century reviewers focused upon the *Four Years in the White House*, made Mary Todd Lincoln its subject, and labeled Keckley as an ignorant or vengeful informant who could not, or did not, write the book herself. Then, and even now, the popular assumption was that Elizabeth Keckley required more than the normal editorial help that publishers regularly afforded their clients.

In the absence of proof to the contrary and given what we know about her personality and previous history, it seems foolish to assume that for such an important act, Madame Keckley would settle for an informant's role. Certainly, she, like most published writers, worked with editors and consultants. And, as the dismay over the unedited letters reveals, some publishing decisions were made without her consent. And were we to learn who made which decisions, we might better understand why her book did not turn out as she had intended.

In a letter to John E. Washington, the author of *They Knew Lincoln,* Mrs. John Brooks declared that she lived at her aunt's boarding house when Keckley wrote *Behind the Scenes.* "I was constantly in her room and the parlor," Brooks says, and Mrs. Keckley was visited by "many abolitionists," and "some of the most celebrated colored men and women of that day." According to Brooks, Elizabeth Keckley . . .

> . . . wrote greatly at night, and every morning many white men would come to see her . . . about the writings. No white women ever came to see her at our house. One man by the name of Redpath would spend several hours every evening with her. Everybody in the house knew that Mrs. Keckley was writing a book on Mrs. Lincoln and that Mr. Redpath was helping her compile it. He was a medium built, red-faced man, and generally wore a reddish brown suit.

James Redpath is certainly a likely suspect. A former correspondent for the New York *Tribune* with a keen interest in politics, Redpath had spent six years in the antebellum South studying slavery and submitting articles that were as controversial as they were widely read. In 1859, he compiled many of those articles into *The Roving Editor, or Talks with Slaves in the Southern States.*

During the Civil War, Redpath had been a Union Army correspondent and he had published a series of inexpensive paperbacks called Books for Camp and Home. Targeting soldiers, women, and students as his primary readership, he sought to keep costs down by concentrating upon reprints of European writers such as Balzac, Hugo, and Swift, which did not enjoy copyright protection in the United States. But Redpath also included works such as *Clotelle,* a novel about slavery by William Wells Brown, who had once been a slave himself, and *Hospital Sketches,* a series of letters written by Louisa May Alcott about her nursing experiences during the war.

Redpath's editorial methods are consistent with those reported by Mrs. Brooks, for he had a reputation for being very energetic and intrusive. For example, Alcott's sketches had previously been published serially in *The Commonwealth.* Nonetheless, for a reprint, Redpath worked "vigorously, sending letters, proof, and notices daily, and making all manner of offers, suggestions, and prophecies concerning the success of the book and its author," according to the author Madeleine Stern. A "concoctor of schemes," Redpath reportedly specialized in "timely works on his side of the political fence, issued them with speed, and lived up to his monetary promises to authors."

It is this last attribute that gives pause. Is it probable that even in his zeal to achieve what he considered the greater political good, he would in fact violate the confidence of an African American woman and that he would deliberately withhold her rightful profits? And, even more tellingly, when reviewers resorted to false and malicious attacks upon Keckley, would he not have come forth to defend her and to acknowledge his own responsibility?

G.W. Carleton's involvement, though inconclusive, is critical to our understanding of what happened to *Behind the Scenes.* Carleton & Company was a respectable and successful establishment that had built its reputation and large profit margin by pioneering innovative production strategies and marketing techniques and by discovering unknown writers whose works fit one of three categories: comedy, moral fiction, and reference books for the nonspecialist. Carleton, for example, had collaborated with Charles G. Browne to publish *Artemus Ward—His Book.* Within six months, this book had sold forty thousand copies, and Carleton & Company quickly became synonymous with "wit and humor." Sentimental fiction, which skirted impropriety with ruffles of moralization, was another specialty of the house. The firm's most famous writer in this genre was Augusta Evans Wilson, whose spectacularly successful novel *St. Elmo* subdues lust though pious lecture. Virtuous Edna counters her would-be seducer with elegant and learned homilies, eventually converting St. Elmo not merely from the error of his ways but into a minister and Edna's "first . . . last . . . and only love." Miss Evans's royalties earned her more than one hundred thousand dollars. And, thirdly, Carleton specialized in history and other reference books designed to give the busy reader digests of helpful information. In 1868, Carleton's list included works such as *Tales from the Operas, Pulpit Pungencies,* and *Handbook of Popular Quotations.* This focus had begun, interestingly enough, when G.W. Carleton in partnership with Edward and George Rudd published *The Wigwam-Edition. The Life, Speeches and Public Services of Abraham Lincoln.* Reputedly the "first campaign biography of Lincoln, the most popular *Life* of the campaign; and . . . the keystone of any Lincolniana collection," this work had appeared only eight years before *Behind the Scenes.*

It is easy to see why an amateur writer such as Elizabeth Keckley would attract this firm's interest. Her book offered a first-person account of undisclosed facts about Abraham Lincoln, as well as other national leaders and important civic events. It should certainly sell well. At the same time, its liberal use of sentimental and sensational rhetoric, its appeals to moral and ethical imperatives, and its avowed positive purpose of helping mend a nation and healing the wounded reputation of the widow of a martyred mythic hero were certainly in the G.W. Carleton tradition. Carleton & Company had another tradition—rapid, assembly-line production. In one famous case, it had established a record by translating 450 pages of Michelet's *La Femme* in three days, and printing and selling twenty thousand copies in less than thirty days.

Elizabeth Keckley declared that she surrendered Mary Todd Lincoln's letters to her publisher upon the condition that they not be printed in their entirety and that comments of a personal nature would be deleted. Why the letters were published as they were is a mystery. Perhaps in the rush to production, someone on the assembly line forgot and no one noticed. What is more clear, however, is that her publisher's advertisements were partly responsible for the book's being read in ways quite different from its author's good intentions. The first pre-publication announcements were staid enough. *American Literary Gazette and Publisher's Circular* for 1 April 1868 reported the forthcoming *Behind the Scenes* in language

Elizabeth Keckley in her later years

Courtesy Moorland-Spingarn Research Center, Howard University

A LITERARY THUNDERBOLT

launched this day from the press of

G. W. CARLETON & CO.

entitled

BEHIND THE SCENES.

By Mrs. ELIZABETH KECKLEY.

For 30 years household slave in the best Southern families, since she purchased her freedom, and during the plotting of the Rebellion Mrs. Jefferson Davis's confidential servant, where, "Behind the Scenes," she heard the first breathings of Secession. Since the commencement of the Rebellion, and up to date, she has been Mrs. Abraham Lincoln's *modiste* (dress maker), confidential friend, and business woman generally; a great portion of her time having been spent in the White House in the President's own family. She has much to say of an interesting, not to say startling nature, in regard to men and things in the White House, Washington, and New York. She discloses the whole history of Mrs. Lincoln's attempt to dispose of her wardrobe, &c.

The work is thoroughly authentic and truthful. 1 vol., cloth, illustrated with portrait of the author. Price $2.

JUST PUBLISHED:

TWO BOOKS BY "BRICK" POMEROY.

NONSENSE—A most laughable book. Illustrated..$1 50
SENSE—A book for Hearts and Homes. Illustrated 1 50

Sold by all Booksellers, and sent by mail on receipt of price, postage free.

G. W. CARLETON & CO., Publishers, N. Y.

"A Literary Thunderbolt"

From the New York Commercial Advertiser, *18 April 1868*

similar to Keckley's own. It was to be a remarkable book, "crowded with incidents of a most romantic as well as tragic interest . . . powerfully and truthfully written." But, a few days later, the *New York Commercial Advertiser* touted the book as "A Literary Thunderbolt" soon to be "launched." This ad identifies Keckley as Mrs. Jefferson Davis's confidential servant, where " 'Behind the Scenes,' she heard the first breathings of Secession" and as "Mrs. Abraham Lincoln's *modiste* . . . confidential friend, and business woman . . . [who] has much to say of an interesting . . . startling nature." Such language reinterprets Keckley's phrase, "truth being thrown to the surface as truth," as revelations of good intentions that ameliorate the bad results of the less-savory meanings of voyeurism, betrayal, and scandal. Soon, G.W. Carleton advertisements had dropped the *Thirty Years a Slave* and renamed the book *White House Revelations or Behind the Scenes* and *Behind the Scenes—The Great Sensational Disclosure by Mrs. Keckley,* thereby effectively erasing Keckley's autobiographical and positive political implications.

Small wonder that reviewers focused more upon the book's sensational and startling revelations and less on its author's life or the book's other concerns.

The reaction of the *New York Citizen* is particularly mysterious. On 18 April 1868, this newspaper reviewed *Behind the Scenes* under the heading "Indecent Publications." Explaining immediately that the caption referred not to "those shameless sheets that are displayed on every newsstand and whose existence is a reproach to our laws and to the police," the writer advises that "indecent" here refers to "a certain class of books which respectable publishers are not ashamed to send forth and advertise." Singling out "respectable publishers" who are unashamed to sell such material is particularly intriguing because Charles G. Halpine, the editor of the *New York Citizen,* was also "Private Miles O'Reilly," one of Carleton & Company's best-selling authors. The writer fiercely attacks Elizabeth Keckley's character, calling her a "traitorous eavesdropper," saying she was "ignorant and vulgar," and a "creature" from whom "all honorable men would turn in disgust." To be asked to buy such a book, the article advises, should be considered an insult.

A week later, the *Citizen* renewed its assault with two long *Behind the Scenes* articles in the same issue. Under a headline repeating the allegation of "indecency," the paper prefaces a letter from Elizabeth Keckley by saying that it was "forwarded to us by the publisher of the volume, with the request that we give it space in our columns." Keckley's letter defends the veracity of her statements and her right "as a free woman" to make them publicly. She details some of the slanderous accusations about Mary Lincoln that her book refutes, asks why such accusations had been published even in the *Citizen* without being denounced as "grossly and shamelessly indecent," and announces her faith that the reading public will recognize that her words are "truth" and that she has "spoken kindly of Mrs. L." The columnist follows the letter with extended comments that do not address Keckley's charges but again attack the character of "the writer" of the book.

This time, however, Keckley is labeled "a servant girl," and the real author, the *Citizen* suggests, is an unidentified man. "The writer of the foregoing letter," the columnist opines, "is evidently totally incapable of understanding how the violation of confidence can be regarded among gentlemen as an indecency and an outrage. . . . He seems to have identified himself so completely with the woman in whose name he writes, as to be unable to comprehend the existence of any higher standard of decency and honor than that which one would naturally expect to find among the slaves on a Southern plantation."

In another section of the paper appears a review of *Behind the Scenes.* It begins "The professed writer of this book is a Negro. . . . The facts—or falsehoods—which she furnished have been thrown together by some literary hack, and the result is the present volume of vulgar, illiterate, ungrammatical twaddle."

We may never know exactly what conspired to turn Keckley's "eventful life" into an "indecent book" by a "literary hack," but from that day until now, many read *Behind the Scenes* as a shameful betrayal of Mary Todd Lincoln with questionable authorship.

At the same time, the letters and certain information found only in *Behind the Scenes* are cited in almost every major study of Mary Todd Lincoln and even in many important biographies of Abraham Lincoln as well. Especially for details about the deaths of Willie and Abraham and the secret history of Mrs. Lincoln's wardrobe, Elizabeth Keckley's *Behind the Scenes* is evidence for works that vary from Carl Sandburg's *Abraham Lincoln* to Jean H. Baker's *Mary Todd Lincoln: A Biography* to the *Records of the Columbia Historical Society.*

It is also interesting to note that while two of the other regularly cited controversial insider-accounts, Ward Hill Lamon's *The Life of Abraham Lincoln* and *Herndon's Life of Abraham Lincoln,* are rarely identified as being ghostwritten, most Lincoln historians mention, if only in passing, that the authorship of *Behind the Scenes* has been questioned.

Few are as expansive as Paul Angle in *A Shelf of Lincoln Books,* but his statement represents the consensus of modern Lincoln scholars:

> The book is obviously ghost-written, yet even this fact, ordinarily damaging, does not impair one's confidence in its essential truthfulness. The author's delineation of Mrs. Lincoln's character has been fully corroborated by later publications, while her account of the wardrobe episode rests on documents the genuineness of which is beyond question. Some allowance should doubtless be made for exaggeration, but the book cannot be heavily discounted, no matter how reluctant one may be to accept its revelations.

* * * *

In memory I have traveled through the shadows and the sunshine of the past. . . . Though poor in worldly goods, I am rich in friendships, and friends are a recompense for all the woes of the darkest pages of life. For sweet friendship's sake, I can bear more burdens than I have borne.

In composing her concluding remarks, Elizabeth Keckley recognized the irony of her position. She had progressed from a slave cabin to the White House, but at this time she was stuck in a rented "garret-like room." She had gone from being property of a struggling entrepreneur to being proprietor of a successful business. Keckley had grandly refused the current president's daughter's patronage because she did not do piece work; now she humbly solicited sewing jobs simply to buy her "daily bread." Keckley's willful, impulsive, but still beloved friend had then fled in dismay back to her Chicago home, leaving Keckley to salvage Mary Lincoln's remaining finery, settle Mary Lincoln's bills, and do what she could to restore their damaged reputations.

Behind the Scenes evidences her stout heart. She had sacrificed her livelihood and was challenging the giants of press and politics to defend a beloved friend and confidante. The book, however, destroyed that friendship and broke its author's heart.

So how are we, as modern readers, to interpret this

saga? Should we read it as a romance? Certainly it contains a hero who experiences strange and wonderful adventures, endures severe and perilous trials, and concludes the quest, rich if not in gold at least in what is more valuable, "sweet friendship." Or, knowing what happened next, should we decide it is an American tragedy?

Like Willie Loman and others, for reasons over which she has minimal control, our protagonist moves from harmony to disharmony, from a comfortable, even enviable, social space to a marginalized and fraught existence. Or, knowing that there are so many unknowns about this book and its author, ought we to class it as a mystery?

For today's readers, "mystery" or even "curiosity" might be tempting choices, for it can be difficult for today's "matter-of-fact reader" to understand the brouhaha this book aroused. And, given the fact that *Behind the Scenes* infuriated many powerful people and engendered a lot of publicity, it seems incredible that its author did not profit financially. "White House informants" are a staple in modern news reporting, and those with particularly sensational revelations generally get sensational sales. Even when compared with other nineteenth-century publications about Abraham Lincoln, *Behind the Scenes* is about as revealing as a Universal Studios tour.

That her involvement in a project to sell a celebrity's clothing or to raise money to support formerly prosperous people would raise concern is indeed puzzling. Mary Todd Lincoln, Elizabeth Keckley, and others knew that this was not unheard of. Nineteenth-century European royalty had found this a rather useful way to clean their closets and replenish their purses. Today, especially, it boggles minds. The auction of Jackie Kennedy Onassis's valuables was a major social event reported as much for who purchased what as for how much they overpaid. In fact, the profits from clothing worn by Pamela Harriman and Diana, Princess of Wales, have changed the way venerable establishments such as Sotheby's and Christie's do business. Even their auction catalogs, some of which bear Forewords by curators of major museums and by other scholars, have become prized collectibles.

We may read *Behind the Scenes* as all these things and more. Certainly, it is a fascinating and valuable account of the Lincoln family and the variety of roles they played and they precipitated in our nation's history. But to read it merely as Lincolniana would be to ignore what it adds to our images of Jefferson Davis, Robert E. Lee, Hugh A. Garland, Horace Greeley, Charles Sumner, and other historical figures.

And it totally obscures the important insights into nineteenth-century African Americans. The parts played by the women of the Colored Baptist Church in Boston, the waiters at the Metropolitan Hotel in New York, and the anonymous "colored man" in New Market comprise a rare behind-the-scenes view of the formal and informal networks that African Americans established among themselves and within the larger mid-nineteenth-century culture.

This seemingly simple volume is actually far more richly complex and versatile than a mere reading as memoir would offer. *Behind the Scenes* is first and finally an autobiography, the personal narrative of an actual individual whose eventful life is offered to us for our pleasure and our instruction. Charles Stansil, a publisher and preacher in Buffalo, New York, recognized this in 1931 when his firm reprinted *Behind the Scenes.* In a brief Foreword, Stansil characterizes Elizabeth Keckley's life as exemplary and commends it as an example to emulate for "the general reader, regardless of race or color." Stansil further states that he reprinted "the book compiled by Elizabeth Keckley," because he wanted the general public to know "something of a character who achieved so much in her day and generation. . . . Although born and reared a slave, . . . [she] was able through force of character and Christian precepts to surmount some of the obstacles to the extent that generations yet unborn may call her blessed, and be inspired with greater love of humanity."

The first words of the Preface to *Behind the Scenes* demonstrate her autobiographical intentions. "I have often been asked to write my life. . . . At last I have acceded." In the tradition of combining explanation and excuse, defense and dissertation employed by Cardinal Newman, Benjamin Franklin, Frederick Douglass, Jarena Lee, Henry Adams, Margaret Mead, Mary

Church Terrell, and countless others, Elizabeth Keckley offers her own *apologia pro vita sua.* "Not altogether a history of myself" suggests that attributes of "memoir" are additional to her personal narrative, that she intends the book to do more than conventional autobiographies.

Keckley's narrative uses the sentimental rhetoric more commonly associated with nineteenth-century women's fiction for nonfictional purposes. She combines elements of several literary genres into an autobiography that is a formal hybrid.

Following the implications of the title and preface, reading the book as it was intended opens the way for several significant interpretations. For example, Mary Todd Lincoln (and certain other characters) functions as a literary foil for the protagonist. That is—in their continual juxtaposition, their different reactions to the same or similar situations—the weaknesses and strengths of each character are a reflection against one another, efficiently revealing multiple images or layers for interpretation.

Mary Todd Lincoln is a victim of malicious forces, but she also victimizes herself by failing to exercise the proper discipline, honesty, and self-reliance. Keckley's "character," her self-discipline, her aptness, her industry and resilience, in contrast, seem all the more admirable.

But, Keckley is not innocent of all that befalls her either. She exhibits many signs of being codependent, enabling and even possibly encouraging Mary Todd

Lincoln's behavior by continually shielding her from the full consequences of her actions.

Were the "imperfect story" entirely unique, the odyssey of one woman who beat the odds of gender, race, and class, Keckley's narrative would be fascinating. But, while unusual, the narrative also suggests that her story is our history. One can read *Behind the Scenes* also as a national autobiography, one written to remind us that our history and our future are interrelated.

Recall that this book was published during the Reconstruction period. Keckley began her testimony with a discourse on the meaning of slavery as an institution. It was "an evil" allowed to grow, a plant which grew to monstrous proportions because its growth went unremarked. The nation, she says, had paid a staggering price for allowing the evil to flourish. Keckley's owner, Hugh A. Garland, had argued masterfully in the Dred Scott case that slaves of African descent had no legitimate claim for freedom. She had persuaded him to acknowledge the validity of hers. Now she may be read as offering her testimony to a passel of Hugh A. Garlands, who advocated restricting citizenship for the freed slaves, arguing, as did Keckley's first mistress, that they were not fit for equality, that they were not (and might not ever be) "worth [their] salt."

Behind the Scenes refutes such arguments and reassures those who have not made up their minds. With her life history and her defense of her friend, she persuasively argues that people of African descent not only have rights that should be respected but that they know and will defend the rights of all people—even "imprudent" widows such as Mary Todd Lincoln.

Frances Smith Foster

Emory University
May 1998

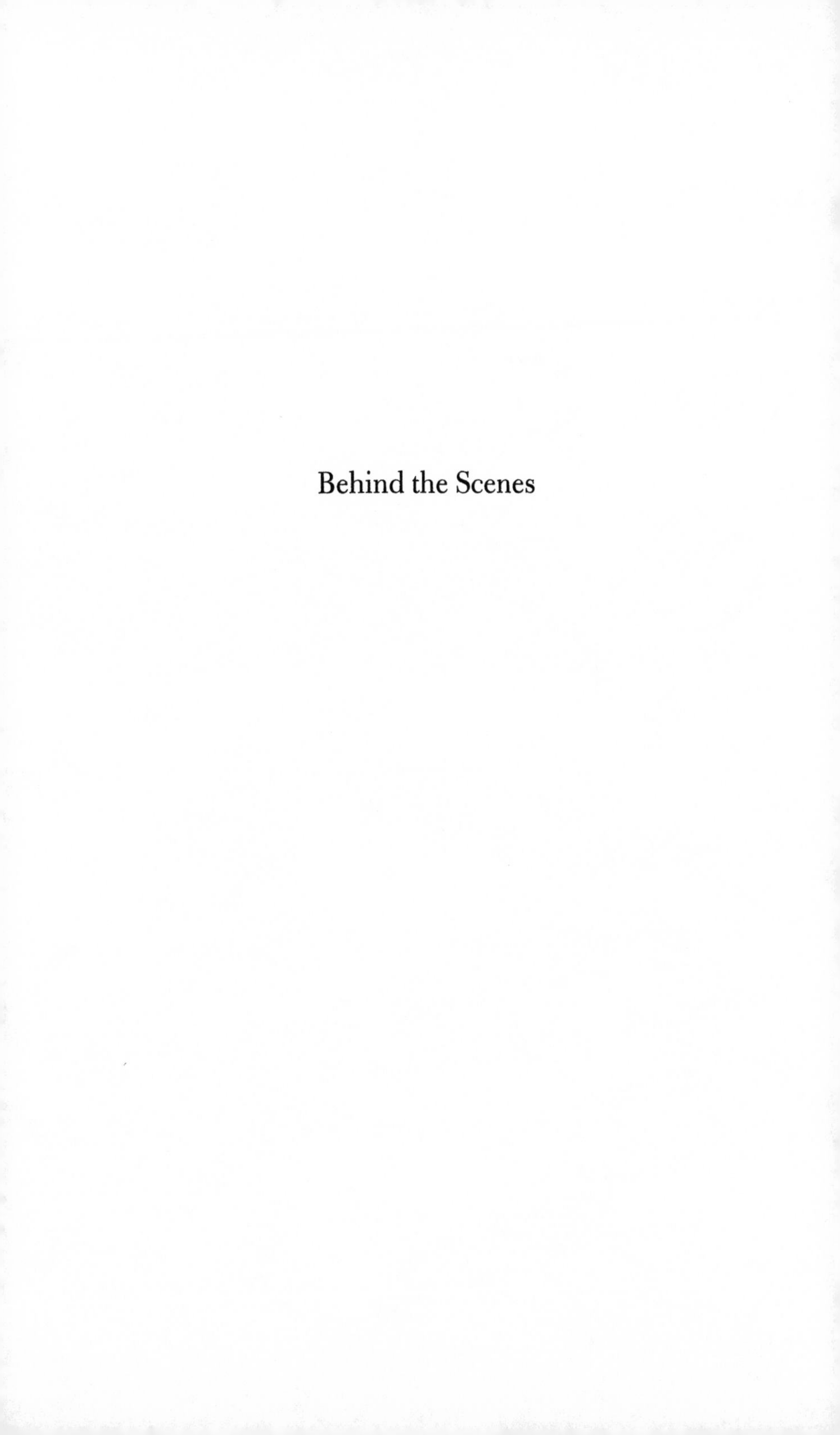

Behind the Scenes

AUTHOR'S PREFACE

I HAVE OFTEN been asked to write my life, as those who know me know that it has been an eventful one. At last I have acceded to the importunities of my friends, and have hastily sketched some of the striking incidents that go to make up my history. My life, so full of romance,[1] may sound like a dream to the matter-of-fact reader; nevertheless, everything I have written is strictly true; much has been omitted, but nothing has been exaggerated. In writing as I have done, I am well aware that I have invited criticism; but before the critic judges harshly, let my explanation be carefully read and weighed.

If I have portrayed the dark side of slavery, I also have painted the bright side. The good that I have said of human servitude should be thrown into the scales with the evil that I have said of it. I have kind, true-hearted friends in the South as well as in the North, and I would not wound those Southern friends by sweeping condemnation, simply because I was once a slave. They were not so much responsible for the curse under which I was born, as the God of nature and the framers of the Constitution for the United States. The law descended to them, and it was but natural that they should recognize it, since it manifestly was in their interest to do so.

[1]Romance: A story in which a hero experiences excitement, adventure, and extraordinary events.

And yet a wrong was inflicted upon me; a cruel custom deprived me of my liberty, and since I was robbed of my dearest right, I would not have been human had I not rebelled against the robbery. God rules the Universe. I was a feeble instrument in His hands, and through me and the enslaved millions of my race, one of the problems was solved that belongs to the great problem of human destiny; and the solution was developed so gradually that there was no great convulsion of the harmonies of natural laws. A solemn truth was thrown to the surface, and what is better still, it was recognized *as a truth* by those who give force to moral laws. An act may be wrong, but unless the ruling power recognizes the wrong, it is useless to hope for a correction of it. Principles may be right, but they are not established within an hour.

The masses are slow to reason, and each principle, to acquire moral force, must come to us from the fire of the crucible; the fire may inflict unjust punishment, but then it purifies and renders stronger the principle not in itself, but in the eyes of those who arrogate judgment to themselves. When the war of the Revolution had established the independence of the American colonies, an evil was perpetrated: Slavery was even more firmly established. And since the evil had been planted, it must pass through certain stages before it could be eradicated. In fact, we give but little thought to the plant of evil until it grows to such monstrous proportions that it overshadows important interests; then the efforts to destroy it become earnest. As one of the victims of slavery I drank of the bitter water; but then, since destiny willed it so, and since I aided in bringing a solemn truth to the surface *as a truth,* perhaps I have no right to complain. Here, as in all things pertaining to life, I can afford to be charitable.

It may be charged that I have written too freely on some questions, especially in regard to Mrs. Lincoln. I do not think so; at least I have been prompted by the purest motive. Mrs. Lincoln, by her own acts, forced herself into notoriety.[2] She stepped beyond the formal lines that hedge about a private life, and invited public criticism. The people have judged her harshly, and no woman was ever more traduced in the public prints of the country. The people knew nothing of the secret history of her transactions; therefore, they judged her by what was thrown to the surface. For an act may be wrong judged purely by itself, but when the motive that prompted the act is understood, it is construed differently. I lay it down as an axiom, that

[2]Mary Todd Lincoln repeatedly stirred criticism for her active interest in politics and imprudent remarks about public figures. She was criticized for actively lobbying her husband and other political leaders on behalf of her friends and relatives and against those she disliked or who offended her. She also violated social and gender protocol by hosting teas in hotels, accepting interviews with newspaper reporters, exceeding congressional budget for redecorating the White House, and wearing elaborate and low-cut gowns. The episode that catalyzed Keckley's memoir was "The Old Clothes Scandal." The newspaper publicity over Mrs. Lincoln's attempt to sell her jewelry and clothing stirred national political and social controversy. Keckley devotes Chapter XV to explaining "The Secret History of Mrs. Lincoln's Wardrobe in New York."

only that is critical in the sight of God where crime is mediated. Mrs. Lincoln may have been imprudent, but since her intentions were good, she should be judged more kindly than she has been. But the world do not know what her intentions were; they have only been made acquainted with her acts without knowing what feeling guided her actions. If the world are to judge her as I have judged her, they must be introduced to the secret history of her transactions.

The veil of mystery must be drawn aside; the origin of a fact must be brought to light with the naked fact itself. If I have betrayed confidence in anything I have published, it is to place Mrs. Lincoln in a better light before the world. A breach of trust—if breach it can be called—of this kind is always excusable. My own character, as well as the character of Mrs. Lincoln, is at stake, since I have been intimately associated with that lady in the most eventful periods of her life. I have been her confidante, and if evil charges are laid at her door, they must also be laid at mine, since I have been a party to all her movements. To defend myself I must defend the lady that I have served.

The world have judged Mrs. Lincoln by the facts that float upon the surface, and through her have partially judged me, and the only way to convince them that wrong was not meditated is to explain the motives that actuated us. I have written nothing that can place Mrs. Lincoln in a worse light than the light in which she now stands; therefore, the secret history that I publish can do her no harm. I have excluded everything of a personal character from her letters; the extracts introduced only refer to public men, and are such as to throw light upon her unfortunate adventure in New York.

These letters were not written for publication, for which reason they are all the more valuable; they are the frank overflowings of the heart, the outcropping of impulse, the key to genuine motives. They prove the motive to have been pure, and if they shall help to stifle the voice of calumny, I am content. I do not forget, before the public journals vilified Mrs. Lincoln, that ladies who moved in the Washington circle in which she moved, freely canvassed her character among themselves. They gloated over many a tale of scandal that grew out of gossip in their own circle. If these ladies could say everything bad of the wife of the president, why should I not be permitted to lay her secret history bare, especially when that history plainly shows that her life, like all lives, has its good side as well as its bad side?

None of us are perfect, for which reason we should heed the voice of charity when it whispers in our ears, "Do not magnify the imperfections of others." Had Mrs. Lincoln's acts never become public property, I should not have published to the world the secret chapters of her life. I am not the special champion of the widow of our lamented president; the reader of the pages that follow will discover that I have written with the utmost frankness in regard to her—have exposed her faults as well as given her credit for honest motives. I wish the world to judge her as she is, free from the exaggeration of praise or scandal, since I have been associated with her in so many things that have provoked hostile criticism; and the judgment that the world may pass upon her, I flatter myself, will present my own actions in a better light.

ELIZABETH KECKLEY

14 Carroll Place, New York
14 March 1868

I

Where I Was Born

My life has been an eventful one. I was born a slave—was the child of slave parents—therefore, I came upon the earth free in God-like thought, but fettered in action. My birthplace was Dinwiddie Court-house, in Virginia. My recollections of childhood are distinct, perhaps for the reason that many stirring incidents are associated with that period. I am now on the shady side of forty, and as I sit alone in my room, my brain is busy, and a rapidly moving panorama brings scene after scene before me, some pleasant and others sad; and when I thus greet old familiar faces, I often find myself wondering if I am not living the past over again. The visions are so terribly distinct that I almost imagine them to be real.

Hour after hour I sit while the scenes are being shifted; and as I gaze upon the panorama of the past, I realize how crowded with incidents my life has been. Every day seems like a romance within itself, and the years grow into ponderous volumes. As I cannot condense, I just omit many strange passages. From such a wilderness of events, it is difficult to make a selection, but as I am not writing altogether the history of myself, I will confine my story to the most important incidents which I believe influenced the moulding of my character.

As I glance over the crowded sea of the past, these incidents stand forth prominently, the guideposts of memory. I presume that I must have been four years old when I first began to remember; at least, I cannot now recall anything occurring previous to this period. My master, Colonel A. Burwell, was somewhat unsettled in his business affairs. While I was yet an infant, he made several removals.

While living at Hampton Sidney College, Prince Edward County, Virginia, Mrs. Burwell gave birth to a daughter, a sweet, black-eyed baby, my earliest and fondest pet. To take care of this baby was my first duty. True, I was but a child myself—only four years old—but then I had been raised in a hardy school—had been taught to rely upon myself, and to prepare myself to render assistance to others. The lesson was not a bitter one, for I was too young to indulge in philosophy, and the precepts that I then treasured and practiced I believe developed those principles of character that have enabled me to triumph over so many difficulties in my life.

Notwithstanding all the wrongs that slavery heaped upon me, I can bless it for one thing—youth's important lesson of self-reliance. The baby was named Elizabeth, and it was pleasant to me to be assigned a duty in connection with it, for the discharge of that duty transferred me from the rude cabin to the household of my master. My simple attire was a short dress and a little white apron. My old mistress encouraged me in rocking the cradle by telling me that if I would watch over the baby well, keep the flies out of its face, and not let it cry, I should be its little maid. This was a golden promise, and I required no better inducement for the faithful performance of my task. I began to rock the cradle most industriously, when lo! out pitched little pet on the floor. I instantly cried out, "Oh! the baby is on the floor"; and, not knowing what to do, I seized the fire-shovel in my perplexity. I was trying to shovel up my tender charge, when my mistress called to me to let the child alone, and then ordered that I be taken out and lashed for my carelessness.

The blows were not administered with a light hand, I assure you, and doubtless the severity of the lashing has made me remember the incident so well. This was the first time I was punished in this cruel way, but not the last. The black-eyed baby that I called my pet grew into a self-willed girl, and in after years was the cause of much trouble to me. I grew strong and healthy, and notwithstanding I knit socks and attended to various kinds of work. I was repeatedly told, even when fourteen years old, that I would never be worth my salt. When I was eight, Mr. Burwell's family consisted of six sons and four daughters, with a large family of servants. My mother was kind and forbearing; Mrs. Burwell, a hard taskmaster; and as mother had so much work to do in making clothes, etc., for the family, besides the slaves, I determined to render her all my assistance, and in rendering such assistance my young energies were taxed to the utmost.

I was my mother's only child, which made her love

for me all the stronger. I did not know much of my father, for he was the slave of another man, and when Mr. Burwell moved from Dinwiddie, he was separated from us, and only allowed to visit my mother twice a year—during the Easter holidays and Christmas. At last Mr. Burwell determined to reward my mother, by making an arrangement with the owner of my father, by which the separation of my parents could be brought to an end. It was a bright day, indeed, for my mother when it was announced that my father was coming to live with us. The old weary look faded from her face, and she worked as if her heart was in every task. But the golden days did not last long. The radiant dream faded all too soon.

In the morning my father called me to him and kissed me, then held me out at arms' length as if he were regarding his child with pride. "She is growing into a large fine girl," he remarked to my mother. "I dun no which I like best, you or Lizzie, as both are so dear to me." My mother's name was Agnes, and my father delighted to call me his "Little Lizzie." While yet my father and mother were speaking hopefully, joyfully of the future, Mr. Burwell came to the cabin with a letter in his hand. He was a kind master in some things, and as gently as possible informed my parents that they must part; for in two hours my father must join his master at Dinwiddie, and go with him to the West, where he had determined to make his future home. The announcement fell upon the little circle in that rude log cabin like a thunderbolt. I can remember the scene as if it were yesterday—how my father cried out against the cruel separation; his last kiss; his wild straining of my mother to his bosom; the solemn prayer to Heaven; the tears and sobs—the fearful anguish of broken hearts. The last kiss, the last good-bye; and he, my father, was gone, gone forever.

The shadow eclipsed even the sunshine, and love brought despair. The parting was eternal. The cloud had no silver lining, but I trust that it will be all silver in heaven. We who are crushed to earth with heavy chains, who travel a weary, rugged, thorny road, groping through midnight darkness on earth, earn our right to enjoy the sunshine in the great hereafter. At the grave, at least, we should be permitted to lay our burdens down, that a new world, a world of brightness, may open to us. The light that is denied us here should grow into a flood of effulgence beyond the dark, mysterious shadows of death. Deep as was the distress of my mother in parting with my father, her sorrow did not screen her from insult. My old mistress said to her: "Stop your nonsense; there is no necessity for you putting on airs. Your husband is not the only slave that has been sold from this family, and you are not the only one that has had to part. There are plenty more men around here, and if you want a husband so badly, stop your crying and go and find another." To these unfeeling words my mother made no reply. She turned away in stoical silence with a curl of that loathing scorn upon her lips, which swelled in her heart.

My father and mother never met again in this world. They kept up a regular correspondence for years, and the most precious mementos of my existence are the faded old letters that he wrote, full of love, and always hoping that the future would bring brighter days. In nearly every letter is a message for me. "Tell my darling little Lizzie," he writes, "to be a good girl, and to learn her book. Kiss her for me, and tell her that I will come to see her some day." Thus he wrote time and time again, but he never came. He lived in hope, but died without ever seeing his wife and child.

I note a few extracts from one of my father's letters to my mother, following copy literally:

Shelbyville, 6 September 1833.

MRS. AGNES HOBBS.

DEAR WIFE: My dear biloved wife I am more than glad to meet with opportunity writee thes few lines to you by my Mistress who ar now about starterng to virginia, and sevl others of my old friends are with her; in compeney Mrs. Ann Rus the wife of master Thos Rus and Dan Woodiard and his family and I am very sorry that I havn the chance to go with them as I feele Determid to see you If life last again. I am now here and out at this pleace so I am not abble to get of at this time. I am write well and hearty and all the rest of masters family. I heard this eveng by Mistress that ar just from theree all sends love to you and all my old friends. I am a living in a town called Shelbyville and I have wrote a greate many letters since Ive beene here and almost been reeady to my selfe that its out of the question to write any more at tall: my dear wife I don't feeld no whys like giving out writing to you as yet and I hope when you get this letter that you be Inncougege to write me a letter. I am well satisfied at my living at this place I am a making money for my own benifit and I hope that its to yours also If I live to Nexct year I shall have my own time from master by giving him 100 and twenty Dollars a year and I thinke I shall be doing good business at that and heve something more thean all that. I hope with gods helpe that I may be abble to rejoys with you on the earth and In heaven lets meet when will I am detemnid to nuver stope praying, not in this earth and I hope to praise god In glory there weel meet to part no more forever. So my dear wife I hope to meet you In paradase to prase god forever * * * I want Elizabeth to be a good girl and not to thinke that because I am bound so fare that gods not abble to open the way * * *

George Pleasant,
Hobbs a servant of Grum.

The last letter that my mother received from my father was dated Shelbyville, Tennessee, 20 March 1839. He writes in a cheerful strain, and hopes to see her soon. Alas! he looked forward to a meeting in vain. Year after year, that was the one great hope that swelled in his heart, but the hope was only realized beyond the dark portals of the grave.

When I was about seven years old, I witnessed, for the first time, the sale of a human being. We were living at Prince Edward, in Virginia, and master had just purchased his hogs for the winter, for which he was unable to pay in full. To escape this embarrassment it became necessary to sell one of the slaves. Little Joe, the son of the cook, was selected as the victim. His mother was ordered to dress him up in his Sunday clothes and send him to the house. He came in with a bright face, was placed in the scales, and was sold, like the hogs, at so much per pound. His mother was kept in ignorance of the transaction, but her suspicions were aroused.

When her son started for Petersburg in the wagon, the truth began to dawn upon her mind, and she pleaded piteously that her boy should not be taken from her; but master quieted her by telling her that he was simply going to town with the wagon, and would be back in the morning. Morning came, but little Joe did not return to his mother. Morning after morning passed, and mother went down to the grave without ever seeing her child again. One day she was whipped for grieving for her lost boy.

Colonel Burwell never liked to see one of his slaves wear a sorrowful face, and those who offended in this particular way were always punished. Alas! the sunny face of the slave is not always an indication of sunshine in the heart. Colonel Burwell at one time owned about seventy slaves, all of which were sold, and in a majority of instances wives were separated from husbands and children from their parents. Slavery in the Border States forty years ago was different from what it was twenty years ago. Time seemed to soften the hearts of master and mistress, and to insure kinder and more humane treatment to bondsmen and bondswomen.

When I was quite a child, an incident occurred that my mother afterward impressed more strongly on my mind. One of my uncles, a slave of Colonel Burwell, lost a pair of ploughlines, and when the loss was made known, the master gave him a new pair and told him that if he did not take care of them, he would punish him severely. In a few weeks the second pair of lines was stolen, and my uncle hung himself rather than meet the displeasure of his master. My mother went to the spring in the morning for a pail of water, and on looking up into the willow tree that shaded the bubbling crystal stream, she discovered the lifeless form of her brother suspended beneath one of the strong branches. Rather than be punished the way Colonel Burwell punished his servants, he took his own life. Slavery had its dark side as well as its bright side.

II

Girlhood and Its Sorrows

I MUST PASS rapidly over the stirring events of my early life. When I was about fourteen years old, I went to live with my master's eldest son, a Presbyterian minister. His salary was small, and he was burdened with a helpless wife, a girl that he had married in the humble walks of life.

She was morbidly sensitive, and imagined that I regarded her with contemptuous feelings because she was of poor parentage. I was their only servant, and a gracious loan at that. They were not able to buy me, so my old master sought to render them assistance by allowing them the benefit of my services. From the very first I did the work of three servants, and yet I was scolded and regarded with distrust. The years passed slowly, and I continued to serve them, and at the same time grew into strong, healthy womanhood. I was nearly eighteen when we removed from Virginia to Hillsboro', North Carolina, where young Mr. Burwell took charge of a church. The salary was small, and we still had to practice the closest economy. Mr. Bingham, a hard, cruel man, the village schoolmaster, was a member of my young master's church, and he was a frequent visitor to the parsonage. She whom I called mistress seemed to be desirous to wreak vengeance on me for something, and Bingham became her ready tool. During this time my master was unusually kind to me; he was naturally a good-hearted man, but was influenced by his wife.

It was Saturday evening, and while I was bending over the bed, watching the baby that I had just hushed into slumber, Mr. Bingham came to the door and asked me to go with him to the study. Wondering what he meant by his strange request, I followed him, and when we had entered the study he closed the door, and in his blunt way remarked: "Lizzie, I am going to flog you." I was thunderstruck, and tried to think if I had been remiss in anything. I could not recollect of doing anything to deserve punishment, and with surprise exclaimed: "Whip me, Mr. Bingham! What for?" "No matter," he replied, "I am going to whip you, so take down your dress this instant."

Recollect, I was eighteen years of age, was a woman fully developed, and yet this man coolly bade me take down my dress. I drew myself up proudly, firmly, and said: "No, Mr. Bingham, I shall not take down my dress before you. Moreover, you shall not whip me unless you prove the stronger. Nobody has a right to whip me but my own master, and nobody shall do so if I can prevent it."

My words seemed to exasperate him. He seized a rope, caught me roughly, and tried to tie me. I resisted with all my strength, but he was the stronger of the two and, after a hard struggle, succeeded in binding my hands and tearing my dress from my back. Then

The Reverend
Robert A. Burwell

Margaret Anna
(Mrs. Reverend Robert) Burwell

The Burwell House in Hillsborough, North Carolina

Courtesy Historic Hillsborough Commission

he picked up a rawhide,[1] and began to ply it freely over my shoulder. With steady hand and practiced eye he would raise the instrument of torture, nerve himself for a blow, and with fearful force the rawhide descended upon the quivering flesh. It cut the skin, raised great welts, and the warm blood trickled down my back. Oh God! I can feel the torture now—the terrible, excruciating agony of those moments. I did not scream; I was too proud to let my tormentor know what I was suffering. I closed my lips firmly, that not even a groan might escape from them, and I stood like a statue while the keen lash cut deep into my flesh.

As soon as I was released, stunned and with pain, bruised, and bleeding, I went home and rushed into the presence of the pastor and his wife, wildly exclaiming: "Master Robert, why did you let Mr. Bingham flog me? What have I done that I should be so punished?"

"Go away," he gruffly answered, "Do not bother me."

I would not be put off thus. "What *have* I done? I *will* know why I have been flogged."

I saw his cheeks flush with anger, but I did not move. He rose to his feet, and on my refusing to go without an explanation, seized a chair, struck me, and felled me to the floor. I rose, bewildered, almost dead with pain, crept to my room, dressed my bruised arms and back as best I could, and then lay down, but not

[1]Rawhide: A rope or whip made of untanned cattle hide used to administer beatings.

to sleep. No, I could not sleep, for I was suffering mental as well as bodily torture. My spirit rebelled against the unjustness that had been inflicted upon me, and though I tried to smother my anger and to forgive those who had been so cruel to me, it was impossible. The next morning I was more calm, and I believe that I could then have forgiven everything for the sake of one kind word.

But the kind word was not proffered, and it may be possible that I grew somewhat wayward and sullen. Though I had faults, I know now, as I felt then, harshness was the poorest inducement for the correction of them. It seems that Mr. Bingham had pledged himself to Mrs. Burwell to subdue what he called my "stubborn pride." On Friday following the Saturday on which I was so savagely beaten, Mr. Bingham again directed me to come to his study. I went, but with the determination to offer resistance should he attempt to flog me again.

On entering the room I found him prepared with a new rope and a new cowhide.[2] I told him that I was ready to die, but that he could not conquer me. In struggling with him I bit his finger severely, when he seized a heavy stick and beat me with it in a shameful manner. Again I went home sore and bleeding, but with pride as strong and defiant as ever. The following Thursday Mr. Bingham again tried to conquer me, but in vain. We struggled, and he struck me many sav-

[2]Cowhide: A whip made of braided leather, prized for its strength and flexibility.

age blows. As I stood bleeding before him, nearly exhausted with his efforts, he burst into tears and declared that it would be a sin to beat me any more. My suffering at last subdued his hard heart; he asked my forgiveness and afterward was an altered man. He was never known to strike one of his servants from that day forward. Mr. Burwell, he who preached the love of Heaven, who glorified the precepts and examples of Christ, who expounded the Holy Scriptures Sabbath after Sabbath from the pulpit, when Mr. Bingham refused to whip me any more, was urged by his wife to punish me himself. One morning he went to the woodpile, took an oak broom, cut the handle off, and with this heavy handle attempted to conquer me. I fought him, but he proved the strongest.

At the sight of my bleeding form, his wife fell upon her knees and begged him to desist. My distress even touched her cold, jealous heart. I was so badly bruised that I was unable to leave my bed for five days. I will not dwell upon the bitter anguish of these hours, for even the thought of them now makes me shudder. The Reverend Mr. Burwell was not yet satisfied. He resolved to make another attempt to subdue my proud, rebellious spirit, made the attempt and again failed, when he told me, with an air of penitence, that he should never strike me another blow; and faithfully he kept his word. These revolting scenes created a great sensation at the time, were the talk of the town and neighborhood, and I flatter myself that the actions of those who had conspired against me were not viewed in a light to reflect much credit upon them.

The savage efforts to subdue my pride were not the only things that brought me suffering and deep mortification during my residence at Hillsboro'. I was regarded as fair-looking for one of my race, and for four years a white man—I spare the world his name—had base designs upon me.[3] I do not care to dwell upon this subject, for it is one that is fraught with pain. Suffice it to say, that he persecuted me for four years, and I—I—became a mother. The child of which he was the father was the only child that I ever brought into the world. If my poor boy ever suffered any humiliating pangs on account of birth, he could not blame his mother, for God knows that she did not wish to give him life; he must blame that society which deemed it no crime to undermine the virtue of girls in my position. Among the old letters preserved by my mother I find the following written by myself while at Hillsboro'. Reverend Robert Burwell is now living (March 1868) at Charlotte, North Carolina:

Hillsboro', 10 April 1838.

MY DEAR MOTHER: I have been intending to write to you for a long time, but numerous things have prevented me. . . .

[3]In the official application for a survivor's pension, Keckley says that Hugh Garland "married" her to his neighbor Alexander Kirkland, that their son was George W.D. Kirkland, that the father did not financially support the child, and that Kirkland died when the boy was eighteen months old. Since it was almost unheard of for a free white man to marry a black slave woman and Keckley includes this as another example of persecution, it is more likely that Keckley was forced to be Kirkland's concubine for four years.

I thought very hard of you for not writing to me, but hope that you will answer this letter as soon as you receive it, and tell me how you like Marshfield, and if you have seen any of my old acquaintances, or if you yet know any of the brick-house people who I think so much of. I want to hear of the family at home very much, indeed. I really believe you and all the family have forgotten me, if not I certainly should have heard from some of you since you left Boyton, if it was only a line; nevertheless I love you all very dearly, and shall, although I may never see you again nor do I ever expect to. Miss Anna is going to Petersburg next winter, but she says that she does not intend to take me; what reason she has for leaving me I cannot tell. I have often wished that I lived where I knew I never could see you, for then I would not have my hopes raised, and to be disappointed in this manner; however, it is said that a bad beginning makes a good ending, but I hardly expect to see that happy day at this place. Give my love to all the family, both white and black. I was very much obliged to you for the presents you sent me last summer, though it is quite late in the day to be thanking for them. Tell Aunt Bella that I was very much obliged to her for her present; I have been so particular with it that I have only worn it once.

There have been six weddings since October; the most respectable[4] one was about a fortnight ago; I was asked to be the first attendant, but, as usual with all my expectations, I was disappointed, for on the wedding day I felt more like being locked up in a three-cornered box than attending a wedding. About a week before Christmas I was bridesmaid for Ann Nash; when the night came I was in quite a trouble; I did not know whether my frock was clean or dirty; I only

[4]Respectable: Worth noting, or particularly special.

had a week's notice and the body and sleeves to make, and only one hour every night to work on it, so you can see with these troubles to overcome my chance was rather slim.

I must now close, although I could fill ten pages with my griefs and misfortunes; no tongue could express them as I feel; don't forget me though; and answer my letters soon. I will write you again, and would write more now, but Miss Anna says it is time I had finished. Tell Miss Elizabeth that I wish she would make haste and get married, for mistress says that I belong to her when she gets married.

I wish you would send me a pretty frock this summer; if you will send it to Mrs. Robertson's, Miss Bet will send it to me.

Farewell, darling mother.
Your affectionate daughter,
ELIZABETH HOBBS.

III

How I Gained My Freedom

THE YEARS passed and brought many changes to me, but on these I will not dwell, as I wish to hasten to the most interesting part of my story. My troubles in North Carolina were brought to an end by my unexpected return to Virginia, where I lived with Mr. Garland, who had married Miss Anne Burwell, one of my old master's daughters. His life was not a prosperous one, and after struggling with the world for several years, he left his native state, a disappointed man. He moved to St. Louis, hoping to improve his fortune in the West; but ill luck followed him there, and he seemed to be unable to escape from the influence of the evil star of his destiny. When his family, myself included, joined him in his new home on the banks of the Mississippi, we found him so poor that he was unable to pay the dues on a letter advertised as in the post office for him. The necessities of the family were so great, that it was proposed to place my mother out at service.[1] The idea was shocking to me.

[1]Out at service: The Garlands intended to rent out Agnes Hobbs's services in order to supplement their income. Also known as "hiring out," it was a common practice among slave owners to rent or lease the labor of their slaves to those who had none of their own or who simply needed temporary help. Given the frightful

Every gray hair in her old head was dear to me, and I could not bear the thought of her going to work for strangers. She had been raised in the family, had watched the growth of each child from infancy to maturity; they had been the objects of her kindest care, and she was wound round about them as the vine winds itself about the rugged oak. They had been the central figures in her dream of life—a dream beautiful to her, since she had basked in the sunshine of no other. And now they proposed to destroy each tendril of affection, to cloud the sunshine of her existence when the day was drawing to a close, when the shadows of solemn night were rapidly approaching. My mother, my poor aged mother, go among strangers to toil for a living! No, a thousand times no! I would rather work my fingers to the bone, bend over my sewing till the film of blindness gathered in my eyes; nay, even beg from street to street. I told Mr. Garland so, and he gave me permission to see what I could do.

I was fortunate in obtaining work, and in a short time I had acquired something of a reputation as a seamstress and dressmaker. The best ladies in St. Louis were my patrons, and, when my reputation was once established, I never lacked for orders. With my needle I kept bread in the mouths of some seventeen persons for two years, five months. While I was working so hard that others might live in comparative com-

---

treatment Keckley experienced when loaned to family and friends, her distress over this plan was based on more than simply being separated from the rest of the family.

fort, and move in those circles of society to which their birth gave them entrance, the thought often occurred to me whether I was really worth my salt or not; and then perhaps the lips curled with a bitter sneer. It may seem strange that I should place so much emphasis upon words thoughtlessly, idly spoken; but then we do many strange things in life, and cannot always explain the motives that actuate us. The heavy task was too much for me, and my health began to give way.

About this time Mr. Keckley, whom I had met in Virginia and learned to regard with more than friendship, came to St. Louis. He then sought my hand in marriage[2]; for a long time I refused to consider his proposal, for I could not bear the thought of bringing children into slavery—of adding one single recruit to the millions bound to hopeless servitude, fettered and shackled with chains stronger and heavier than manacles of iron. I made a proposition to buy myself and son; the proposition was bluntly declined, and I was commanded never to broach the subject again. I would not be put off thus, for hope pointed to a freer, brighter life in the future. Why should my son be held in slavery?

I often asked myself this. He came into the world

[2]Slaves were legal property and could not enter into legal contracts of any kind, including marriage. However, they were generally encouraged to "marry" informally for, by law, all children followed the condition of their mothers. Though his father was white and free, Keckley's son was, as was his mother, a slave. He was known as "Garland's George" until after she purchased his freedom.

through no will of mine, and yet, God only knows how I loved him. The Anglo-Saxon blood as well as the African flowed in his veins; the two currents commingled—one singing of freedom, the other silent and sullen with generations of despair. Why should not the Anglo-Saxon triumph—why should it be weighed down with the rich blood typical of the tropics? Must the life-current of one race bind the other race in chains as strong and enduring as if there had been no Anglo-Saxon taint? By the laws of God and nature, as interpreted by man, one-half of my boy was free, and why should not this fair birthright of freedom remove the curse from the other half—raise it into the bright, joyous sunshine of liberty? I could not answer these questions of my heart that almost maddened me, and I learned to regard human philosophy with distrust. Much as I respected the authority of my master, I could not remain silent on a subject that so nearly concerned me. One day, when I insisted on knowing whether he would permit me to purchase myself, and what price I must pay for myself, he turned to me in a petulant manner, thrust his hand into his pocket, drew forth a bright silver quarter of a dollar, and proffering it to me, said: "Lizzie, I have told you often not to trouble me with such a question. If you really wish to leave me, take this: it will pay the passage of yourself and boy on this ferry-boat, and when you are on the other side of the river you will be free.[3] It is by far the

[3]The Mississippi River divided Missouri (where slavery was legal) from Illinois (a free state). The proximity between the

cheapest way to accomplish that which you desire."

I looked at him in astonishment, and earnestly replied: "No, master, I do not wish to be free in such a manner. If such had been my wish, I should never have troubled you about obtaining your consent to my purchasing myself. I can cross the river any day, as you well know, and have frequently done so, but will never leave you in such a manner. By the laws of the land I am your slave—you are my master, and I will only be free by such means as the laws of the country provide." He expected this answer, and I knew that he was pleased. Some time afterward he told me that he had reconsidered the question; that I had served his family faithfully; that I deserved my freedom, and that he would take twelve hundred dollars for myself and the boy. This was joyful intelligence, and the reflection of hope gave a silver lining to the dark cloud of my life—faint, it is true, but still a silver lining.

Taking a prospective glance at liberty, I consented to marry Keckley.[4] The wedding was a great event in

---

two states made it relatively easy for some slaves to seek refuge among anti-slavery communities. However, the proximity between the two states made it easy to be kidnapped into slavery also. Even with documents identifying them as "free," no African American was safe from accusations of being a runaway. Without legal manumission documents, Keckley's "freedom" would have been even more perilous. (See Historical Introduction for more information on this subject.)

[4]As shown earlier, despite the lack of legal sanction, slaves generally solemnized their marriages with wedding ceremonies. Sometimes this was as simple as gathering friends for a meal

the family. The ceremony took place in the parlor, in the presence of the family and a number of guests. Mr. Garland gave me away, and the pastor, Bishop Hawks, who had solemnized the bridals of Mr. G.'s own children, performed the ceremony.

The day was a happy one, but it faded all too soon. Mr. Keckley—let me speak kindly of his faults—proved dissipated, and a burden instead of a helpmate. More than all, I learned that he was a slave instead of a free man, as he represented himself to be. With the simple explanation that I lived with him eight years, I will let charity draw around him the mantle of silence.

I went to work in earnest to purchase my freedom, but the years passed, and I was still a slave. Mr. Garland's family claimed so much of my attention—in fact, I supported them—that I was not able to accumulate anything.

In the meantime, Mr. Garland died and Mr. Burwell, a Mississippi planter, came to St. Louis to settle up the estate. He was a kind-hearted man, and said I should be free, and would afford me every facility to raise the necessary amount to pay the price of my liberty. Several schemes were urged upon me by my friends. At last I formed a resolution to go to New York, to state my case, and to appeal to the benevo-

---

highlighted by the couple's jumping over a broom to symbolize their setting up housekeeping together. It was not uncommon for favored slaves, however, to have elaborate weddings, which were condoned, attended, and sometimes performed and financed by their owners.

lence of the people.[5] The plan seemed feasible, and I made preparations to carry it out. When I was almost ready to turn my face northward, Mrs. Garland told me that she would require the names of six gentlemen who would vouch for my return, and become responsible for the amount at which I was valued. I had many friends in St. Louis, and, as I believed that they had confidence in me, I felt that I could readily obtain the names desired. I started out, stated my case, and obtained five signatures to the paper, and my heart throbbed with pleasure, for I did not believe that the sixth would refuse me. I called, he listened patiently, then remarked:

"Yes, yes, Lizzie; the scheme is a fair one, and you shall have my name. But I shall bid you good-bye when you start."

"Good-bye for a short time," I ventured to add.

"No, good-bye for all time," and he looked at me as if he would read my very soul with his eyes. I was startled. "What do you mean, Mr. Farrow? Surely you do not think that I do not mean to come back?"

"No."

"No, what then?"

"Simply this: you *mean* to come back, that is, you

[5]As early as 1730, there were highly publicized cases of individual slaves who had managed to raise money to buy themselves or loved ones by personally soliciting contributions from antislavery groups and sympathetic individuals. In the antebellum period, this became a viable option for those few slaves who had the financial resources and social contacts to gain audience with the people who might be persuaded to help them.

mean so now, but you never will. When you reach New York, the abolitionists will tell you what savages we are, and they will prevail on you to stay there; and we shall never see you again."

"But I assure you, Mr. Farrow, you are mistaken. I not only *mean* to come back, but I *will* come back, and pay every cent of the twelve hundred dollars for myself and child."

I was beginning to feel sick at heart, for I could not accept the signature of this man when he had no faith in my pledges. No; slavery, eternal slavery rather than be regarded with distrust by those whose respect I esteemed.

"But—I am not mistaken," he persisted. "Time will show. When you start for the North I shall bid you good-bye."

The heart grew heavy. Every ray of sunshine was eclipsed. With humbled pride, weary step, tearful face, and a dull, aching pain, I left the house. I walked along the street mechanically. The cloud had no silver lining now. The rosebuds of hope had withered and died without lifting up their heads to receive the dew kiss of morning. There was no morning for me—all was night, dark night.

I reached my own home and, weeping, threw myself upon the bed. My trunk was packed, my luncheon was prepared by Mother, the cars were ready to bear me where I would not hear the clank of chains, where I would breathe the free, invigorating breezes of the glorious North. I had dreamed such a happy dream, in imagination had drunk of the water, the pure, sweet, crystal water of life, but now—now—the flower had withered before my eyes; darkness had settled down upon me like a pall, and I was left alone with cruel mocking shadows.

The first paroxysm of grief was scarcely over when a carriage stopped in front of the house; Mrs. Le Bourgois, one of my kind patrons, got out of it and entered the door. She seemed to bring sunshine with her handsome cheery face.

She came to where I was, and in her sweet way said:

"Lizzie, I hear that you are going to New York to beg for money to buy your freedom. I have been thinking over the matter, and told Ma it would be a shame to allow you to go north to beg for what we should give you. You have many friends in St. Louis, and I am going to raise the twelve hundred dollars required among them. I have two hundred dollars put away for a present; am indebted to you one hundred dollars; Mother owes you fifty dollars, and will add another fifty to it; and as I do not want the present, I will make the money a present to you. Don't start for New York now until I see what I can do among your friends."

Like a ray of sunshine she came, and like a ray of sunshine she went away. The flowers no longer were withered, drooping. Again they seemed to bud and grow in fragrance and beauty. Mrs. Le Bourgois, God bless her dear good heart, was more than successful. The twelve hundred dollars were raised, and at last my son and I were free. Free, free! what a glorious ring to the word. Free! the bitter heart-struggle was over. Free! the soul could go out to heaven and to God with no chains to clog its flight or pull it down. Free! the earth wore a brighter look, and the very stars seemed to sing with joy. Yes, free! free by the laws of man and the smile of God—and heaven bless them who made me so!

The following, copied from the original papers contain, in brief, the history of my emancipation:

27 June 1855.

I PROMISE to give Lizzie and her son George their freedom, on the payment of $1,200.

ANNE P. GARLAND.

LIZZY: I send you this note to sign for the sum of $75, and when I give you the whole amount you will then sign the other note for $100.

ELLEN M. DOAN.

St. Louis, 13 August 1855.

I HAVE received of Lizzy Keckley $950, which I have deposited with Darby & Barksdale for her—$600 on 21 July, $300 on 27 and 28 July, and $50 on 13 August 1855.

I have and shall make use of said money for Lizzy's benefit, and hereby guarantee to her one percent per month—as much more as can be made she shall have. The one percent, as it may be checked out, I will be responsible for myself, as well as for the whole amount, when it shall be needed by her.

WILLIS L. WILLIAMS.

KNOW ALL men by these presents, that for and in consideration of the love and affection we bear toward our sister, Anne P. Garland, of St. Louis, Missouri, and for the further consideration of $5 in hand paid, we hereby sell and convey unto her, the said Anne P. Garland, a Negro woman named Lizzie, and a Negro boy, her son, named George; said Lizzie now resides at St. Louis, and is a seamstress, known there as Lizzie Garland, the wife of a yellow man named James, and called James Keckley; said George is a bright mulatto boy, and is known in St. Louis as Garland's George.

We warrant these two slaves to be slaves for life, but make no representations as to age or health.

Witness our hands and seals, this 10th day of August, 1855.

JAS. R. PUTNAM
E. M. PUTNAM
A. BURWELL.

The State of Mississippi,
Warren County,
City of Vicksburg.

BE IT REMEMBERED, that on the tenth day of August, in the year of our Lord one thousand eight hundred and fifty-five, before me, Francis N. Steele, a Commissioner, resident in the city of Vicksburg, duly commissioned and qualified by the executive authority and under the laws of the State of Missouri, to take the acknowledgment of deed, etc.,to be used or recorded therein, personally appeared James R. Putnam and E. M. Putnam, his wife, and Armistead Burwell, to me known to be the individuals named in, and who executed the foregoing conveyance, and acknowledged that they executed the same for the purposes therein mentioned; and the E. M. Putnam being by me examined apart from her husband, and being fully acquainted with the contents of the foregoing conveyance, acknowledged that she executed the same freely, and relinquished her dower,[6] and any other claim she might have in and to the property therein mentioned, freely, and without fear, compulsion, or undue influence of her said husband.

In witness whereof I have hereunto set my hand and affixed my official seal, this 10th day of August, A.D. 1855.

F. N. STEELE
Commissioner for Missouri.

KNOW ALL MEN by these presents, that I, Anne P. Garland, of the County and City of St. Louis, State of Missouri, for and in consideration of the sum of twelve hundred dollars, to me in hand paid this day in cash, hereby emancipate my Negro woman Lizzie and her son George; the said Lizzie is known in St. Louis as the wife of James, who is called James Keckley; is of light complexion, about thirty-

[6]Even though Elizabeth Keckley and her son George lived with Anne Garland, three Burwell children apparently had inherited them in common. James Putnam, as Elizabeth Burwell Putnam's husband, had legal control over his wife's property, but, since Keckley was property obtained outside her marriage ("dower"), he could not dispose of it without his wife's consent. Thus, the certification and bill of sale from the other three owners were necessary before Anne Garland could sell Elizabeth Keckley and her son to themselves.

Know all men by these presents, that I, Ann P. Garland of the County and City of St. Louis, State of Missouri, for and in Consideration of the sum of twelve hundred dollars, to me in hand paid this day in cash, hereby emancipate my negro woman Lizzie and her son George — the said Lizzie is known in St. Louis, as the wife of James, who is called James Keckelly, is of light complexion, about thirty seven — years of age, by trade a dress-maker, and called by those who know her, <u>Garland's Lizzie</u> — the said boy George, is the only Child of Lizzie, is about sixteen years of age, and is almost white, and called by those who know him, <u>Garland's George</u>.

Witness my hand and seal this 13th day of November A.D. 1855.

Witness

Anne P. Garland (Seal)

John Wickham

Willy L. Williams

[illegible] Circuit Court October Term 1855

November 15th 1855

State of Missouri ss.

Manumission of Elizabeth Keckley and her son, George Garland, 1855

Courtesy Missouri Historical Society

seven years of age, by trade a dressmaker, and called by those who know her Garland's Lizzie. The said boy, George, is the only child of Lizzie, is about sixteen years of age, and is almost white, and called by those who know him Garland's George. Witness my hand and seal, this 13th day of November A.D. 1855.

ANNE P. GARLAND
Witness: JOHN WICKHAM
WILLIS L. WILLIAMS.

In St. Louis Circuit Court, October Term, 1855.
15 November 1855.
State of Missouri, County of St. Louis.

BE IT REMEMBERED, that on this fifteenth day of November, eighteen hundred and fifty-five, in open court came John Wickham and Willis L. Williams, these two subscribing witnesses, examined under oath to that effect, proved the execution and acknowledgment of said deed by Anne P. Garland to Lizzie and her son George, which said proof of acknowledgment is entered on the record of the court of that day.

In testimony whereof I hereto set my hand and affix the seal of said court, at office in the City of St. Louis, the day and year last aforesaid.

WM. J. HAMMOND, *Clerk.*

State of Missouri, County of St. Louis.

I, WM. J. HAMMOND, Clerk of the Circuit Court within and for the county aforesaid, certify the foregoing to be a true copy of a deed of emancipation from Anne P. Garland to Lizzie and her son George, as fully as the same remain in my office. In testimony whereof I hereto set my hand and affix the seal of said court, at the office in the City of St. Louis, this fifteenth day of November, 1855.

Wm. J. Hammond, *Clerk.*
By Wm. A. Pennington, D.C.

State of Missouri, County of St. Louis.

I, the undersigned Recorder of said county, certify that the foregoing instrument of writing was filed for record in my office on the 14th day of November, 1855; it is truly recorded in Book No. 169, page 288.

Witness my hand and official seal, date last aforesaid.

C. Keemle, *Recorder.*

IV

In the Family of Senator Jefferson Davis

THE TWELVE hundred dollars with which I purchased the freedom of myself and son I consented to accept only as a loan. I went to work in earnest, and in a short time repaid every cent that was so kindly advanced by my lady patrons of St. Louis. All this time my husband was a source of trouble to me, and a burden as well.

Too close occupation with my needle had its effects upon my health, and feeling exhausted with work, I determined to make a change. I had a conversation with Mr. Keckley; informed him that since he persisted in dissipation we must separate[1]; that I was going north, and that I should never live with him again, at least until I had good evidence of his reform. He was rapidly debasing himself, and although I was willing to work for him, I was not willing to share his degradation. Poor man; he had his faults, but over these faults death has drawn a veil. My husband is now sleeping in his grave, and in the silent grave I would bury all unpleasant memories of him.

I left St. Louis in the spring of 1860, taking the cars

[1]Though she was as discreet about the failings of her husband in her life as she is in her book, most sources indicate that James Keckley was an alcoholic.

direct for Baltimore, where I stopped six weeks, attempting to realize a sum of money by forming classes of young colored women, and teaching them my system of cutting and fitting dresses. The scheme was not successful, for after six weeks of labor and vexation, I left Baltimore with scarcely money enough to pay my fare to Washington.

Arriving in the capital, I sought and obtained work at two dollars and a half per day. However, as I was notified that I could only remain in the city ten days without obtaining a license to do so, such being the law, and as I did not know to whom to apply to for assistance, I was very troubled. I had to have someone vouch to the authorities that I was a free woman. My means were too scanty, and my profession much too precarious to warrant my purchasing a license. In my perplexity I called on a lady for whom I was sewing, Miss Ringold, a member of General Mason's family, from Virginia. I stated my case, and she kindly volunteered to render me all the assistance in her power. She called on Mayor Burritt with me, and Miss Ringold succeeded in making an arrangement for me to remain in Washington without paying the sum required for a license; moreover, I was not to be molested. I rented apartments in a good locality, and soon had a good run of custom.

The summer passed, winter came, and I was still in Washington. Mrs. Davis, wife of Senator Jefferson Davis, came from the South in November of 1860 with her husband. Learning that Mrs. Davis wanted a modiste,[2] I presented myself, and was employed by her on the recommendation of one of my patrons and her intimate friend, Mrs. Captain Hetsill. I went to the house to work, but finding that they were such late risers, and as I had to fit many dresses on Mrs. Davis, I told her that I should prefer giving half the day to her, working the other in my own room for some of my other lady patrons. Mrs. D. consented to the proposition, and it was arranged that I should come to her own house every day after noon.

It was the winter before the breaking out of that fierce and bloody war between the two sections of the country; as Mr. Davis occupied a leading position, his house was the resort of politicians and statesmen from the South. Almost every night, as I learned from the servants and other members of the family, secret meetings were held at the house; and some of these meetings were protracted to a very late hour. The prospects of war were freely discussed in my presence by Mr. and Mrs. Davis and their friends. The holidays were approaching, and Mrs. Davis kept me busy in manufacturing articles of dress for herself and children. She desired to present Mr. Davis on Christmas with a handsome dressing gown. The material was purchased, and for weeks the work had been under

[2]Modiste: Unlike tailors and seamstresses who merely made clothing, a modiste was also a designer and fashion expert. Keckley's use of the term is appropriate with her description of her own careful screening of clients and her later refusal to "cut and fit" a dress for President Johnson's daughter.

way. Christmas Eve came, and the gown had been laid aside so often that it was still unfinished. I saw that Mrs. D. was anxious to have it completed, so I volunteered to remain and work on it. Wearily, the hours dragged on, but there was no rest for my busy fingers. I persevered in my task, notwithstanding my head was aching. Mrs. Davis was busy in the adjoining room, arranging the Christmas tree for the children. I looked at the clock, and the hands pointed to a quarter of twelve. I was arranging the cords on the gown when the senator came in; he looked somewhat careworn, and his step seemed to be a little nervous. He leaned against the door, and expressed his admiration of the Christmas tree, but there was no smile on his face. Turning round, he saw me sitting in the adjoining room, and quickly exclaimed:

"That you, Lizzie! Why are you here so late? Still at work; I hope that Mrs. Davis is not too exacting!"

"No, sir," I answered. "Mrs. Davis was very anxious to have this gown finished tonight, and I volunteered to remain and complete it."

"Well, well, the case must be urgent," and he came slowly toward me, took the gown in his hand, and asked the color of the silk, as he said the gaslight was so deceptive to his old eyes.

"It is a drab changeable silk, Mr. Davis," I answered; and might have added that it was rich and handsome, but did not, well knowing that he would make the discovery in the morning.

He smiled curiously, but turned and walked from

the room without another question. He inferred that the gown was for him, that it was to be the Christmas present from his wife, and he did not wish to destroy the pleasure that she would experience in believing that the gift would prove a surprise. In this respect, as in many others, he always appeared to me as a thoughtful, considerate man in the domestic circle. As the clock struck twelve, I finished the gown, little dreaming of the future that was before it. It was worn, I have not the shadow of a doubt, by Mr. Davis during the stormy years that he was the president of the Confederate States.

The holidays passed, and before the close of January the war was discussed in Mr. Davis's family as an event certain to happen in the future. Mrs. Davis was warmly attached to Washington, and I often heard her say that she disliked the idea of breaking up old associations, and going south to suffer from trouble and deprivation. One day, while discussing the question in my presence with one of her intimate friends, she exclaimed: "I would rather remain in Washington and be kicked about, than go south and be Mrs. President." Her friend expressed surprise at the remark and Mrs. Davis insisted that the opinion was an honest one. While dressing her one day, she said to me: "Lizzie, you are so very handy that I should like to take you south with me."

"When do you go south, Mrs. Davis?" I inquired.

"Oh, I cannot tell just now, but it will be soon. You know there is going to be war, Lizzie?"

"No!"

"But I tell you yes."

"Who will go to war?" I asked.

"The North and South," was her ready reply.

"The Southern people will not submit to the humiliating demands of the Abolition party; they will fight first."

"And which do you think will whip?"

"The South, of course. The South is impulsive, is in earnest, and the Southern soldiers will fight to conquer. The North will yield, when it sees the South is in earnest, rather than engage in a long and bloody war."

"But, Mrs. Davis, are you certain that there will be war?"

"Certain!—I know it. You had better go south with me; I will take good care of you. Besides, when the war breaks out, the colored people will suffer in the North. The Northern people will look upon them as the cause of the war, and I fear, in their exasperation, will be inclined to treat you harshly. Then, I may come back to Washington in a few months, and live in the White House. The Southern people talk of choosing Mr. Davis for their president. In fact, it may be considered settled that he will be their president. As soon as we go south and secede from the other states, we will raise an army and march on Washington, and then I shall live in the White House."

I was bewildered with what I heard. I had served Mrs. Davis faithfully, and she had learned to place the greatest confidence in me. At first I was almost tempted to go south with her, for her reasoning seemed plausible. At the time the conversation was closed, with my promise to consider the question.

I thought over the question much, and the more I thought, the less inclined I felt to accept the proposition so kindly made by Mrs. Davis. I knew the North to be strong, and believed that the people would fight for the flag that they pretended to venerate so highly. The Republican party had just emerged from a heated campaign, flushed with victory, and I could not think that the hosts composing the party would quietly yield all they had gained in the presidential canvass. A show of war from the South, I felt, would lead to actual war in the North; and with the two sections bitterly arrayed against each other, I preferred to cast my lot among the people of the North.

I parted with Mrs. Davis kindly, half promising to join her in the South if further deliberation should induce me to change my views. A few weeks before she left Washington, I made two chintz[3] wrappers for her. She said that she must give up expensive dressing for a while; and that she, with the Southern people, now that war was imminent, must learn to practice lessons of economy. She left some fine needlework in my

[3]Chintz: An inexpensive cotton print fabric, used today more often for draperies or furniture coverings. Keckley notes that it was one of these less expensive dressing gowns that was later exhibited as the disguise Jefferson Davis reportedly wore when he tried to escape capture after the fall of the Confederate capital at Richmond.

hands, which I finished, and forwarded to her at Montgomery, Alabama, in the month of June, through the assistance of Mrs. Emory, one of her oldest and best friends.

Since bidding them good-bye at Washington, early in the year 1860, I have never met any of the Davis family. Years of excitement, years of bloodshed, and hundreds of thousands of graves intervene between the months I spent in the family and now. The years have brought many changes; and in view of these terrible changes even I, who was once a slave, who have been punished with the cruel lash, who have experienced the heart and soul tortures of a slave's life, can say to Mr. Jefferson Davis, "Peace! you have suffered! Go in peace."

In the winter of 1865 I was in Chicago, and one day visited the great charity fair held for the benefit of the families of those soldiers who were killed or wounded during the war. In one part of the building was a wax figure of Jefferson Davis, wearing over his other garments the dress in which it was reported that he was captured. There was always a great crowd around this figure, and I was naturally attracted toward it. I worked my way to the figure, and in examining the dress made the pleasing discovery that it was one of the chintz wrappers that I had made for Mrs. Davis, a short time before she departed from Washington for the South. When it was announced that I recognized the dress as one that I had made for the wife of the late Confederate president, there was great cheering and

"I thought your Government was more magnanimous than to hunt down *women* and children."

Jefferson Davis, as caricatured in his attempt to elude capture by the Union army

Courtesy Illinois State Historical Library

excitement, and I at once became an object of the deepest curiosity. Great crowds followed me, and in order to escape from the embarrassing situation I left the building.

I believe it now is pretty well established that Mr. Davis had on a waterproof cloak instead of a dress, as first reported, when he was captured. This does not invalidate any portion of my story. The dress on the wax figure at the fair in Chicago unquestionably was one of the chintz wrappers that I made for Mrs. Davis in Washington; and I infer, since it was not found on the body of the fugitive president of the South, it was taken from the trunks of Mrs. Davis, captured at the same time. Be this as it may, the coincidence is none the less striking and curious.

Jeff. Davis at Bryan Hall.

I hereby certify that I, Elizabeth Keckley, was originally dress-maker for Mrs. Jefferson Davis; that I have recently been dress-maker for Mrs. President Lincoln, and have attended her from Washington to Chicago; that I have seen the figure of Jefferson Davis now on exhibition at Trophy Hall, and recognize the *dress* upon said figure as one made by me for Mrs. Jefferson Davis, and worn by her. ELIZABETH KECKLEY.

Chicago, June 6th, 1865.

Witnesses: F. P. Fisher, Mrs. C. A. Lamb, Mrs. J. B. Bradwell.

"I hereby certify . . . "

From the Chicago Evening Journal, *7 June 1865*

V

My Introduction to Mrs. Lincoln

EVER SINCE arriving in Washington I had a very great desire to work for the ladies of the White House, and to accomplish this end I was ready to make almost any sacrifice consistent with propriety. Work came in slowly, and I was beginning to feel very much embarrassed, for I did not know how I was to meet the bills staring me in the face. It is true, the bills were small, but then they were formidable to me, who had little or nothing to pay them with. While I was in this situation, I called at the Ringolds', where I met Mrs. Captain Lee. Mrs. L. was in a state bordering on excitement, as the great event of the season, the dinner party given in honor of the Prince of Wales, was soon to come off, and she must have a dress suitable for the occasion. The silk had been purchased, but a dressmaker had not yet been found. Miss Ringold recommended me, and I then received the order to make the dress.

When I called on Mrs. Lee the next day, her husband was in the room, and handing me a roll of bank bills, amounting to one hundred dollars, he requested me to purchase the trimmings, and to spare no expense in making a selection. With the money in my pocket I went out in the street, entered the store of

Harper & Mitchell, and asked to look at their laces. Mr. Harper waited on me himself, and was polite and kind. When I asked permission to carry the laces to Mrs. Lee, in order to learn whether she could approve my selection or not, he gave a ready assent. When I reminded him that I was a stranger, and that the goods were valuable, he remarked that he was not afraid to trust me—that he believed my face was the index to an honest heart.

It was pleasant to be spoken to thus, and I shall never forget the kind words of Mr. Harper. I often recall them, for they are associated with the dawn of a brighter period in my dark life. I purchased the trimmings, and Mr. Harper allowed me a commission of twenty-five dollars on the purchase. The dress was done in time, and it gave complete satisfaction. Mrs. Lee attracted great attention at the dinner party, and her elegant dress proved a good card for me. I received numerous orders, and was relieved from all pecuniary embarrassments. One of my patrons was Mrs. General McClean, a daughter of General Sumner. One day when I was very busy, Mrs. McC. drove up to my apartments, came in where I was engaged with my needle, and in her emphatic way said:

"Lizzie, I am invited to dine at Willard's[1] on next

[1]The Willard Hotel, located on the corner of Fourteenth and Pennsylvania, was a gathering place for the Washington in-crowd. President and Mrs. Lincoln stayed there before the inaugural. It is reported that the Willard brothers sometimes fed fifteen hundred people in one day.

Sunday, and positively I have not a dress fit to wear on the occasion. I have just purchased material, and you must commence work on it right away."

"But Mrs. McClean," I replied, "I have more work now promised than I can do. It is impossible for me to make a dress for you to wear on Sunday next."

"Pshaw! Nothing is impossible. I must have the dress made by Sunday," and she spoke with some impatience.

"I am sorry," I began, but she interrupted me.

"Now don't say no again. I tell you that you must make the dress. I have often heard you say that you would like to work for the ladies of the White House. Well, I have it in my power to obtain you this privilege. I know Mrs. Lincoln well, and you shall make a dress for her provided you finish mine in time to wear at dinner on Sunday."

The inducement was the best that could have been offered. I would undertake the dress if I should have to sit up all night—every night—to make my pledge good. I sent out and employed assistants, and, after much worry and trouble, the dress was completed to the satisfaction of Mrs. McClean. It appears that Mrs. Lincoln had upset a cup of coffee on the dress she designed wearing on the evening of the reception after the inauguration of Abraham Lincoln as president of the United States, which rendered it necessary that she should have a new one for the occasion. On asking Mrs. McClean who her dressmaker was, that lady promptly informed her, "Lizzie Keckley."

"Lizzie Keckley? The name is familiar to me. She used to work for some of my lady friends in St. Louis, and they spoke well of her. Can you recommend her to me?"

"With confidence. Shall I send her to you?"

"If you please. I shall feel under many obligations for your kindness."

The next Sunday Mrs. McClean sent me a message to call at her house at four o'clock p.m., that day. As she did not state why I was to call, I determined to wait till Monday morning.

Monday morning came, and nine o'clock found me at Mrs. McC.'s house. The streets of the capital were thronged with people, for this was Inauguration Day. A new president, a man of the people from the broad prairie of the West, was to accept the solemn oath of office; was to assume the responsibilities attached to the high position of chief magistrate of the United States. Never was such deep interest felt in the inauguration proceedings as was felt today; for threats of assassination had been made, and every breeze from the south came heavily laden with the rumors of war. Around Willard's hotel swayed an excited crowd, and it was with the utmost difficulty that I worked my way to the house on the opposite side of the street, occupied by the McCleans. Mrs. McClean was out, but presently an aide of General McClean's staff called, and informed me that I was wanted at Willard's. I crossed the street, and on entering the hotel was met by Mrs. McClean, who greeted me:

A section of Pennsylvania Avenue, including the Harper & Mitchell store

Courtesy Historical Society of Washington, D.C

Willard Hotel, Washington, D.C.
Courtesy Willard Inter-Continental Washington

"Lizzie, why did you not come yesterday, as I requested? Mrs. Lincoln wanted to see you, but I fear that now you are too late."

"I am sorry, Mrs. McClean. You did not say what you wanted with me yesterday, so I judged that this morning would do as well."

"You should have come yesterday," she insisted. "Go up to Mrs. Lincoln's room"—giving me the number—"she may find use for you yet."

With a nervous step I passed on, and knocked at Mrs. Lincoln's door. A cheery voice bade me come in, and a lady, inclined to stoutness, about forty years of age, stood before me.

"You are Lizzie Keckley, I believe." I bowed assent. "The dressmaker that Mrs. McClean recommended."

"Yes, madam."

"Very well; I have not time to talk to you now, but would like to have you call at the White House, at eight o'clock tomorrow morning, where I shall then be."

I bowed myself out of the room, and returned to my apartments. The day passed slowly, for I could not help but speculate in relation to the appointed interview for the morrow. My long-cherished hope was about to be realized, and I could not rest.

Tuesday morning, at eight o'clock, I crossed the threshold of the White House for the first time. I was shown into a waiting room, and informed that Mrs. Lincoln was at breakfast. While in the waiting room, I found no less than three mantua-makers waiting for an interview with the wife of the new president. It seems that Mrs. Lincoln had told several of her lady friends that she had urgent need for a dressmaker and that each of these friends had sent her mantua-maker[2] to the White House. Hope fell at once. With so many rivals for the position sought after, I regarded my chances for success as extremely doubtful. I was the last one summoned to Mrs. Lincoln's presence. All the others had a hearing, and were dismissed. I went upstairs timidly, and entering the room with nervous step, discovered the wife of the president standing by a window, looking out, and engaged in lively conversation with a lady, a Mrs. Grimsly, as I afterward learned. Then Mrs. L. came forward, and greeted me warmly.

"You have come at last. Mrs. Keckley, who have you worked for in the city?"

"Among others, Mrs. Senator Davis has been one of my best patrons," was my reply.

"Mrs. Davis! So you have worked for her, have you? Of course you gave satisfaction; so far, good. Can you do my work?"

"Yes, Mrs. Lincoln," I replied immediately. "Will

[2]Mantua-maker: In the late eighteenth century, a mantua was a loose-fitting gown that generally opened in the front to reveal a nice petticoat. By the mid-nineteenth century, the term referred more exclusively to fashionable formal dresses, often adorned with ruffles and flounces, darts and ribbons, laces, bows, and other elaborate details. Only the most highly skilled and creative dressmakers could make these tightly fitted bodices and skirts, which used as much as ten yards of material.

Mary Todd Lincoln, 1862

Photograph by Mathew Brady; courtesy Missouri Historical Society

you have very much work for me to do for you?"

"That, Mrs. Keckley, will depend altogether upon your prices. I trust that your terms are reasonable. I cannot afford to be extravagant. We are just from the West, and are poor. If you do not charge too much, I shall be able to give you all my work."

"I do not think there will be any difficulty about charges, Mrs. Lincoln; my terms are reasonable."

"Well, if you will work cheap, you shall have plenty to do. I can't afford to pay big prices, so I frankly tell you so in the beginning."

The terms were satisfactorily arranged, and I measured Mrs. Lincoln, took the dress with me, a bright rose-colored moiré-antique, and returned the next day to fit it on her. A number of ladies were in the room, all making preparations for the levee[3] to come off on Friday night. These ladies, I learned, were relatives of Mrs. L.'s, Mrs. Edwards and Mrs. Kellogg, her own sisters, and Elizabeth Edwards and Julia Baker, her nieces.

Mrs. Lincoln this morning was dressed in a cashmere wrapper, quilted down the front; and she wore a simple headdress. The other ladies wore morning robes.

I was already hard at work on the dress, when I was

[3]Levee: Originally, a formal morning reception, often held in the private chambers of monarchs or titled gentry and restricted to men. In the United States, it came to mean a formal reception hosted by the president or high-ranking government officials at any time of day.

informed that the levee had been postponed from Friday night till Tuesday night. This, of course, gave me more time to complete my task. Mrs. Lincoln sent for me, and suggested some alteration in style, which was made. She also requested that I make a waist of blue watered silk for Mrs. Grimsly, as work on the dress would not require all my time.

Tuesday evening came, and I had taken the last stitches on the dress. I folded it and carried it to the White House, with the waist for Mrs. Grimsly. When I went upstairs, I found the ladies in a terrible state of excitement. Mrs. Lincoln was protesting that she could not go down, for the reason that she had nothing to wear.

"Mrs. Keckley, you have disappointed me—deceived me. Why do you bring my dress at this late hour?"

"Because I have just finished it, and I thought I should be in time."

"But you are not in time, Mrs. Keckley; you have bitterly disappointed me. I have no time now to dress, and, what is more, I will not dress, and go downstairs."

"I am sorry if I have disappointed you, Mrs. Lincoln, for I intended to be in time. Will you let me dress you? I can have you ready in a few minutes."

"No, I won't be dressed. I will stay in my room. Mr. Lincoln can go down with the other ladies."

"But there is plenty of time for you to dress, Mary," joined in Mrs. Grimsly and Mrs. Edwards. "Let Mrs.

Grand White House reception, 1865

From Frank Leslie's Illustrated Newspaper; *courtesy Library of Congress*

Keckley assist you, and she will soon have you ready."

Thus urged, she consented. I dressed her hair, and arranged the dress on her. It fitted nicely, and she was pleased. Mr. Lincoln came in, threw himself on the sofa, laughed with Willie and little Tad, and then commenced pulling on his gloves, quoting poetry all the while.

"You seem to be in a poetical mood tonight," said his wife.

"Yes, Mother, these are poetical times" was his pleasant reply. "I declare, you look charming in that dress. Mrs. Keckley has met with great success." And then he proceeded to compliment the other ladies.

Mrs. Lincoln looked elegant in her rose-colored moiré-antique. She wore a pearl necklace and had pearl earrings, pearl bracelets, and red roses in her hair. Mrs. Baker was dressed in lemon-colored silk; Mrs. Kellogg in a drab silk, ashes of rose; Mrs. Edwards in brown and black silk; Miss Edwards in crimson, and Mrs. Grimsly in blue watered silk. Just before starting downstairs, Mrs. Lincoln's lace handkerchief was the object of search. It had been displaced by Tad, who was mischievous and hard to restrain. The handkerchief found, all became serene. Mrs. Lincoln took the president's arm, and with smiling face led the train below. I was surprised at her grace and composure. I had heard so much in current and malicious report of her low life, of her ignorance and vulgarity, that I expected to see her embarrassed on this occasion. Report, I soon saw, was wrong. No queen, accustomed to the usages of royalty all her life, could have comported herself with more calmness and dignity than did the wife of the president. She was confident and self-possessed, and confidence always gives grace.[4]

This levee was a brilliant one, and the only one of the season. I became the regular modiste of Mrs. Lincoln. I made fifteen or sixteen dresses for her during the spring and early part of the summer, when she left Washington, spending the hot weather at Saratoga, Long Branch, and other places. In the meantime, I was employed by Mrs. Senator Douglas, one of the loveliest ladies that I ever met; Mrs. Secretary Welles; Mrs. Secretary Stanton, and others. Mrs. Douglas always dressed in deep mourning with excellent taste and several of the leading ladies of Washington society were extremely jealous of her superior attractions.

[4]Mary Todd was one of more than a dozen children reared by a Lexington, Kentucky, banker. While her family was middle class with pretensions to aristocracy (Dolly Todd, the wife of former President Madison, was a distant relative), they were not known as intellectuals, and many of them were slaveholders. That, combined with her reputation for being outspoken and having emotional outbursts, and having arrived in D.C. from the wilderness of Springfield, Illinois, fueled continual rumors that she was gauche and ill-prepared to be a first lady.

VI

Willie Lincoln's Deathbed

MRS. LINCOLN returned to Washington in November, and again duty called me to the White House. The war was now in progress, and every day brought stirring news from the front—the front, where the Gray opposed the Blue, where flashed the bright saber in the sunshine, where were heard the angry notes of battle, the deep roar of cannon, and the fearful rattle of musketry; where new graves were being made every day, where brother forgot a mother's early blessing and sought the life-blood of brother, and friend raised the deadly knife against friend.

Oh, the front, with its stirring battle-scenes! Yes! oh, the front, with its ghastly heaps of dead! The life of the nation was at stake; and when the land was full of sorrow, there could not be much gaiety at the capital. The days passed quietly with me. I soon learned that some people had an intense desire to penetrate the inner circle of the White House. No president and his family, heretofore occupying this mansion, ever excited so much curiosity as the present incumbents.

Mr. Lincoln had grown up in the wilds of the West, and evil report had said much of him and his wife.[1]

[1]"Evil report . . .": Kentucky-born President Lincoln was a Republican lawyer from the frontier state of Illinois, and his family

The polite world was shocked, and the tendency to exaggerate intensified curiosity. As soon as it was known that I was the modiste of Mrs. Lincoln, parties crowded around and affected friendship for me, hoping to induce me to betray the secrets of the domestic circle. One day a woman, I will not call her a lady, drove up to my rooms, gave me an order to make a dress, and insisted on partly paying me in advance. She called on me every day, and was exceedingly kind. When she came to take her dress away, she cautiously remarked:

"Mrs. Keckley, you know Mrs. Lincoln?"

"Yes."

"You are her modiste, are you not?"

"Yes."

"You know her very well; do you not?"

"I am with her every day or two."

"Don't you think you would have some influence with her?"

"I cannot say. Mrs. Lincoln, I presume, would listen to anything I should suggest, but whether she would be influenced by a suggestion of mine is another question."

"I am sure that you could influence her, Mrs. Keckley. Now listen; I have a proposition to make. I have a

---

was barely middle class, if that. Tidewater gentry of Washington, D.C., disdained Republicans, Yankees, and Westerners. Political party, geographical origins, and family origins combined to create expectations and rumors that the Lincolns were poor, gauche, and social upstarts.

great desire to become an inmate of the White House. I have heard so much of Mr. Lincoln's goodness that I should like to be near him; and if I can enter the White House no other way, I am willing to go as a menial. My dear Mrs. Keckley, will you not recommend me to Mrs. Lincoln as a friend of yours out of employment, and ask her to take me as a chambermaid? If you will do this, you shall be well rewarded. It may be worth several thousand dollars to you in time."

I looked at the woman in amazement. A bribe, and to betray the confidence of my employer! Turning to her with a glance of scorn, I said:

"Madam, you are mistaken in regard to my character. Sooner than betray the trust of a friend, I would throw myself into the Potomac River. I am not so base as that. Pardon me, but there is the door, and I trust that you will never enter my room again."

She sprang to her feet in deep confusion, and passed through the door, murmuring: "Very well; you will live to regret your action today."

"Never, never!" I exclaimed, and closed the door after her with a bang. I afterwards learned that this woman was an actress, and that her object was to enter the White House as a servant, learn its secrets, and then publish a scandal to the world. I do not give her name, for such publicity would wound the sensitive feelings of friends, who would have to share her disgrace, without being responsible for her faults.

I simply record the incident to show how I often was approached by unprincipled parties. It is not necessary to say that I indignantly refused every bribe offered.

The first public appearance of Mrs. Lincoln that winter was at the reception on New Year's Day. This reception was shortly followed by a brilliant levee. The day after the levee I went to the White House, and while fitting a dress to Mrs. Lincoln, she said:

"Lizabeth"—she had learned to drop the E—"Lizabeth, I have an idea. These are war times and we must be as economical as possible. You know the president is expected to give a series of state dinners every winter, and these dinners are very costly. Now, I want to avoid this expense; my idea is, that if I give three large receptions, the state dinners can be scratched from the programme. What do you think, Lizabeth?"

"I think that you are right, Mrs. Lincoln."

"I am glad to hear you say so. If I can make Mr. Lincoln take the same view of the case, I shall not fail to put the idea into practice."

Before I left her room that day, Mr. Lincoln came in. She at once stated the case to him. He pondered the question a few moments before answering.

"Mother, I am afraid your plan will not work."

"But it *will* work, if you will only determine that it *shall* work."

"It is breaking in on the regular custom," he mildly replied.

"But you forget, Father, these are war times, and old customs can be done away with for the once. The idea truly is much more economical, you must admit."

"Yes, Mother, but we must think of something besides economy."

"I do think of something else. Public receptions are more democratic than stupid state dinners—are more in keeping with the spirit of the institutions of our country, as you would say if called upon to make a stump speech. There are a great many strangers in the city, foreigners and others, whom we can entertain at our receptions, but whom we cannot invite to any of our dinners."

"I believe you are right, Mother. You argue the point well. I think that we shall have to decide on the receptions."

So the day was carried. The question was decided, and arrangements were made for the first reception. It now was January, and cards were issued for February.

The children, Tad and Willie, were constantly receiving presents.[2] Willie was so delighted with a little pony, that he insisted on riding it every day. The weather was changeable, and exposure resulted in a severe cold, which deepened into fever. He was very sick, and I was summoned to his bedside. It was sad to see the poor boy suffer. Always of a delicate constitution, he could not resist the strong inroads of the disease.

[2]Thomas (Tad) Lincoln was about eight years old and William Wallace (Willie) Lincoln was eleven. The Lincolns were known as indulgent parents who appreciated those who appreciated their children.

The days dragged wearily by, and he grew weaker and more shadow-like. He was his mother's favorite child, and she doted on him. It grieved her heart sorely to see him suffer. When able to be about, he was almost constantly by her side.

When I would go in her room, almost always I found blue-eyed Willie there, reading from an open book, or curled up in a chair with pencil and paper in hand.

He had decidedly a literary taste, and was a studious boy. A short time before his death he wrote this simple little poem:

Washington D.C.,
30 October 1861.

DEAR SIR: I enclose you my first attempt at poetry.

Yours truly,
WM. W. LINCOLN.

To the Editor of the National Republican.

LINES
ON THE DEATH OF
COLONEL EDWARD BAKER[3]

There was no patriot like Baker,
So noble and so true;
He fell as a soldier on the field,
His face to the sky of blue.

[3]Edward D. Baker had been a close friend of Abraham Lincoln since his days in Springfield, Illinois. The Lincolns had named their second son after him. Colonel Baker had spent the afternoon at the White House the day before he was killed at the Battle of Ball's Bluff.

His voice is silent in the hall
Which oft his presence graced;
No more he'll hear the loud acclaim
Which rang from place to place.

No squeamish notions filled his breast,
The Union was his theme;
No surrender and no compromise,
His day-thought and night's dream.

His Country has *her* part to pay
To'rds those he has left behind;
His widow and his children all,
She must always keep in mind.

Finding that Willie continued to grow worse, Mrs. Lincoln determined to withdraw her cards of invitation and postpone the reception. Mr. Lincoln thought that the cards had better not be withdrawn. At least he advised that the doctor be consulted before any steps were taken. Accordingly, Dr. Stone was called in. He pronounced Willie better, and said that there was every reason for an early recovery. He thought, since the invitations had been issued, it would be best to go on with the reception. Willie, he insisted, was in no immediate danger. Mrs. Lincoln was guided by these counsels, and no postponement was announced. On the evening of the reception, Willie was suddenly taken worse. His mother sat by his bedside a long while, holding his feverish hand in her own, and watching his labored breathing. The doctor claimed there was no cause for alarm. I arranged Mrs. Lincoln's hair, then assisted her to dress. Her dress was white satin, trimmed with black lace. The trail was very long, and as she swept through the room, Mr. Lincoln was standing with his back to the fire, his hands behind him, and his eyes on the carpet. His face wore a thoughtful, solemn look. The rustling of the satin dress attracted his attention. He looked at it a few moments; then, in his quaint, quiet way remarked—

"Whew! our cat has a long tail tonight."

Mrs. Lincoln did not reply. The president added:

"Mother, it is my opinion, if some of that tail was nearer the head, it would be in better style"; and he glanced at her bare arms and neck. She had a beautiful neck and arm, and low dresses were becoming to her. She turned away with a look of offended dignity, and presently took the president's arm, and both went downstairs to their guests, leaving me alone with the sick boy.

The reception was a large and brilliant one, and the rich notes of the Marine Band in the apartments below came to the sickroom in soft, subdued murmurs, like the wild, faint sobbing of far-off spirits. Some of the young people had suggested dancing, but Mr. Lincoln met the suggestion with an emphatic veto. The brilliance of the scene could not dispel the sadness that rested upon the face of Mrs. Lincoln. During the evening she came upstairs several times, and stood by the bedside of the suffering boy. She loved him with a mother's heart, and her anxiety was great.

The night passed slowly; morning came, and Willie

was worse. He lingered a few days, and died. God called the beautiful spirit home, and the house of joy was turned into the house of mourning. I was worn out with watching, and was not in the room when Willie died, but was immediately sent for. I assisted in washing him and dressing him, and then laid him on the bed, when Mr. Lincoln came in. I never saw a man so bowed down with grief.[4] He came to the bed, lifted the cover from the face of his child, gazed at it long and earnestly, murmuring, "My poor boy, he was too good for this earth. God has called him home. I know that he is much better off in heaven, but then we loved him so. It is hard, hard to have him die!"

Great sobs choked his utterance. He buried his head in his hands, and his tall frame was convulsed with emotion. I stood at the foot of the bed, my eyes full of tears, looking at the man in silent, awe-stricken wonder. His grief unnerved him, and made him a weak, passive child.

I did not dream that his rugged nature could be so moved. I shall never forget those solemn moments—genius and greatness weeping over love's idol lost. There is a grandeur as well as a simplicity about the picture that will never fade. With me it is immortal—I really believe that I shall carry it with me across the dark, mysterious river of death.

[4]Not only were the Lincolns doting parents, but Willie was the second son who had died in childhood. Their son Edward Baker Lincoln had died after a brief illness shortly after his fourth birthday.

Mrs. Lincoln's grief was inconsolable. The pale face of her dead boy threw her into convulsions. Around him love's tendrils had been twined, and now that he was dressed for the tomb, it was like tearing the tendrils out of the heart by their roots. Willie, she often said, if spared by Providence, would be the hope and stay of her old age. But Providence had not spared him. The light faded from his eyes, and the death-dew had gathered on his brow.

In one of her paroxysms of grief the president kindly bent over his wife, took her by the arm, and gently led her to the window. With a stately, solemn gesture, he pointed to the lunatic asylum.

"Mother, do you see that large white building on the hill yonder? Try and control your grief, or it will drive you mad, and we may have to send you there."

Mrs. Lincoln was so completely overwhelmed with sorrow that she did not attend the funeral.

Willie was laid to rest in the cemetery, and the White House was draped in mourning. Black crepe everywhere met the eye, contrasting strangely with the gay and brilliant colors of a few days before. Party dresses were laid aside, and everyone who crossed the threshold of the presidential mansion spoke in subdued tones when they thought of the sweet boy at rest—

"Under the sod and the dew."

Previous to this I had lost my son.[5] Leaving Wilber-

[5]Keckley's son, George Kirkland, had enlisted in the Union army as a white man. He was killed 10 August 1861 at the Battle of Wilson's Creek.

force, he went to the battlefield with the three-month troops,[6] and was killed in Missouri—found his grave on the battlefield where the gallant General Lyon fell. It was a sad blow to me, and the kind, womanly letter that Mrs. Lincoln wrote to me when she heard of my bereavement was full of golden words of comfort.

Nathaniel Parker Willis,[7] the genial poet, now sleeping in his grave, wrote this beautiful sketch of Willie Lincoln, after the sad death of the bright-eyed boy:

THIS LITTLE FELLOW had his acquaintances among his father's friends, and I chanced to be one of them. He never failed to seek me out in the crowd, shake hands, and make some pleasant remark; and this, in a boy of ten years of age, was, to say the least, endearing to a stranger. But he had more than mere affectionateness. His self-possession—*aplomb,* as the French call it—was extraordinary. I was one day passing the White House, when he was outside with a play-fellow on the sidewalk. Mr. Seward drove in, with

[6]Three-month troops (aka "ninety-day men"): Enlisted for that amount of time. Especially at the beginning of the war, many citizens and state officials (on both sides) were convinced the war would be swiftly won. Federal officials and Lincoln were not so sure and tried to encourage longer enlistments. But a great many of those first seventy-five thousand who answered Lincoln's 15 April 1861 call were "three-month troops."

[7]Nathaniel Parker Willis (1806–1867) was a popular nineteenth-century poet and journalist. He founded *American Monthly Magazine* and contributed travel sketches of his European tours to various periodicals. The brother of best-selling author Fanny Fern (Sara Payson Willis), N.P. Willis was a frequent visitor to the Lincoln household.

Prince Napoleon[8] and two of his *suite* in the carriage; and, in a mock-heroic way—terms of intimacy evidently existing between the boy and the secretary—the official gentleman took off his hat, and the Napoleon did the same, all making the young Prince President a ceremonious salute. Not a bit staggered with the homage, Willie drew himself up to his full height, took off his little cap with graceful self-possession, and bowed down formally to the ground, like a little ambassador. They drove past, and he went on unconcernedly with his play: the impromptu readiness and good judgment being clearly a part of his nature. His genial and open expression of countenance was nonetheless ingenuous and fearless for a certain tincture of fun; and it was in this mingling of qualities that he so faithfully resembled his father.

With all the splendor that was around this little fellow in his new home, he was so bravely and beautifully *himself*—and that only. A wild flower transplanted from the prairie to the hothouse, he retained his prairie habits, unalterably pure and simple, till he died. His leading trait seemed to be a fearless and kindly frankness, willing that everything should be as different as it pleased, but resting unmoved in his own conscious single-heartedness. I found I was studying him irresistibly, as one of the sweet problems of childhood that the world is blessed with in rare places; and the news of his death (I was absent from Washington, on a visit to my own children, at the time) came to me like a knell heard unexpectedly at a merry-making.

On the day of the funeral I went before the hour, to take

[8]Prince Napoleon (Napoleon Joseph Charles Paul Bonaparte), 1822–1891, was son of Jerome, brother of Napoleon I. He toured the United States in 1861, visited Lincoln, and was given safe passage to tour Confederate states.

a near farewell look at the dear boy; for they had embalmed him to send home to the West—to sleep under the sod of his own valley—and the coffin-lid was to be closed before the service. The family had just taken their leave of him, and the servants and nurses were seeing him for the last time—and with tears and sobs wholly unrestrained, for he was loved like an idol by every one of them. He lay with eyes closed—his brown hair parted as we had known it—pale in the slumber of death; but otherwise unchanged, for he was dressed as if for the evening, and held in one of his hands, crossed upon his breast, a bunch of exquisite flowers—a message coming from his mother, while we were looking upon him, that those flowers might be preserved for her. She was lying in her bed, worn out with grief and over-watching.

The funeral was very touching. Of the entertainments in the East Room, the boy had been—for those who now assembled more especially—a most life-giving variation. With his bright face, and his apt greetings and replies, he was remembered in every part of that crimson-curtained hall, built only for pleasure—of all the crowds, each night, certainly the one least likely to be death's first mark. He was his father's favorite. They were intimates—often seen hand in hand. And there sat the man, with a burden on his brain at which the world marvels—bent now with the load at both heart and brain—staggering under a blow like the taking from him of his child! His men of power sat around him—McClellan, with a moist eye when he bowed to the prayer, as I could see from where I stood; and Chase and Seward with their austere features at work; and senators, and ambassadors, and soldiers, all struggling with their tears—great hearts sorrowing with the president as a stricken man and a brother. That God may give him strength for all his burdens is, I am sure, at present the prayer of a nation.

This sketch was very much admired by Mrs. Lincoln. I copy it from the scrapbook in which she pasted it, with many tears, with her own hands.

VII

Washington in 1862–1863

In the summer of 1862, freedmen began to flock into Washington from Maryland and Virginia.[1] They came with a great hope in their hearts and with all their worldly goods on their backs. Fresh from the bonds of slavery, fresh from the benighted regions of the plantation, they came to the capital looking for liberty, and many of them not knowing it when they found it.

Many good friends reached forth kind hands, but the North is not warm and impulsive. For one kind word spoken, two harsh ones were uttered; there was something repelling in the atmosphere, and the bright joyous dreams of freedom to the slave faded—were

[1]Long before the Emancipation Proclamation of 1863, numerous slaves had taken advantage of the turmoil to escape to the North. Others were freed when the Union army captured territory. The government declared captured slaves (like the animals, crops, real estate, and other Confederate property) "contraband" of the war. Some worked (with and without pay) for the military. But most were left to fend for themselves. Communities, particularly those bordering the Confederacy, were inundated with penniless and homeless refugees, but few people would employ them. Government agencies were exceedingly slow to respond to their plights. Keckley organized her friends, most of whom were women with whom she attended the Fifteenth Street Presbyterian Church, to help feed, clothe, and employ the newly freed slaves.

sadly altered, in the presence of that stern, practical mother, reality. Instead of flowery paths, days of perpetual sunshine, and bowers hanging with golden fruit, the road was rugged and full of thorns, the sunshine was eclipsed by shadows, and the mute appeals for help too often were answered by cold neglect. Poor dusky children of slavery, men and women of my own race—the transition from slavery to freedom was too sudden for you! The bright dreams were too rudely dispelled; you were not prepared for the new life that opened before you, and the great masses of the North learned to look upon your helplessness with indifference—learned to speak of you as an idle, dependent race. Reason should have prompted kinder thoughts. Charity is ever kind.

One fair summer evening, I was walking the streets of Washington, accompanied by a friend, when a band of music was heard in the distance. We wondered what it could mean, and curiosity prompted us to find out its meaning. We quickened our steps, and discovered that it came from the house of Mrs. Farnham. The yard was brilliantly lighted, ladies and gentlemen were moving about, and the band was playing some of its sweetest airs. We approached the sentinel on duty at the gate, and asked what was going on. He told us that it was a festival given for the benefit of the sick and wounded soldiers in the city. This suggested an idea to me.

If the white people can give festivals to raise funds for the relief of suffering soldiers, why should not the well-to-do colored people go to work to do something for the benefit of the suffering blacks? I could not rest. The thought was ever present with me, and the next Sunday I made a suggestion in the colored church[2] that a society of colored people be formed to labor for the benefit of the unfortunate freedmen. The idea proved popular, and in two weeks the "Contraband Relief Association" was organized, with forty working members.

In September of 1862, Mrs. Lincoln left Washington for New York, and requested me to follow her in a few days and join her at the Metropolitan Hotel. I was glad of the opportunity to do so, for I thought that in New York I would be able to do something in the interests of our society. Armed with credentials, I took the train for New York and went to the Metropolitan, where Mrs. Lincoln had secured accommodations for me. The next morning I told Mrs. Lincoln of my project; and she immediately headed my list with a subscription of two hundred dollars. I circulated among the colored people, and got them thoroughly interested in the subject, when I was called to Boston by Mrs. Lincoln, who wished to visit her son,

[2]The colored church: Keckley was a member of the Fifteenth Street Presbyterian Church, probably the most prestigious and politically active African American church in Washington, D.C. Most of the elite White House staff belonged to this congregation, which, from March 1864 to October 1866, during the Civil War, was pastored by the radical abolitionist, Henry Highland Garnet. Garnet is mentioned later as one of the African American leaders enlisted to help raise funds for Mary Lincoln's support.

Robert, attending college in that city[3]. I met Mr. Wendell Phillips,[4] and other Boston philanthropists who gave me all the assistance in their power.

We held a mass meeting at the Colored Baptist Church. Reverend Mr. Grimes, in Boston, raised a sum of money and organized there a branch society. The society was organized by Mrs. Grimes, wife of the pastor, assisted by Mrs. Martin, wife of Reverend Stella Martin. This branch of the main society, during the war, was able to send us over eighty large boxes of goods, contributed exclusively by the colored people of Boston. Returning to New York, we held a successful meeting at the Shiloh Church, Reverend Henry Highland Garnet, pastor.

The Metropolitan Hotel, at that time as now, employed colored help. I suggested the object of my mission to Robert Thompson, steward of the hotel, who immediately raised quite a sum of money among the dining-room waiters. Mr. Frederick Douglass[5] contributed two hundred dollars, besides lecturing for us. Other prominent colored men sent in liberal contributions. From England a large quantity of stores was received. Mrs. Lincoln made frequent contribu-

[3]Robert Todd Lincoln was attending Harvard College.

[4]A leader of the American Anti-Slavery Society, Phillips had been initally skeptical about Lincoln's presidency, but once convinced of his sincerity, he became a firm ally.

[5]Frederick Douglass had been a fugitive slave whose eloqence and courage led to a meteoric rise in abolitionist circles, ownership of internationally circulated newspapers, and national prominence as an African American spokesperson on every major issue.

tions, as also did the president. In 1863 I was re-elected president of the association, which office I continue to hold.

For two years after Willie's death, the White House was the scene of no fashionable display. The memory of the dead boy was duly respected.

In some things Mrs. Lincoln was an altered woman. Sometimes, when in her room, with no one present but myself, the mere mention of Willie's name would excite her emotion, and any trifling memento that recalled him would move her to tears. She could not bear to look upon his picture; and after his death she never crossed the threshold of the Guest's Room in which he died, or the Green Room in which he was embalmed. There was something supernatural in her dread of these things, and something that she could not explain. Tad's nature was the opposite of Willie's, and he was regarded as his father's favorite child. His black eyes fairly sparkled with mischief.

The war progressed, fair fields had been stained with blood, thousands of brave men had fallen, and thousands of eyes were weeping for the fallen at home. There were desolate hearthstones in the South as well as in the North, and as the people of my race watched the sanguinary struggle, the ebb and flow of the tide of battle, they lifted their faces Zionward, as if they hoped to catch a glimpse of the Promised Land beyond the sulphurous clouds of smoke that shifted now and then but to reveal ghastly rows of new-made graves. Sometimes the very life of the nation seemed to tremble with the fierce shock of arms. In 1863, the Confederates were flushed with victory, and sometimes it looked as if the proud flag of the Union, the glorious old Stars and Stripes, must yield half its nationality to the tri-barred flag that floated grandly over long columns of gray. These were sad, anxious days to Mr. Lincoln, and those who saw the man in privacy only could tell how much he suffered.

One day he came into the room where I was fitting a dress on Mrs. Lincoln. His step was slow and heavy, and his face sad. Like a tired child he threw himself upon a sofa, and shaded his eyes with his hands. He was a complete picture of dejection. Mrs. Lincoln, observing his troubled look, asked: "Where have you been, Father?"

"To the War Department," was the brief, almost sullen answer.

"Any news?"

"Yes, plenty of news, but no good news. It is dark, dark everywhere."

He reached forth one of his long arms, and took a small Bible from a stand near the head of the sofa, opened the pages, and soon was absorbed in reading them. A quarter of an hour passed, and on glancing at the sofa, the face of the president seemed more cheerful. The dejected look was gone; in fact, the countenance was lighted up with new resolution and hope. The change was so marked that I could not but wonder at it, and wonder led to the desire to know what book of the Bible afforded so much comfort.

Making the search for a missing article an excuse, I walked gently around the sofa, and looking into the open book, I discovered that Mr. Lincoln was reading that divine comforter, Job. He read with Christian eagerness, and the courage and hope that he derived from the inspired pages made him a new man. I almost imagined that I could hear the Lord speaking to him from out of the whirlwind of battle: "Gird up thy loins now like a man: I will demand of thee, and declare thou unto me." What a sublime picture was this! A ruler of a mighty nation going to the pages of the Bible with simple Christian earnestness for comfort and courage, and finding both in the darkest hours of a nation's calamity. Ponder it, O ye scoffers at God's Holy Word, and then hang your heads for very shame!

Frequent letters were received warning Mr. Lincoln of assassination, but he never gave a second thought to the mysterious warnings. The letters, however, sorely troubled his wife. She seemed to read impending danger in every rustling leaf, in every whisper of the wind.

"Where are you going now, Father?" she would say to him, as she observed him putting on his overshoes and shawl.

"I am going over to the War Department, Mother, to try and learn some news."

"But, Father, you should not go out alone. You know you are surrounded with danger."

"All imagination. What does anyone want to harm me for? Don't worry about me, Mother, as if I were a little child, for no one is going to molest me"; and with a confident, unsuspecting air he would close the door behind him, descend the stairs, and pass out to his lonely walk.

For weeks, when trouble was anticipated, friends of the president would sleep in the White House to guard him from danger. Robert would come home every few months, bringing new joy to the family circle. He was very anxious to quit school and enter the army, but the move was sternly opposed by his mother.

"We have lost one son, and his loss is as much as I can bear, without being called upon to make another sacrifice," she would say, when the subject was under discussion.

"But many a poor mother has given up all her sons," mildly suggested Mr. Lincoln, "and our son is not more dear to us than the sons of other people are to their mothers."

"That may be; but I cannot bear to have Robert exposed to danger. His services are not required in the field, and the sacrifice would be a needless one."

"The services of every man who loves his country are required in this war. You should take a liberal instead of a selfish view of the question, Mother."

Argument at last prevailed, and permission was granted Robert to enter the army. With the rank of captain and A.D.C.,[6] he went into the field, and he remained in the army until the very close of the war.

[6]Lincoln personally requested General U.S. Grant to assign Robert to his staff. A.D.C. probably stands for "aide de camp," but

I well recollect a little incident that gave me a clearer insight into Robert's character. He was at home at the time the Tom Thumb combination was at Washington[7]. The marriage of little Hop-o'-my-thumb—actually Charles Stratton—to Miss Warren created no little excitement, and even the people of Washington participated in the general curiosity. Some of Mrs. Lincoln's friends made her believe that it was the duty of Mrs. Lincoln to show some attention to the remarkable dwarfs. Tom Thumb had been caressed by royalty in the Old World, and why should not the wife of the president of his native country smile upon him also? Verily, duty is one of the greatest bugbears in life. A hasty reception was arranged, and cards of invitation issued. I had dressed Mrs. Lincoln, and she was ready to go below and receive her guests, when Robert entered his mother's room.

"You are at leisure this afternoon, are you not, Robert?"

Robert Lincoln was officially appointed as captain and assistant adjutant general of volunteers.

[7]Tom Thumb is a folk figure of very diminutive stature and a term often applied to male dwarfs amd pygmies. Charles Sherwood Stratton, a three-foot, four-inch, seventy-pound adult, was exhibited by P.T. Barnum as "Tom Thumb." Barnum orchestrated his marriage on 10 February 1863 to another little person, Lavinia Warren, into a national sensation, complete with an elaborate wedding at Grace Episcopal Church in New York City. Mary Lincoln was persuaded that it would be good public relations to acknowledge the national obsession with this couple by inviting them to stay at the White House and by hosting an informal reception as well.

"Yes, Mother."

"Of course, you will dress and come downstairs."

"No, Mother, I do not propose to assist in entertaining Tom Thumb. My notions of duty, perhaps, are somewhat different from yours."

Robert had a lofty soul, and he could not stoop to all of the follies and absurdities of the ephemeral current of fashionable life.

Mrs. Lincoln's love for her husband sometimes prompted her to act very strangely. She was extremely jealous of him, and if a lady desired to court her displeasure, she could select no surer way to do it than to pay marked attention to the president. These little jealous streaks often were a source of perplexity to Mr. Lincoln. If it was a reception for which they were dressing, he would come into her room to conduct her downstairs, and while pulling on his gloves ask, with a merry twinkle in his eyes:

"Well, Mother, who must I talk with tonight—shall it be Mrs. D.?"

"That deceitful woman! No, you shall not listen to her flattery."

"Well, then, what do you say to Miss C.?[8] She is too young and handsome to practice deceit."

"Young and handsome, you call her! You should not judge beauty for me. No, she is in league with Mrs. D., and you shall not talk with her."

"Well, Mother, I must talk with someone. Is there

[8]Probably Kate Chase, the daughter of Lincoln's Secretary of the Treasury, Salmon P. Chase.

Grand Presidential Party at the White House, 1862:
(from left) Mrs. George McClellan, Mary Todd Lincoln, and Mrs. Senator Crittenden

From Frank Leslie's Illustrated Newspaper, 22 *February 1862; courtesy University of Chicago Library*

anyone that you do not object to?" trying to button his glove, with a mock expression of gravity.

"I don't know as it is necessary that you should talk to anybody in particular. You know well enough, Mr. Lincoln, that I do not approve of your flirtations with silly women, just as if you were a beardless boy, fresh from school."

"But, Mother, I insist that I must talk with somebody. I can't stand around like a simpleton, and say nothing. If you will not tell me who I may talk with, please tell me who I may *not* talk with."

"There is Mrs. D. and Miss C. in particular. I detest them both. Mrs. B. also will come around you, but you need not listen to her flattery. These are the ones in particular."

"Very well, Mother; now that we have settled the question to your satisfaction, we will go downstairs"; and always with stately dignity, he proffered his arm and led the way.

VIII

Candid Opinions

Often Mr. and Mrs. Lincoln discussed the relations of Cabinet officers and gentlemen prominent in politics, in my presence. I soon learned that the wife of the president had no love for Mr. Salmon P. Chase, at that time secretary of the treasury. She was well versed in human character, was somewhat suspicious of those by whom she was surrounded, and often her judgment was correct. Her intuition about the sincerity of individuals was more accurate than that of her husband. She looked beyond, and read the reflection of action in the future.

Her hostility to Mr. Chase was very bitter. She claimed that he was a selfish politician instead of a true patriot, and warned Mr. Lincoln not to trust him too far. The daughter of the secretary was quite a belle in Washington, and Mrs. Lincoln, who was jealous of the popularity of others, had no desire to build up her social position through political favor to her father. Miss Chase, now Mrs. Senator Sprague, was a lovely woman, and was worthy of all the admiration she received. Mr. Lincoln was more confiding than his wife. He never suspected the fidelity of those who claimed to be his friends. Honest himself, and frank as a child, he never dreamed of questioning the sincerity of others.

"Father, I do wish that you would inquire a little into the motives of Chase," said his wife one day.

The president was lying carelessly upon a sofa, holding a newspaper in his hands. "Mother, you are too suspicious. I give you credit for sagacity, but you are disposed to magnify trifles. Chase is a patriot, and one of my best friends."

"Yes, one of your best friends because it is in his interest to be so. He is anything for Chase. If he thought he could make anything by it, he would betray you to-morrow."

"I fear that you are prejudiced against the man, Mother. I know that you do him injustice."

"Mr. Lincoln, you are either blind or will not see. I am not the only one that has warned you against him."

"True, I receive letters daily from all parts of the country, telling me not to trust Chase; but then these letters are written by the political enemies of the secretary, and it would be unjust and foolish to pay any attention to them."

"Very well, you will find out some day, if you live long enough, that I have read the man correctly. I only hope that your eyes may not be opened to the truth when it is too late." The president, as far as I could judge from his conversation with his wife, continued to confide in Mr. Chase to the time of his tragic death.

Mrs. Lincoln was especially severe on Mr. Wm. H. Seward, secretary of state. She but rarely lost an opportunity to say an unkind word of him. One morning I went to the White House somewhat earlier than usual.

Mr. Lincoln was sitting in a chair, reading a paper, and stroking with one hand the head of little Tad. I was basting a dress for Mrs. Lincoln. A servant entered, and handed the president a letter brought by a messenger.

He broke the seal, and when he had read the contents his wife asked: "Who is the letter from, Father?"

"Seward; I must go over and see him today."

"Seward! I wish you had nothing to do with that man. He cannot be trusted."

"You say the same of Chase. If I listened to you, I should soon be without a cabinet."

"Better be without it than to confide in some of the men that you do. Seward is worse than Chase. He has no principle."

"Mother, you are mistaken; your prejudices are so violent that you do not stop to reason. Seward is an able man, and the country as well as myself can trust him."

"Father, you are too honest for this world! You should have been born a saint. You will generally find it a safe rule to distrust a disappointed, ambitious politician. It makes me mad to see you sit still and let that hypocrite, Seward, twine you around his finger as if you were a skein of thread."

"It is useless to argue the question, Mother. You cannot change my opinion."

Mrs. Lincoln prided herself upon her ability to read character. She was shrewd and far-seeing, and had no patience with the frank, even the confiding nature of the president.

When Andrew Johnson was urged for military governor of Tennessee, Mrs. Lincoln bitterly opposed the appointment. "He is a demagogue," she said, almost fiercely, "and if you place him in power, Mr. Lincoln, mark my words, you will rue it some day."

General McClellan, when made commander-in-chief, was the idol of the soldiers. Never was a general more universally popular. "He is a humbug," remarked Mrs. Lincoln one day in my presence.

"What makes you think so, Mother?" inquired the president good-naturedly.

"Because he talks so much and does so little. If I had the power I would very soon take off his head, and put some energetic man in his place."

"But I regard McClellan as a patriot and an able soldier. He has been much embarrassed. The troops are raw, and the subordinate officers inclined to be rebellious. There are too many politicians in the army with shoulder-straps. McClellan is young and popular, and they are jealous of him. They will kill him off if they can."

"McClellan can make plenty of excuse for himself; therefore, he needs no advocate in you. If he would only do something, and not promise so much, I might learn to have a little faith in him. I tell you he is a humbug, and you will have to find some man to take his place, that is, if you wish to conquer the South."

Mrs. Lincoln could not tolerate General Grant. "He is a butcher," she would often say, "and is not fit to be at the head of an army."

"But he has been very successful in the field," argued the president.

"Yes, he generally manages to claim a victory, but such a victory! He loses two men to the enemy's one. He has no management, no regard for life. If the war should continue four years longer, and he should remain in power, he would depopulate the North. I could fight an army as well myself. According to his tactics, there is nothing under the heavens to do but to march a new line of men in front of the rebel breastworks to be shot down as fast as they take their position, and keep marching until the enemy grows tired of the slaughter. Grant, I repeat, is an obstinate fool and a butcher."

"Well, Mother, supposing that we give you command of the army," replied the president. "No doubt you would do much better than any general that has been tried." There was a twinkle in the eyes, and a ring of irony in the voice.

I have often heard Mrs. Lincoln say that if Grant should ever be elected president of the United States, she would desire to leave the country, and remain absent during his term of office.[1]

It was well-known that Mrs. Lincoln's brothers were in the Confederate army, and for this reason it was often charged that her sympathies were with the South. Those who made the hasty charge were never more widely mistaken.

[1]Grant was elected to the first of his two terms as president in 1868, so Mary Lincoln had to tolerate him as president (she survived until 1882).

One morning, on my way to the White House, I heard that Captain Alexander Todd, one of her brothers, had been killed. I did not like to inform Mrs. Lincoln of his death, judging that it would be painful news to her. I had been in her room but a few minutes when she said, with apparent unconcern, "Lizzie, I have just heard that one of my brothers has been killed in the war."

"I also heard the same, Mrs. Lincoln, but hesitated to speak of it, for fear the subject would be a painful one to you."

"You need not hesitate. Of course, it is but natural that I should feel for one so nearly related to me, but not to the extent that you suppose. He made his choice long ago. He decided against my husband, and through him against me. He has been fighting against us; and since he chose to be our deadly enemy, I see no special reason why I should bitterly mourn his death."

I felt relieved, and in subsequent conversations learned that Mrs. Lincoln had no sympathy for the South. "Why should I sympathize with the rebels," she would say; "are they not against me? They would hang my husband tomorrow if it were in their power, and perhaps gibbet me with him. How then can I sympathize with a people at war with me and mine?" She always objected to being thought Southern in feeling.

Mr. Lincoln was generous by nature, and though his whole heart was in the war, he could not but respect the valor of those opposed to him. His soul was too great for narrow, selfish views of partisanship. Brave by nature himself, he honored bravery in others, even his foes. Time and again I have heard him speak in the highest terms of the soldierly qualities of such brave Confederate generals as Lee, Stonewall Jackson, and Joseph E. Johnson. Jackson was his ideal soldier. "He is a brave, honest, and a Presbyterian soldier," were his words; "what a pity that we should have to fight such a gallant fellow! If we only had such a man to lead the armies of the North, the country would not be appalled with so many disasters."

As this is a rambling chapter, I will here record an incident showing his feeling toward Robert E. Lee. The very morning of the day on which he was assassinated, his son, Captain Robert Lincoln, came into the room with a portrait of General Lee in his hand. The president took the picture, laid it on a table before him, scanned the face thoughtfully, and said: "It is a good face; it is the face of a noble, noble, brave man. I am glad that the war is over at last." Looking up at Robert, he continued: "Well, my son, you have returned safely from the front. The war is now closed, and we soon will live in peace with the brave men that have been fighting against us. I trust that the era of good feeling has returned, and that henceforth we shall live in peace." His face was more cheerful than I had seen it for a long while, and he seemed to be in a generous, forgiving mood.

IX

Behind the Scenes

SOME OF the freedmen and freedwomen had exaggerated ideas of liberty. To them it was a beautiful vision, a land of sunshine, rest, and glorious promise. They flocked to Washington, and since their extravagant hopes were not realized, it was but natural that many of them should bitterly feel their disappointment. The colored people are wedded to associations, and when you destroy these, you destroy half of the happiness of their lives. They make a home, and are so fond of it that they prefer it, squalid though it be, to the comparative ease and luxury of a shifting, roaming life. Well, the emancipated slaves, in coming North, left old associations behind them, and the love for the past was so strong that they could not find much beauty in the new life so suddenly opened to them.

Thousands of the disappointed huddled together in camps, and fretted and pined like children for the "good old times." In visiting them in the interests of the Relief Society, of which I was president, they would crowd around me with pitiful stories of distress. Often I heard them declare that they would rather go back to slavery in the South, and be with their old masters, than to enjoy the freedom of the North. I believe they were sincere, since dependence had become a part of their second nature, and independence brought with it the cares and vexations of poverty.

I was very much amused one day at the grave complaints of a good old simple-minded woman, fresh from a life of servitude. She had never ventured beyond a plantation until coming North. The change was too radical for her, and she could not exactly understand it. She thought, as many others thought, that Mr. and Mrs. Lincoln were the government, and that the president and his wife had nothing to do but to supply the extravagant wants of everyone that applied to them. The wants of this old woman, however, were not very extravagant.

"Why, Missus Keckley," said she to me one day, "I is been here eight months, and Missus Lingom ain't even give me one shife. Bliss God, childen, if I had ar know dat de government, and Mister and Missus Government, was going to do dat ar way, I neber would 'ave comed here in God's wurld. My old missus us't gib me two shifes eber year."

I could not restrain a laugh at the grave manner in which this good old woman entered her protest. Her idea of freedom was two or more old shifts every year. Northern readers may not fully recognize the pith of the joke. On the Southern plantation, the mistress, according to established custom, every year made a present of certain undergarments to her slaves, articles which were always anxiously looked forward to, and thankfully received. The old woman had been in the habit of receiving annually two shifts from her mistress, and she thought the wife of the president of the United States very mean for overlooking this established custom of the plantation.

While some of the emancipated blacks pined for the old associations of slavery and refused to help themselves, others went to work with commendable energy, and planned with remarkable forethought. They built themselves cabins, and each family cultivated for itself a small patch of ground. The colored people are fond of domestic life, and with them domestication means happy children, a fat pig, a dozen or more chickens, and a garden. Whoever visits the Freedmen's Village now in the vicinity of Washington will discover all of these evidences of prosperity and happiness. Good teachers, white and colored, are employed, and whole brigades of bright-eyed dusky children are there taught the common branches of education. These children are studious, and the teachers inform me that their advancement is rapid. I number among my personal friends twelve colored girls employed as teachers in the schools at Washington.

The Colored Mission Sabbath School, established through the good influence of General Brown at the Fifteenth Street Presbyterian Church, is always an object of great interest to the residents of the capital, as well as to the hundreds of strangers visiting the city.

In 1864, the receptions again commenced at the White House. For the first two years of Mr. Lincoln's administration, the president selected a lady to join in the promenade with him, which left Mrs. Lincoln free to choose an escort from among the distinguished gentlemen that always surrounded her on such occasions. This custom at last was discontinued by Mrs. Lincoln.

"Lizabeth!"—I was sewing in her room, and she was seated in a comfortable armchair— "Lizabeth, I have been thinking over a little matter. As you are well aware, the president, at every reception, selects a lady to lead the promenade with him. Now it occurs to me that this custom is an absurd one. On such occasions our guests recognize the position of the president as first of all; consequently, he takes the lead in everything; well, now, if they recognize his position, they should also recognize mine. I am his wife, and should lead with him. And yet he offers his arm to any other lady in the room, making her first with him and placing me second. The custom is an absurd one, and I mean to abolish it. The dignity that I owe to my position, as Mrs. President, demands that I should not hesitate any longer to act."

Mrs. Lincoln kept her word. Ever after this, she either led the promenade with the president, or the president walked alone or with a gentleman. The change was much remarked, but the reason why it was made, I believe, was never generally known.

In 1864, much doubt existed in regard to the re-election of Mr. Lincoln, and the White House was besieged by all grades of politicians. Mrs. Lincoln was often blamed for having a certain class of men around her.

"I have an object in view, Lizabeth," she said to me in reference to this matter. "In a political canvass it is policy to cultivate every element of strength. These men have influence, and we require influence to re-elect Mr. Lincoln. I will be clever to them until after the election, and then, if we remain at the White House, I will drop every one of them, and let them know very plainly that I only made tools of them. They are an unprincipled set, and I don't mind a little double-dealing with them."

"Does Mr. Lincoln know what your purpose is?" I asked.

"God! no; he would never sanction such a proceeding, so I keep him in the dark, and will tell him of it when all is over. He is too honest to take the proper care of his own interests, so I feel it to be my duty to electioneer for him."

Mr. Lincoln, as everyone knows, was far from handsome. He was not admired for his graceful figure and finely moulded face, but for the nobility of his soul and the greatness of his heart. His wife was different. He was wholly unselfish in every respect, and I believe that he loved the mother of his children very tenderly. He asked nothing but affection from her, but did not always receive it. When in one of her wayward, impulsive moods, she was apt to say and do things that wounded him deeply. If he had not loved her, she would have been powerless to cloud his thoughtful face, or gild it with a ray of sunshine as she pleased. We are indifferent to those we do not love, and certainly the president was not indifferent to his wife. She often wounded him in unguarded moments, but calm reflection never failed to bring regret.

Mrs. Lincoln was extremely anxious that her husband should be re-elected president of the United States. In endeavoring to make a display becoming her exalted position, she had to incur many expenses. Mr. Lincoln's salary was inadequate to meet them, and she was forced to run in debt, hoping that good fortune would favor her and enable her to extricate herself from an embarrassing situation. She bought the most expensive goods on credit, and, in the summer of 1864, enormous unpaid bills stared her in the face.

"What do you think about the election, Lizabeth?" she said to me one morning.

"I think that Mr. Lincoln will remain in the White House four years longer," I replied, looking up from my work.

"What makes you think so? Somehow I have learned to fear that he will be defeated."

"Because he has been tried, and has proved faithful to the best interests of the country. The people of the North recognize in him an honest man, and they are willing to confide in him, at least until the war has been brought to a close. The Southern people made his election a pretext for rebellion, and now to replace him by someone else, after years of sanguinary war, would look too much like a surrender of the North. So, Mr. Lincoln is certain to be re-elected. He represents a principle, and to maintain this principle the loyal people of the loyal states will vote for him, even if he had no merits to commend him."

"Your view is a plausible one, Lizabeth, and your confidence gives me new hope. If he should be defeated, I do not know what would become of us all. To me, to him, there is more at stake in this election than he dreams of."

"What can you mean, Mrs. Lincoln? I do not comprehend."

"Simply this. I have contracted large debts, of which he knows nothing, and which he will be unable to pay if he is defeated."

"What are your debts, Mrs. Lincoln?"

"They consist chiefly of store bills. I owe altogether about twenty-seven thousand dollars; the principal portion at Stewart's in New York. You understand, Lizabeth, that Mr. Lincoln has but little idea of the expense of a woman's wardrobe. He glances at my rich dresses, and is happy in the belief that the few hundred dollars that I obtain from him supply all my wants. I must dress in costly materials. The people scrutinize every article that I wear with critical curiosity. The very fact of having grown up in the West subjects me to more searching observation," she noted. "To keep up appearances, I must have money—more than Mr. Lincoln can spare for me. He is too honest to make a penny outside of his salary; consequently

I had, and still have, no alternative but to run in debt."

"And Mr. Lincoln does not even suspect how much you owe?"

"God, no!"—this was a favorite expression of hers—"and I would not have him suspect. If he knew that his wife were involved to the extent that she is, the knowledge would drive him mad. He is so sincere and straightforward himself that he is shocked by the duplicity of others. He does not know a thing about any debts, and I value his happiness, not to speak of my own, too much to allow him to know anything. This is what troubles me so much. If he is re-elected, I can keep him in ignorance of my affairs; but if he is defeated, then the bills will be sent in and he will know all"; and something like a hysterical sob escaped her.

Mrs. Lincoln sometimes feared that the politicians would get hold of the particulars of her debts, and use them in the presidential campaign against her husband; and when this thought occurred to her, she was almost crazy with anxiety and fear.

When in one of these excited moods, she would fiercely exclaim—"The Republican politicians must pay my debts. Hundreds of them are getting immensely rich off the patronage of my husband, and it is but fair that they should help me out of my embarrassment. I will make a demand of them, and when I tell them the facts, they cannot refuse to advance whatever money I require."

Liberty Medallion Quilt, made by Elizabeth Keckley, ca. 1870, silk, 85-½ inches square, pieced, appliquéd, and embroidered

Courtesy Kentucky Quilt Project

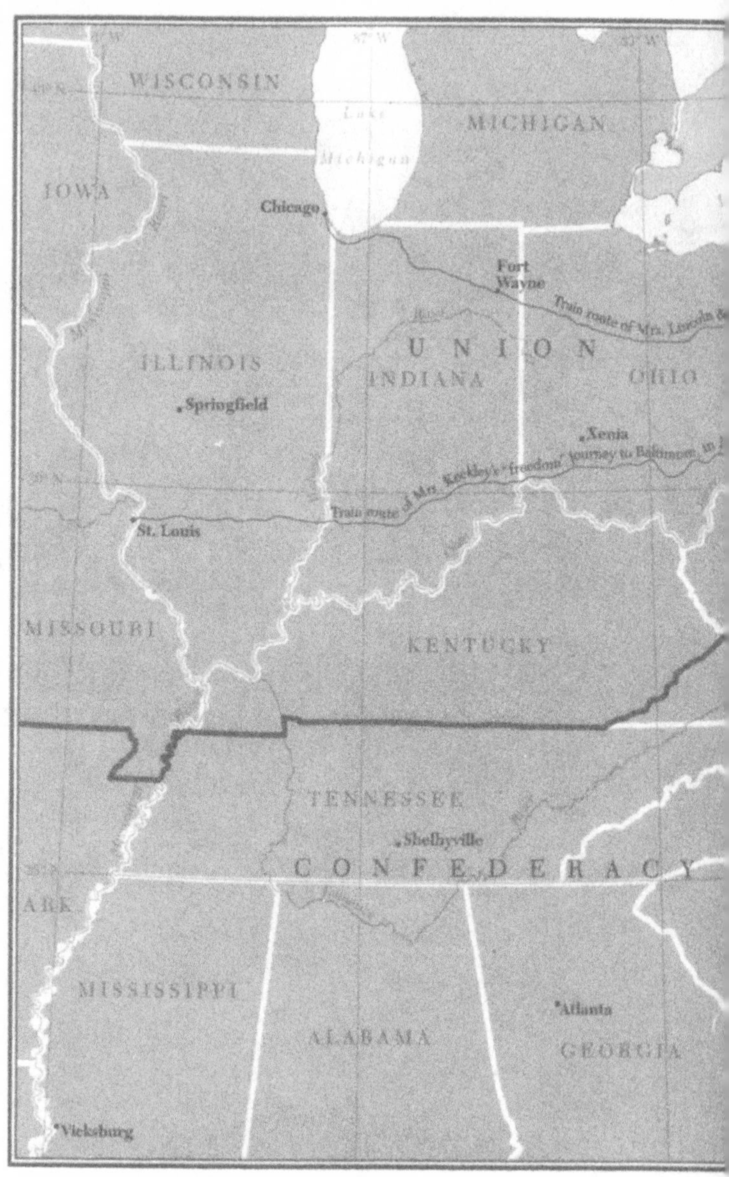
WISCONSIN
MICHIGAN
Lake Michigan
IOWA
Chicago
Fort Wayne
Train route of Mrs. Lincoln
U N I O N
ILLINOIS
INDIANA
OHIO
Springfield
Xenia
Train route of Mrs. Keckley's "freedom" journey to Baltimore
St. Louis
MISSOURI
KENTUCKY
TENNESSEE
Shelbyville
C O N F E D E R A C Y
ARK.
MISSISSIPPI
ALABAMA
Atlanta
GEORGIA
Vicksburg

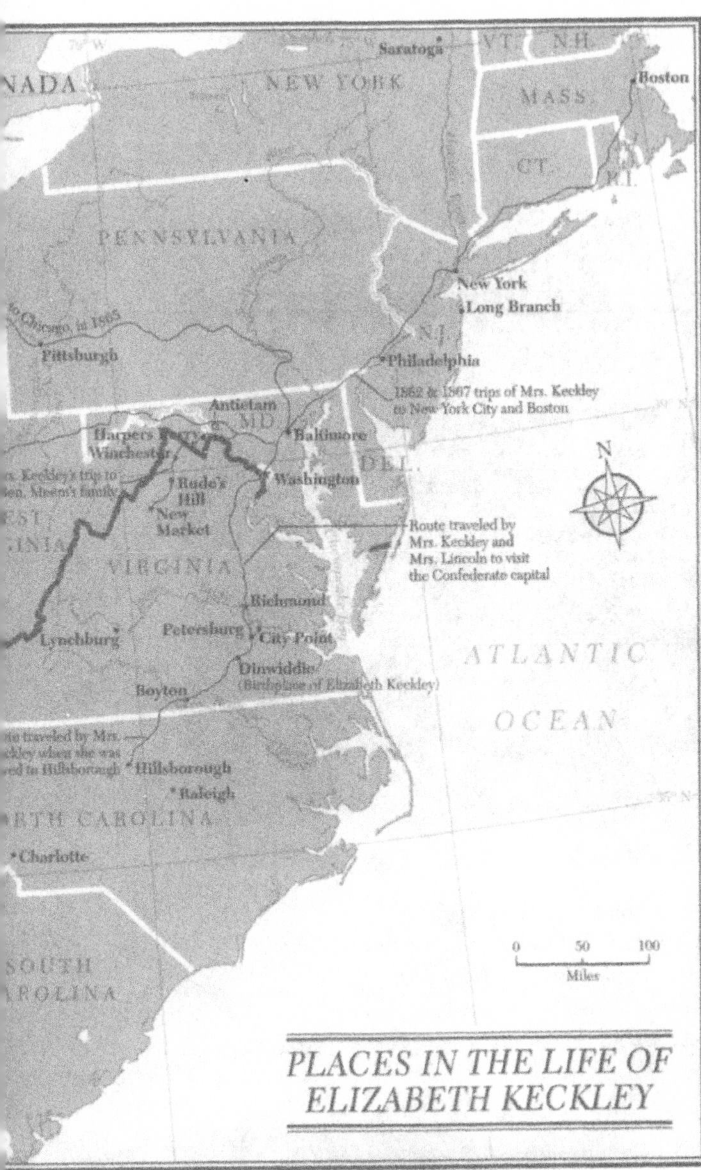

Saratoga
VT.
N.H.
NEW YORK
Boston
MASS.
CT.
R.I.
PENNSYLVANIA
New York
Long Branch
N.J.
Pittsburgh
Philadelphia
1862 & 1867 trips of Mrs. Keckley to New York City and Boston
Antietam
MD
Harpers Ferry
Baltimore
Winchester
DEL.
Washington
Rude's Hill
New Market
Route traveled by Mrs. Keckley and Mrs. Lincoln to visit the Confederate capital
VIRGINIA
Richmond
Lynchburg
Petersburg
City Point
Dinwiddie
(Birthplace of Elizabeth Keckley)
Boyton
ATLANTIC
OCEAN
Hillsborough
Raleigh
Charlotte
0 50 100
Miles
PLACES IN THE LIFE OF ELIZABETH KECKLEY

A Lincoln family portrait:
Mary Todd, Willie, Robert, Tad, and President Abraham Lincoln;
painting by Francis B. Carpenter

Courtesy of the Collection of The New-York Historical Society

Color image shows fabric detail from the only extant authenticated dress made by Elizabeth Keckley for Mary Todd Lincoln; the dress, now altered and preserved, is on exhibit at the Smithsonian Institution

Photograph by Mathew Brady; fabric swatch courtesy Smithsonian Institution

The Republican Court in the Days of Lincoln, *oil on canvas by Peter J. Rothermel, 1867*

Courtesy White House Historical Association

Elizabeth Keckley, photographed in New York City, 1860s

Courtesy Moorland-Spingarn Research Center, Howard University

X

The Second Inauguration

MRS. LINCOLN came to my apartments one day toward the close of the summer of 1864 to consult me in relation to a dress. And here let me remark I never approved of ladies attached to the presidential household coming to my rooms. I always thought that it would be more consistent with their dignity to send for me and let me come to them, instead of their coming to me. I may have peculiar notions about some things, and this may be regarded as one of them. No matter, I have recorded my opinion. I cannot forget the associations of my early life. Well, Mrs. Lincoln came to my rooms, and, as usual, she had much to say about the presidential election.

After some conversation, she asked: "Lizzie, where do you think I will be this time next summer?"

"Why, in the White House, of course."

"I cannot believe so. I have no hope of the reelection of Mr. Lincoln. The canvass is a heated one, the people begin to murmur at the war, and every vile charge is brought against my husband."

"No matter," I replied, "Mr. Lincoln will be reelected. I am so confident of it, that I am tempted to ask a favor of you."

"A favor! Well, if we remain in the White House, I

shall be able to do you many favors. What is the special favor?"

"Simply this, Mrs. Lincoln—I should like for you to make me a present of the right-hand glove that the president wears at the first public reception after his second inaugural."

"You shall have it in welcome. It will be so filthy when he pulls it off, I shall be tempted to take the tongs and put it in the fire. I cannot imagine, Lizabeth, what you want with such a glove."

"I shall cherish it as a precious memento of the second inauguration of the man who has done so much for my race. He has been a Jehovah to my people—has lifted them out of bondage, and directed their footsteps from darkness into light. I shall keep the glove, and hand it down to posterity."

"You have some strange ideas, Lizabeth. Never mind, you shall have the glove; that is, if Mr. Lincoln continues president after the fourth of March next."

I held Mrs. Lincoln to her promise. That glove is now in my possession, bearing the marks of the thousands of hands that grasped the honest hand of Mr. Lincoln on that eventful night. Alas! it has become a prouder, sadder memento than I ever dreamed—prior to making the request—it would be.

In due time the election came off, and all of my predictions were verified. The loyal states decided that Mr. Lincoln should continue at the nation's helm. Autumn faded, winter dragged slowly by, and still the country resounded with the clash of arms. The South

The Second Inauguration of Abraham Lincoln, 4 March 1865

Courtesy National Archives

was suffering, yet suffering was borne with heroic determination, and the army continued to present a bold, defiant front. With the first early breath of spring, thousands of people gathered in Washington to witness the second inauguration of Abraham Lincoln as president of the United States. It was a stirring day in the national capital, and one that will never fade from the memory of those who witnessed the imposing ceremonies.

The morning was dark and gloomy; clouds hung like a pall in the sky, as if portending some great disaster. But when the president stepped forward to receive the oath of office, the clouds parted, and a ray of sunshine streamed from the heavens to fall upon and gild his face. It is also said that a brilliant star was seen at noonday.

It was the noonday of life with Mr. Lincoln, and the star, as viewed in the light of subsequent events, was emblematic of a summons from on high. This was Saturday, and on Monday evening I went to the White House to dress Mrs. Lincoln for the first grand levee. While arranging Mrs. L.'s hair, the president entered the room. It was the first time I had seen him since the inauguration, and I went up to him, proffering my hand with words of congratulation.

He grasped my outstretched hand warmly, and held it while he spoke: "Thank you. Well, Madam Elizabeth"—he always called me Madam Elizabeth—"I don't know whether I should feel thankful or not. The position brings with it many trials. We do not know what we are destined to pass through. But God will be with us all. I put my trust in God." He dropped my hand, and with solemn face walked across the room and took his seat on the sofa.

Prior to this I had congratulated Mrs. Lincoln, and she had answered with a sigh, "Thank you, Elizabeth; but now that we have won the position, I almost wish it were otherwise. Poor Mr. Lincoln is looking so broken-hearted, so completely worn out, I fear he will not get through the next four years." Was it a presentiment that made her take a sad view of the future? News from the front was never more cheering. On every side the Confederates were losing ground, and the lines of blue were advancing in triumph.

As I would look out my window almost every day, I could see the artillery going past on its way to the open space of ground, to fire a salute in honor of some new victory. From every point came glorious news of the success of the soldiers that fought for the Union. And yet, in their private chamber, away from the curious eyes of the world, the president and his wife wore sad, anxious faces.

I finished dressing Mrs. Lincoln, and she took the president's arm and went below. It was one of the largest receptions ever held in Washington. Thousands crowded the halls and rooms of the White House, eager to shake Mr. Lincoln by his hand, and receive a gracious smile from his wife. The jam was terrible, and the enthusiasm great. The president's hand was well shaken, and the next day, on visiting

Mrs. Lincoln, I received the soiled glove that Mr. Lincoln had worn on his right hand that night.

Many colored people were in Washington, and large numbers had desired to attend the levee, but orders were issued not to admit them. A gentleman, a member of Congress, on his way to the White House, recognized Mr. Frederick Douglass, the eloquent colored orator, on the outskirts of the crowd.

"How do you do, Mr. Douglass? A fearful jam tonight. You are going in, of course?"

"No—that is, no to your last question."

"Not going in to shake the president by the hand! Why, pray?"

"The best reason in the world. Strict orders have been issued not to admit people of color."

"It is a shame, Mr. Douglass, that you should thus be placed under ban. Never mind; wait here, and I will see what can be done."

The gentleman entered the White House, and working his way to the president, asked permission to introduce Mr. Douglass to him.

"Certainly," said Mr. Lincoln. "Bring Mr. Douglass in, by all means. I shall be glad to meet him."

The gentleman returned, and soon Mr. Douglass stood face to face with the president. Mr. Lincoln pressed his hand warmly, saying: "Mr. Douglass, I am glad to meet you. I have long admired your course, and I value your opinions highly."

Mr. Douglass was very proud of the manner in which Mr. Lincoln received him. On leaving the

White House he came to a friend's house where a reception was being held, and he related the incident with great pleasure to myself and others.

On the Monday following the reception at the White House, everybody was busy preparing for the grand inaugural ball to come off that night. I was in Mrs. Lincoln's room the greater portion of the day. While dressing her that night, the president came in, and I remarked to him how much Mr. Douglass had been pleased on the night he was presented to Mr. Lincoln. Mrs. L. at once turned to her husband with the inquiry, "Father, why was not Mr. Douglass introduced to me?"

"I do not know. I thought he was presented."

"But he was not."

"It must have been an oversight then, Mother, I am sorry you did not meet him."

I finished dressing her for the ball and then I accompanied her to the door. She was dressed magnificently, and entered the ballroom leaning on the arm of Senator Sumner, a gentleman that she very much admired. Mr. Lincoln walked into the ballroom accompanied by two gentlemen. This ball closed the season. It was the last time that the president and his wife ever appeared in public (until the assassination night).

Some days after, Mrs. Lincoln, with a party of friends, went to City Point on a visit.

Mrs. Lincoln had returned to Washington prior to the second of April. On Monday, 3 April, Mrs. Secretary Harlan came into my room with material for a dress. While conversing with her, I saw artillery pass the window; and as it was on its way to fire a salute, I inferred that good news had been received at the War Department. My reception room was on one side of the street, and my workroom on the other side. Inquiring the cause of the demonstration, we were told that Richmond had fallen.[1] Mrs. Harlan took one of my hands in each of her own, and we rejoiced together. I ran across to my workroom, and on entering it, discovered that the girls in my employ also had heard the good news. They were particularly elated, as it was reported that the rebel capital had surrendered to colored troops. I had promised my employees a holiday when Richmond should fall; and now that Richmond had fallen, they reminded me of my promise.

I recrossed to my reception room, and Mrs. Harlan told me that the good news was enough for her—she could afford to wait for her dress and to give the girls a holiday and a treat, by all means. She returned to her house, and I joined my girls in the joy of the long-promised holiday. We wandered about the streets of the city with happy faces and hearts overflowing with joy. The clerks in the various departments also enjoyed a holiday, and they improved it by getting gloriously fuddled. Toward evening I saw S., and many other usually clear-headed men, in the street in a confused, uncertain state of mind.

[1]Richmond was the capital of the Confederacy. Its capture signaled Union victory in the Civil War.

Mrs. Lincoln had invited me to accompany her to City Point. I went to the White House and told her that if she intended to return, I would regard it as a privilege to go with her, as City Point was near Petersburg, my old home. Mrs. L. said she would be delighted to take me with her; so it was arranged that I should accompany her.

A few days after, we were on board the steamer en route for City Point. Mrs. Lincoln was joined by Mrs. Secretary Harlan and daughter, Senator Sumner, and several other gentlemen.

Prior to this, Mr. Lincoln had started for City Point, and before we reached our destination, he had visited Richmond, Petersburg, and other points. We arrived on Friday, and Mrs. Lincoln was much disappointed when she learned that the president had visited the late Confederate capital, as she had greatly desired to be with him when he entered the conquered stronghold. It was immediately arranged that the entire party on board the *River Queen* should visit Richmond and other points with the president.

The next morning, after the arrangement was perfected, we were steaming up James River—the river that so long had been impassable, even to our gunboats. The air was balmy, and the banks of the river were beautiful and fragrant with the first sweet blossoms of spring. For hours I stood on deck, breathing the pure air and viewing the landscape on either side of the majestically flowing river. Here stretched fair fields, emblematic of peace—and here deserted camps and frowning forts, speaking of the stern vicissitudes of war. Alas! how many changes had taken place since my eye had wandered over the classic fields of dear old Virginia! A birthplace is always dear, no matter under what circumstances you were born, since it revives in memory the golden hours of childhood, free from philosophy, and the warm kiss of a mother. I wondered if I should catch a glimpse of a familiar face. I wondered what had become of those I had once known—had they fallen in battle, been scattered by the relentless tide of war, or were they still living as they lived when last I saw them? I wondered, now that Richmond had fallen, and Virginia had been restored to the clustering stars of the Union, if the people would come together in the bonds of peace; and as I gazed and wondered, the *River Queen* rapidly carried us to our destination.

The presidential party were all curiosity on entering Richmond. They drove about the streets of the city and examined every object of interest. The Capitol presented a desolate appearance—desks broken and papers scattered promiscuously in the hurried flight of the Confederate Congress. I picked up a number of papers, and, by curious coincidence, the resolution prohibiting free colored people from entering the state of Virginia. In the Senate chamber I sat in the chair that Jefferson Davis sometimes occupied; also in the chair of their vice president, Alexander H. Stephens. We paid a visit to the mansion occupied by Mr. Davis and family during the war, and the ladies who were in charge of it scowled darkly upon our party as we inspected the different rooms. After a delightful visit we returned to City Point.

That night, in the cabin of the *River Queen,* smiling faces gathered around the dinner table. One of the guests was a young officer attached to the Sanitary Commission. He was seated near Mrs. Lincoln, and, by way of pleasantry, remarked: "Mrs. Lincoln, you should have seen the president the other day, on his triumphal entry into Richmond. He was the cynosure of all eyes. The ladies kissed their hands to him, and greeted him with waving handkerchiefs. He is quite a hero when surrounded by pretty young ladies."

The young officer suddenly paused with a look of embarrassment. Mrs. Lincoln turned to him with flashing eyes, with the remark that his familiarity was offensive to her. Quite a scene followed, and I do not think that the captain who incurred Mrs. Lincoln's displeasure will ever forget that memorable evening in the cabin of the *River Queen,* at City Point.

Saturday morning the whole party decided to visit Petersburg, and I was only too eager to accompany them.

When we arrived at the city, numbers crowded around the train, and a little ragged Negro boy ventured timidly into the car occupied by Mr. Lincoln and immediate friends, and in replying to numerous questions, used the word "tote."

"Tote," remarked Mr. Lincoln, "what do you mean by tote?"

"Why, massa, to tote um on your back."

"Very definite, my son; I presume when you tote a thing, you carry it. By the way, Sumner," turning to the senator, "what is the origin of tote?"

"Its origin is said to be African. The Latin word *totum,* from *totus,* means all—an entire body—the whole."

"But my young friend here did not mean an entire body, or anything of the kind, when he said he would tote my things for me," interrupted the president.

"Very true," continued the senator. "He used the word tote in the African sense, to carry, to bear. Tote in this sense is defined in our standard dictionaries as a colloquial word of the Southern states, used especially by the Negroes."

"Then you regard the word as a good one?"

"Not elegant, certainly. For myself, I should prefer a better word; but since it has been established by usage, I cannot refuse to recognize it."

Thus the conversation proceeded in pleasant style.

Getting out of the car, the president and those with him went to visit the forts and other scenes, while I wandered off by myself in search of those whom I had known in other days. War, grim-visaged war, I soon discovered had brought many changes to the city so well known to me in the days of my youth. I found a number of old friends, but the greater portion of the population were strange to me. The scenes suggested painful memories, and I was not sorry to turn my back again upon the city. A large, peculiarly shaped oak tree, I well remember, attracted the particular attention of the president; it grew upon the outskirts of Petersburg, and as he had discovered it on his first visit, a few days previous to the second, he insisted that the party should go with him to take a look at the isolated and magnificent specimen of the stately grandeur of the forest. Every member of the party was only too willing to accede to the president's request, and the visit to the oak was made, and much enjoyed.

On our return to City Point from Petersburg the train moved slowly, and the president, observing a terrapin[2] basking in the warm sunshine on the wayside, had the conductor stop the train, and had one of the brakemen bring the terrapin in to him. The movements of the ungainly little animal seemed to delight him, and he amused himself with it until we reached James River, where our steamer lay. Tad stood near, and joined in the happy laugh with his father.

For a week the *River Queen* remained in James River, anchored the greater portion of the time at City Point, and a pleasant and memorable week it was to all on board. During the whole of this time a yacht lay in the stream about a quarter of a mile distant, and its peculiar movements attracted our attention. General Grant and Mrs. Grant were on our steamer several times, and many distinguished officers of the army also were entertained by the president and his party.

[2]Terrapin: A turtle. The Lincolns collected a large menagerie of animals, most of which generally had free range of the White House property.

Mr. Lincoln, when not off on an excursion of any kind, lounged about the boat, talking familiarly with everyone that approached him.

The day before we started on our journey back to Washington, Mr. Lincoln was engaged in reviewing the troops in camp. He returned to the boat in the evening, with a tired, weary look.

"Mother," he said to his wife, "I have shaken so many hands today that my arms ache tonight. I almost wish that I could go to bed now."

As the twilight shadows deepened, the lamps were lighted, and the boat was brilliantly illuminated; as it lay in the river, decked with many-colored lights, it looked like an enchanted floating palace. A military band was on board, and as the hours lengthened into night, it discoursed sweet music. Many officers came on board to say good-bye, and the scene was a brilliant one indeed. About ten o'clock Mr. Lincoln was called upon to make a speech. Rising to his feet, he said: "You must excuse me, ladies and gentlemen. I am too tired to speak tonight. On next Tuesday night I make a speech in Washington, at which time you will learn all I have to say. And now, by way of parting from the brave soldiers of our gallant army, I call upon the band to play 'Dixie.'[3] It has always been a favorite of mine, and since we have captured it, we have a perfect right to enjoy it."

[3]Dixie was a name for the South, especially the Confederate states. The song, written by Daniel D. Emmett (1815–1904), became synonymous with the rebel cause.

On taking his seat the band at once struck up with "Dixie," that sweet, inspiring air; and when the music died away, there were clapping of hands and other manifestations of applause.

At eleven o'clock the last good-bye was spoken, the lights were taken down, the *River Queen* rounded out into the water, and we were on our way back to Washington. We arrived at the capital at six o'clock on Sunday evening, where the party separated, each going to his and her own home. This was one of the most delightful trips of my life, and I always revert to it with feelings of genuine pleasure.

XI

The Assassination of President Lincoln

I HAD NEVER heard Mr. Lincoln make a public speech, and, knowing the man so well, was very anxious to hear him. On the morning of the Tuesday after our return from City Point, Mrs. Lincoln came to my apartments, and before she drove away, I asked permission to come to the White House that night and hear Mr. Lincoln speak.

"Certainly, Lizabeth; if you take any interest in political speeches, come and listen in welcome."

"Thank you, Mrs. Lincoln. May I trespass further on your kindness by asking permission to bring a friend with me?"

"Yes, bring your friend also. By the way, come in time to dress me before the speaking commences."

"I will be in time. You may rely upon that. Good morning," I added, as she swept from my room and, passing out into the street, entered her carriage and drove away.

About seven o'clock that evening I entered the White House. As I went upstairs, I glanced into Mr. Lincoln's room through the half-open door, and seated by a desk was the president, looking over his notes and muttering to himself. His face was thoughtful, his manner abstracted, and I knew, as I paused a moment to watch him, that he was rehearsing the part that he was to play in the great drama soon to commence.

Proceeding to Mrs. Lincoln's apartment, I worked with busy fingers, and in a short time her toilette was completed.

Great crowds began to gather in front of the White House, and loud calls were made for the president. The band stopped playing, and as he advanced to the center window over the door to make his address, I looked out and never before saw such a mass of heads. It was like a black, gently swelling sea. The swaying motion of the crowd, in the dim uncertain light, was like the rising and falling of billows—like the ebb and flow of the tide upon the stranded shore of the ocean. Close to the house the faces were plainly discernible, but they faded into mere ghostly outlines on the outskirts of the assembly; and what added to the weird, spectral beauty of the scene was the confused hum of voices that rose above the sea of forms, sounding like the subdued, sullen roar of an ocean storm, or the wind sighing through the dark lonely forest. It was a grand and imposing scene, and when the president, with pale face and his soul flashing through his eyes, advanced to speak, he looked more like a demigod than a man crowned with the most fleeting days of mortality.

The moment the president appeared at the window he was greeted with a storm of applause, and voices re-echoed the cry, "A light! a light!" A lamp was

FRANK LESLIE'S ILLUSTRATED NEWSPAPER

NEW YORK, APRIL 29, 1865.

ABRAHAM LINCOLN.

The Martyr President.

The assassination of President Lincoln

From Frank Leslie's Illustrated Newspaper, *29 April 1865; courtesy University of Chicago Library*

brought, and little Tad at once rushed to his father's side, exclaiming: "Let me hold the light, Papa! Let me hold the light!"

Mrs. Lincoln directed that the wish of her son be gratified, and the lamp was transferred to his hands. The father and son standing there in the presence of thousands of free citizens, the one lost in a chain of eloquent ideas, the other looking up into the speaking face with a proud, manly look, formed a beautiful and striking tableau.

There were a number of distinguished gentlemen, as well as ladies, in the room, nearly all of whom remarked the picture.

I stood a short distance from Mr. Lincoln, and as the light from the lamp fell full upon him, making him stand out boldly in the darkness, a sudden thought struck me, and I whispered to the friend at my side: "What an easy matter would it be to kill the president as he stands there! He could be shot down from the crowd, and no one be able to tell who fired the shot."

I do not know what put such an idea into my head, unless it was the sudden remembrance of the many warnings that Mr. Lincoln had received.

The next day, I made mention to Mrs. Lincoln of the idea that had impressed me so strangely the night before, and she replied with a sigh:

"Yes, yes, Mr. Lincoln's life is always exposed. Ah, no one knows what it is to live in constant dread of some fearful tragedy. The president has been warned so often, that I tremble on every public occasion. I have a presentiment that he will meet with a sudden and violent end. I pray God to protect my beloved husband from the hands of the assassin."

Mr. Lincoln was fond of pets. He had two goats that knew the sound of his voice, and when he called them, they would come bounding to his side. In the warm, bright days, he and Tad would sometimes play in the yard with these goats for an hour at a time. One Saturday afternoon I went to the White House to dress Mrs. Lincoln. I had nearly completed my task, when the president came in. It was a bright day, and walking to the window, he looked down into the yard, smiled, and, turning to me, asked:

"Madam Elizabeth, you are fond of pets, are you not?"

"O yes, sir," I answered.

"Well, come here and look at my two goats. I believe they are the kindest and best goats in the world. See how they sniff the clear air, and skip and play in the sunshine. Whew! what a jump," he exclaimed as one of the goats made a lofty spring. "Madam Elizabeth, did you ever before see such an active goat?" Musing a moment, he continued: "He feeds on my bounty and jumps with joy. Do you think we could call him a bounty-jumper? But I flatter the bounty-jumper.[1] My goat is far above him. I would rather wear his horns and hairy coat through life than demean my-

[1]A "bounty" was paid for enlisting in the military. Bounty-jumpers served long enough to collect their bonuses, deserted, and enlisted again.

self to the level of the man who plunders the national treasury in the name of patriotism. The man who enlists into the service for a consideration, and deserts the moment he receives his money but to repeat the play, is bad enough; but the men who manipulate the grand machine and who simply make the bounty-jumper their agent in an outrageous fraud are far worse. They are beneath the worms that crawl in the dark hidden places of earth."

His lips curled with haughty scorn, and a cloud was gathering on his brow. Only a moment the shadow rested on his face. Just then both goats looked up at the window and shook their heads as if they would say, "How d'ye do, old friend?"

"See, Madam Elizabeth," exclaimed the president in a tone of enthusiasm, "my pets recognize me. How earnestly they look! There they go again; what jolly fun!" and he laughed outright as the goats bounded swiftly to the other side of the yard. Just then Mrs. Lincoln called out, "Come, Lizabeth; if I get ready to go down this evening I must finish dressing myself, or you must stop staring at those silly goats."

Mrs. Lincoln was not fond of pets, and she could not understand how Mr. Lincoln could take so much delight in his goats. After Willie's death, she could not bear the sight of anything he loved, not even a flower. Costly bouquets were presented to her, but she turned from them with a shudder, and either placed them in a room where she could not see them, or threw them out of the window. She gave every one of Willie's toys—everything connected with him—away. She said she could not look upon them without thinking of her poor dead boy, and to think of him, in his white shroud and cold grave, was maddening. I never in my life saw a more peculiarly constituted woman. Search the world over, and you will not find her counterpart.

After Mr. Lincoln's death, the goats that he loved so well were given away—I believe to Mrs. Lee, *née* Miss Blair, one of the few ladies with whom Mrs. Lincoln was on intimate terms in Washington.

During my residence in the capital I made my home with Mr. and Mrs. Walker Lewis,[2] people of my own race and friends in the truest sense of the word.

The days passed without any incident of particular note disturbing the current of life. Then on Friday morning, 14 April—alas! what American does not remember the day—I saw Mrs. Lincoln for a moment. She told me that she was to attend the theatre that night with the president, but I was not summoned to assist her in making her toilette. Sherman had swept from the northern border of Georgia through the heart of the Confederacy down to the sea, striking the death-blow to the rebellion. Grant had pursued General Lee beyond Richmond, and the army of Virginia, which had made such stubborn

[2]Mr. and Mrs. Walker Lewis were prominent caterers in Washington, D.C., members of the Fifteenth Street Presbyterian Church, and leaders of the free African American community. Keckley lived with them at 1017 12th Street and was godmother to their daughter, Alberta Elizabeth Lewis-Savoy.

resistance, was crumbling. Fort Sumter had fallen; the stronghold first wrenched from the Union, and which had braved the fury of federal guns for so many years, was restored to the Union; the end of the war was near at hand, and the great pulse of the loyal North thrilled with joy. The dark war-cloud was fading, and a white-robed angel seemed to hover in the sky, whispering, "Peace—peace on earth, goodwill toward men!" Sons, brothers, fathers, friends, sweethearts were coming home. Soon the white tents would be folded, the volunteer army be disbanded, and tranquillity again reign. Happy, happy day!—happy at least to those who fought under the banner of the Union. There was great rejoicing throughout the North. From the Atlantic to the Pacific, flags were gaily thrown to the breeze, and at night every city blazed with its tens of thousand lights.

But scarcely had the fireworks ceased to play, and the lights been taken down from the windows, when the lightning flashed the most appalling news over the magnetic wires. "The president has been murdered!" spoke the swift-winged messenger, and the loud huzza died upon the lips. A nation suddenly paused in the midst of festivity, and stood paralyzed with horror.

Oh, memorable day! oh, memorable night! Never before was joy so violently contrasted with sorrow. At eleven o'clock at night I was awakened by an old friend and neighbor, Miss M. Brown, with the startling intelligence that the entire cabinet had been assassinated and Mr. Lincoln shot, but not mortally wounded. When I heard the words I felt as if the blood had been frozen in my veins, and that my lungs must collapse for the want of air. Mr. Lincoln shot! the Cabinet assassinated!

What could it mean? The streets were alive with wondering, awe-stricken people. Rumors flew thick and fast, and the wildest reports came with every new arrival. The words were repeated with blanched cheeks and quivering lips. I waked Mr. and Mrs. Lewis, and told them that the president was shot, and that I must go to the White House. I could not remain in a state of uncertainty. I felt that the house would not hold me. They tried to quiet me, but gentle words could not calm the wild tempest. They quickly dressed themselves, and we sallied out into the street to drift with the excited throng. We walked rapidly toward the White House, and on our way passed the residence of Secretary Seward, which was surrounded by armed soldiers, keeping back all intruders with the point of the bayonet.

We hurried on, and as we approached the White House, saw that it, too, was surrounded with soldiers. Every entrance was strongly guarded, and no one was permitted to pass. The guard at the gate told us that Mr. Lincoln had not been brought home, but refused to give any other information. More excited than ever, we wandered down the street. Grief and anxiety were making me weak, and as we joined the outskirts of a large crowd, I began to feel as meek and humble as a penitent child. A gray-haired old man was passing. I caught a glimpse of his face, and it seemed so full of kindness and sorrow that I gently touched his arm, and imploringly asked:

"Will you please, sir, to tell me whether Mr. Lincoln is dead or not?"

"Not dead," he replied, "but dying. God help us!" and with a heavy step he passed on.

"Not dead, but dying! Then indeed God help us!"

We learned that the president was mortally wounded—that he had been shot down in his box at the theatre, and that he was not expected to live till morning. We returned home with heavy hearts. I could not sleep. I wanted to go to Mrs. Lincoln, as I pictured her wild with grief; but then I did not know where to find her, and I must wait till morning. Never did the hours drag so slowly. Every moment seemed an age, and I could do nothing but walk about and hold my arms in mental agony.

Morning came at last, and a sad morning was it. The flags that floated so gaily yesterday now were draped in black, and hung in silent folds at half-mast. The president was dead, and a nation was mourning for him. Every house was draped in black, and every face wore a solemn look. People spoke in subdued tones, and glided whisperingly, wonderingly, silently about the streets.

About eleven o'clock on Saturday morning, a carriage drove up to the door, and a messenger asked for "Elizabeth Keckley."

"Who wants her?" I asked.

"I come from Mrs. Lincoln. If you are Mrs. Keckley, come with me immediately to the White House."

I hastily put on my shawl and bonnet, and was driven at a rapid rate to the White House.

Everything about the building was sad and solemn. I was quickly shown to Mrs. Lincoln's room, and on entering, saw Mrs. L. tossing uneasily about upon a bed. The room was darkened, and the only person in it besides the widow of the president was Mrs. Secretary Welles, who had spent the night with her. Bowing to Mrs. Welles, I went to the bedside.

"Why did you not come to me last night, Elizabeth—I sent for you?" Mrs. Lincoln asked in a low whisper.

"I did try to come to you, but I could not find you," I answered, as I laid my hand upon her hot brow.

I afterwards learned that when she had partially recovered from the first shock of the terrible tragedy in the theatre, Mrs. Welles asked: "Is there no one, Mrs. Lincoln, that you desire to have with you in this terrible affliction?"

"Yes, send for Elizabeth Keckley. I want her just as soon as she can be brought here."

Three messengers, it appears, were successively dispatched for me, but all of them mistook the number and failed to find me.

Shortly after entering the room on Saturday morning, Mrs. Welles excused herself, as she said she must go to her own family, and I was left alone with Mrs. Lincoln.

She was nearly exhausted with grief, and when she became a little quiet, I asked and received permission to go into the Guest's Room, where the body of the president lay in state. When I crossed the threshold of the room, I could not help recalling the day on which I had seen little Willie lying in his coffin where the body of his father now lay. I remembered how the president had wept over the pale beautiful face of his gifted boy, and now the president himself was dead. The last time I saw him he spoke kindly to me, but alas! the lips would never move again. The light had faded from his eyes, and when the light went out, the soul went with it. What a noble soul was his—noble in all the noble attributes of God! Never did I enter the solemn chamber of death with such palpitating heart and trembling footsteps as I entered it that day.

No common mortal had died. The Moses of my people had fallen in the hour of his triumph. Fame had woven her choicest chaplet[3] for his brow. Though the brow was cold and pale in death, the chaplet should not fade, for God had studded it with the glory of the eternal stars.

When I entered the room, the members of the cabinet and many distinguished officers of the army were grouped around the body of their fallen chief. They made room for me, and, approaching the body, I lifted the white cloth from the white face of the man whom I had worshipped as an idol—who I looked upon as a

[3]Chaplet: A wreath of honor, often constructed of flowers or laurel leaves.

demigod. Notwithstanding the violence of the death of the president, there was something beautiful as well as grandly solemn in the expression of the placid face. There lurked the sweetness and gentleness of childhood, and the stately grandeur of god-like intellect. I gazed long at the face, and turned away with tears in my eyes and a choking sensation in my throat. Ah! never was a man so widely mourned before. The whole world bowed their heads in grief when Abraham Lincoln died.

Returning to Mrs. Lincoln's room, I found her in a new paroxysm of grief. Robert was bending over his mother with tender affection, and little Tad was crouched at the foot of the bed with a world of agony in his young face. I shall never forget the scene—the wails of a broken heart, the unearthly shrieks, the terrible convulsions, the wild, tempestuous outbursts of grief from the soul. I bathed Mrs. Lincoln's head with cold water, and soothed the terrible tornado as best I could. Tad's grief at his father's death was as great as the grief of his mother, but her terrible outbursts awed the boy into silence. Sometimes he would throw his arms around her neck, and exclaim, between his broken sobs, "Don't cry so, Mamma! Don't cry, or you will make me cry, too! You will break my heart."

Mrs. Lincoln could not bear to hear Tad cry, and when he would plead to her not to break his heart, she would calm herself with a great effort, and clasp her child in her arms.

Every room in the White House was darkened, and

everyone spoke in subdued tones and moved about with muffled tread. The very atmosphere breathed of the great sorrow that weighed heavily upon each heart. Mrs. Lincoln never left her room, and while the body of her husband was being borne in solemn state from the Atlantic to the broad prairies of the West, she was weeping with her fatherless children in her private chamber. She denied admittance to almost everyone, and I was her only companion, except her children, in the days of her great sorrow.

There were many surmises as to who was implicated with J. Wilkes Booth in the assassination of the president. A new messenger had accompanied Mr. and Mrs. Lincoln to the theatre on that terrible Friday night. It was the duty of this messenger to stand at the door of the box during the performance, and thus guard the inmates from all intrusion. It appears that the messenger was carried away by the play, and so neglected his duty that Booth gained easy admission to the box. Mrs. Lincoln firmly believed that this messenger was implicated in the assassination plot.

One night I was lying on a lounge near the bed occupied by Mrs. Lincoln. One of the servants entered the room, and Mrs. L. asked: "Who is on watch ?"

"The new messenger" was the reply.

"What! the man who attended us to the theatre on the night my dear, good husband was murdered! He, I believe, is one of the murderers. Tell him to come in to me."

The messenger had overheard Mrs. Lincoln's

words through the half-open door, and when he came in he was trembling violently.

She turned to him fiercely: "So you are on guard tonight—on guard in the White House after helping to murder the president!"

"Pardon me, but I did not help to murder the president. I could never stoop to murder—much less to the murder of so good and great a man as the president."

"But it appears that you did stoop to murder."

"No, no! don't say that," he broke in. "God knows that I am innocent."

"I don't believe you. Why were you not at the door to keep the assassin out when he rushed into the box?"

"I did wrong, I admit, and I have bitterly repented it, but I did not help to kill the president. I did not believe that anyone would try to kill so good a man in such a public place, and the belief made me careless. I was attracted by the play, and did not see the assassin enter the box."

"But you should have seen him. You had no business to be careless. I shall always believe that you are guilty. Hush! I shan't hear another word," she exclaimed, as the messenger essayed to reply. "Go now and keep your watch," she added, with an imperious wave of her hand. With mechanical step and white face the messenger left the room, and Mrs. Lincoln fell back on her pillow, covered her face with her hands, and commenced sobbing.

Robert was very tender to his mother in the days of her sorrow. He suffered deeply, as his haggard face indicated, but he was ever manly and collected when in the presence of his mother.

Mrs. Lincoln, who was extremely nervous, refused to have anybody about her but myself. Many ladies called, but she received none of them. Had she been less secluded in her grief, perhaps she would have had many warmer friends today than she has. But far be it from me to harshly judge the sorrow of anyone. Could the ladies who called to condole with Mrs. Lincoln after the death of her husband and who were denied admittance to her room have seen how completely prostrated she was with grief, they would have learned to speak more kindly of her. Often at night, when Tad would hear her sobbing, he would get up and come to her bed in his white sleeping clothes: "Don't cry, Mamma; I cannot sleep if you cry! Papa was good, and he has gone to heaven. He is happy there. He is with God and brother Willie. Don't cry, Mamma, or I will cry too." The closing appeal always proved the most effectual, as Mrs. Lincoln could not bear to hear her child cry.

Tad had been petted by his father, but petting could not spoil such a manly nature as his. He seemed to realize that he was the son of a president—to realize it in its loftiest and noblest sense. One morning, while being dressed, he looked up at his nurse, and said: "Pa is dead. I can hardly believe that I shall never see him again. I must learn to take care of myself now."

He looked thoughtful a moment, then added, "Yes, Pa is dead, and I am only Tad Lincoln now, little Tad, like other little boys. I am not a president's son now. I won't have many presents any more. Well, I will try and be a good boy, and will hope to go some day to Pa and brother Willie, in heaven." He was a brave, manly child, and knew that influence had passed out of their hands with the death of his father, and that his position in life was altered. He seemed to feel that people petted him and gave him presents because they wanted to please the president of the United States.

From that period forward he became more independent, and in a short time learned to dispense with the services of a nurse. While in Chicago, I saw him get out his clothes one Sunday morning and dress himself, and the change was such a great one to me—for while in the White House servants obeyed his every nod and bid—that I could scarcely refrain from shedding tears. Had his father lived, I knew it would have been different with his favorite boy. Tad roomed with Robert, and he always took pride in pleasing his brother.

After the committee had started west with the body of the president, there was quite a breeze of excitement for a few days as to where the remains should be interred. Secretary Stanton and others held frequent conferences with Robert, Mr. Todd, Mrs. Lincoln's cousin, and Dr. Henry,[4] an old schoolmate and friend of Mr. Lincoln. The city authorities of Springfield had

[4]Dr. Anson G. Henry, friend and physician to both Lincolns.

purchased a beautiful plat of ground in a prosperous portion of the city, and work was rapidly progressing on the tomb, when Mrs. Lincoln made strenuous objection to the location. She declared that she would stop the body in Chicago before it should be laid to rest in the lot purchased for the purpose by the city of Springfield. She gave as a reason that it was her desire to be laid by the side of her husband when she died, and that such would be out of the question in a public place of the kind. As is well known, the difficulty was finally settled by placing the remains of the president in the family vault at Oak Ridge, a charming spot for the home of the dead.

After the president's funeral Mrs. Lincoln rallied and began to make preparations to leave the White House. One day she suddenly exclaimed: "God, Elizabeth, what a change! Did ever woman have to suffer so much and experience so great a change? I had an ambition to be Mrs. President; that ambition has been most gratified, and now I must step down from the pedestal. My poor husband! Had he never been president, he might be living today. Alas! all is over with me!"

Folding her arms for a few moments, she rocked back and forth, then commenced again, more vehemently than ever: "My God, Elizabeth, I can never go back to Springfield! No, never, until I go in my shroud to be laid by my dear husband's side, and may heaven speed that day! I should like to live for my sons, but life is so full of misery that I would rather die." And then she would go off into a fit of hysterics.

XII

Mrs. Lincoln Leaves the White House

FOR FIVE WEEKS, Mrs. Lincoln was confined to her room. Packing afforded quite a relief, as it so closely occupied us that we had not much time for lamentation. Letters of condolence were received from all parts of the country, and even from foreign potentates, but Mr. Andrew Johnson, the successor of Mr. Lincoln, never called on the widow, or even so much as wrote a line expressing sympathy for her grief and the loss of her husband. Robert called on him one day to tell him that his mother would turn the White House over to him in a few days, and he never even so much as inquired after their welfare. Mrs. Lincoln firmly believes that Mr. Johnson was concerned in the assassination plot.

In packing, Mrs. Lincoln gave away everything intimately connected with the president, as she said that she could not bear to be reminded of the past. The articles were given to those who were regarded as the warmest of Mr. Lincoln's admirers. All of the presents passed through my hands. The dress that Mrs. Lincoln wore on the night of the assassination was given to Mrs. Slade, who was the wife of an old and faithful messenger.

The cloak, stained with the president's blood, was

given to me, as also was the bonnet worn on the same memorable night. Afterwards I received the comb and brush that Mr. Lincoln used during his residence at the White House. With this same comb and brush I had often combed his head. When almost ready to go down to a reception, he would turn to me with a quizzical look: "Well, Madam Elizabeth, will you brush my bristles down tonight?"

"Yes, Mr. Lincoln."

Then he would take his seat in an easy-chair, and sit quietly while I arranged his hair. As may well be imagined, I was only too glad to accept this comb and brush from the hands of Mrs. Lincoln. The cloak, bonnet, comb, and brush, the glove worn at the first reception after the second inaugural, and Mr. Lincoln's overshoes, also given to me, I have donated since for the benefit of Wilberforce University, a colored college near Xenia, Ohio, destroyed by fire on the night that the president was murdered.[1]

There was much surmise, when Mrs. Lincoln left the White House, what her fifty or sixty boxes, not to count her score of trunks, could contain. Had the government not been so liberal in furnishing the boxes, it is possible that there would have been less demand for so much transportation.

[1]Wilberforce University, founded first in 1846 as the Ohio African University and later owned by the African Methodist Episcopal Church, was the major institution of higher education for African Americans. It was rebuilt after the fire and continues in operation to this day. Elizabeth Keckley taught domestic science there in 1892–93.

The boxes were loosely packed, and many of them with articles not worth carrying away. Mrs. Lincoln had a passion for hoarding old things, believing that they were "handy to have about the house."

The bonnets that she brought with her from Springfield, in addition to every one purchased during her residence in Washington, were packed in the boxes and transported to Chicago. She remarked that she might find use for the material some day, and it was prudent to look to the future. I am sorry to say that Mrs. Lincoln's foresight in regard to the future was only confined to cast-off clothing, as she owed, at the time of the president's death, different store bills amounting to seventy thousand dollars. Mr. Lincoln knew nothing of these bills, and the only happy feature of his assassination was that he died in ignorance of them. Had he known to what extent his wife was involved, the fact would have embittered the only pleasant moments of his life. I disclose this secret in regard to Mrs. Lincoln's debts in order to explain why she should subsequently have labored under pecuniary embarrassment. The children, as well as herself, had received a vast number of presents during Mr. Lincoln's administration, and these presents constituted a large item in the contents of the boxes. The only article of furniture, so far as I know, taken away from the White House by Mrs. Lincoln, was a little dressing stand used by the president. I recollect hearing him say one day:

"Mother, this little stand is so handy, and suits me

so well, that I do not know how I shall get along without it when we move away from here." He was standing before a mirror, brushing his hair, when he made the remark.

"Well, Father," Mrs. Lincoln replied, "if you like the stand so well, we will take it with us when we go away."

"Not for the world," he exclaimed; but she interrupted him:

"I should like to know what difference it makes if we put a better one in its place."

"That alters the question. If you will put a stand in its place worth twice as much as this one, and the commissioner consents, then I have no objection."

Mrs. Lincoln remembered these words, and, with the consent of the commissioner, took the stand to Chicago with her for the benefit of little Tad. Another stand, I must not forget to add, was put in its place.

It is charged that a great deal of furniture was lost from the White House during Mr. Lincoln's occupation of it. Very true, and it can be accounted for in this way: In some respects, to put the case very plainly, Mrs. Lincoln was "penny wise and pound foolish." When she moved into the White House, she had discharged the steward, whose business it was to look after the affairs of the household. When the steward was dismissed, there was no one to superintend affairs, and the servants carried away many pieces of furniture. In this manner the furniture rapidly disappeared.

Robert was frequently in the room where the boxes were being packed, and he tried without avail to influence his mother to set fire to her vast stores of old goods. "What are you going to do with that old dress, Mother?" he would ask.

"Never mind, Robert, I will find use for it. You do not understand this business."

"And what is more, I hope I never may understand it. I wish to heaven the car would take fire in which you place these boxes for transportation to Chicago, and burn all of your old plunder up"; and then, with an impatient gesture, he would turn on his heel and leave the room.

"Robert is so impetuous," his mother would say to me, after the closing of the door. "He never thinks about the future. Well, I hope that he will get over his boyish notions in time."

Many of the articles that Mrs. Lincoln took away from the White House were given, after her arrival in Chicago, for the benefit of charity fairs.

At last everything was packed, and the day for departure for the West came. I can never forget that day because it was so unlike the day when the president's body was borne from the hall in grand and solemn state. Then thousands gathered to bow the head in reverence as the plumed hearse drove down the line. There was all the pomp of military display—drooping flags, battalions with reversed arms, and bands playing dirge-like airs. Now, the wife of the president was leaving the White House, and there was scarcely a friend to tell her good-bye. She passed down the public stairway, entered her carriage, and quietly drove to the depot where we took the cars. The silence was almost painful.

It had been arranged that I should go to Chicago. When Mrs. Lincoln first suggested her plan, I strongly objected; but I had been with her so long that she had acquired great power over me.

"I cannot go west with you, Mrs. Lincoln," I said, when the idea was first advanced.

"But you must go to Chicago with me, Elizabeth; I cannot do without you."

"You forget my business, Mrs. Lincoln. I cannot leave it. Just now I have the spring trousseau to make for Mrs. Douglas, and I have promised to have it done in less than a week."

"Never mind. Mrs. Douglas can get someone else to make her trousseau. You may find it to your interest to go. I am very poor now, but if Congress makes an appropriation for my benefit, you shall be well rewarded."

"It is not the reward, but—" I commenced, by way of reply, but she stopped me:

"Now don't say another word about it, if you do not wish to distress me. I have determined that you shall go to Chicago with me, and you *must* go."

When Mrs. Douglas learned that Mrs. Lincoln wished me to accompany her west, she sent me word: "Never mind me. Do all you can for Mrs. Lincoln. My heart's sympathy is with her."

The Hyde Park Hotel, Chicago

Courtesy Chicago Historical Society

Finding that no excuse would be accepted, I made preparations to go to Chicago with Mrs. L. The green car had specially been chartered for us, and in this we were conveyed to the West. Dr. Henry accompanied us, and he was remarkably attentive and kind. The first night out, Mrs. Lincoln had a severe headache; and while I was bathing her temples, she said to me:

"Lizabeth, you are my best and kindest friend, and I love you as my best friend. I wish it were in my power to make you comfortable for the balance of your days. If Congress provides for me, depend upon it, I will provide for you."

The trip was devoid of interest. We arrived in Chicago without accident or delay, and apartments were secured for us at the Tremont House, where we remained one week. At the expiration of this time Mrs. Lincoln decided that living at the hotel was attended with too much expense, so it was arranged that we should go to the country. Rooms were selected at Hyde Park, a summer resort.

Robert and Tad accompanied their mother to Hyde Park. We arrived about three o'clock in the afternoon of Saturday. The place had just been opened the summer before, and there was a newness about everything. The accommodations were not first-class, the rooms being small and plainly furnished. It was a lively day for us all. Robert occupied himself unpacking his books, and arranging them on the shelves in the corner of his small but neat room. I assisted him, he talking pleasantly all the while. When we were through, he folded his arms, stood off a little distance from the mantel, with an abstracted look as if he were thinking of the great change in his fortunes—contrasting the present with the past. Turning to me, he asked: "Well, Mrs. Keckley, how do you like our new quarters?"

"This is a delightful place, and I think you will pass your time pleasantly," I answered.

He looked at me with a quizzical smile, then remarked: "You call it a delightful place! Well, perhaps it is. Since you do not have to stay here, you can safely say as much about the charming situation as you please. I presume that I must put up with it, because mother's pleasure must be consulted before my own. But candidly, I would almost as soon be dead as be compelled to remain three months in this dreary house."

He seemed to feel what he said, and going to the window, he looked out upon the view with moody countenance. I passed into Mrs. Lincoln's room and found her lying upon the bed, sobbing as if her heart would break.

"What a dreary place, Lizzie! and to think that I should be compelled to live here because I have not the means to live elsewhere. Oh! what a sad change has come to us all."

I had listened to her sobbing for eight weeks; therefore, I was never surprised to find her in tears. Tad was the only cheerful one. He was a child of sunshine; nothing seemed to dampen the ardor of his spirits.

Sunday was a very quiet day. I looked out of my window in the morning, upon the beautiful lake that formed one of the most delightful views from the house. The wind was just strong enough to ripple the broad bosom of the water, and each ripple caught a jewel from the sunshine and threw it sparkling up toward the sky. Here and there a sailboat silently glided into view or sank below the faint blue line that marked the horizon—glided and melted away like the spectral shadows that sometimes haunt the white snow fields in the cold, tranquil light of a winter's moon. As I stood by my window that morning looking out upon the lake, my thoughts were etherealized—the reflected sunbeams suggested visions of crowns studded with the jewels of eternal life, and I wondered how anyone could call Hyde Park a dreary place. I had seen so much trouble in my life that I was willing to sink into a passive slumber—slumber anywhere, so the great longing of the soul was gratified—rest.

Robert spent the day in his room with his books, while I remained in Mrs. Lincoln's room, talking with her, contrasting the present with the past, and drawing plans for the future. She held no communication, by letter or otherwise, with any of her relatives or old friends, saying that she wished to lead a secluded life for the summer.

Old faces, she claimed, would only bring back memories of scenes that she desired to forget; and new faces, she felt assured, could not sympathize with her distress, or add to the comforts of her situation.

On Monday morning, Robert was getting ready to ride into Chicago, as business called him to the city.

"Where you goin', brother Bob?"—Tad generally called Robert, brother Bob.

"Only into town!" was the brief reply.

"Mayn't I go with you?"

"Ask mother. I think that she will say no."

Just then Mrs. Lincoln came in, and Tad ran to her, with the eager question:

"Oh, Ma! can't I go to town with brother Bob? I want to go so badly."

"Go to town! No; you must stay and keep me company. Besides, I have determined that you shall get a lesson every day, and I am going to commence today with you."

"I don't want to get a lesson—I won't get a lesson," broke in the impetuous boy. "I don't want to learn my book; I want to go to town!"[2]

"I suppose you want to grow up to be a great dunce. Hush, Tad; you shall not go to town until you have said a lesson"; and the mother looked resolute.

"May I go after I learn my book?" was the next question.

"Yes; if Robert will wait for you."

"Oh, Bob will wait; won't you, Bob?"

[2]Tad Lincoln, a lively and fun-loving child, was not fond of books and, after the death of Willie, his doting parents had dismissed the tutor and relieved Tad of any requirements for formal education. He was illiterate until he was sent to a private school in Chicago when he was twelve years old.

"No, I cannot wait; but the landlord is going in this afternoon, and you can go with him. You must do as Mother tells you, Tad. You are getting to be a big boy now, and must start to school next fall; and you would not like to go to school without knowing how to read."

"Where's my book, Ma? Get my book quick. I will say my lesson," and he jumped about the room, boisterously, boy-like.

"Be quiet, Tad. Here is your book, and we will now begin the first lesson," said his mother, as she seated herself in an easy-chair.

Tad had always been much humored by his parents, especially by his father. He suffered from a slight impediment in his speech and had never been made to go to school; consequently his book knowledge was very limited.

I knew that his education had been neglected, but had no idea he was so deficient as the first lesson at Hyde Park proved him to be.

Drawing a low chair to his mother's side, he then opened his book, and began to slowly spell the first word, "A-P-E."

"Well, what does A-P-E spell?"

"Monkey" was the instant rejoinder. The word was illustrated by a small wood-cut of an ape, which looked to Tad's eyes very much like a monkey; and his pronunciation was guided by the picture, and not by the sounds of the different letters.

"Nonsense!" exclaimed his mother. "A-P-E does not spell monkey."

"Does spell monkey! Isn't that a monkey?" and Tad pointed triumphantly to the picture.

"No, it is not a monkey."

"Not a monkey! What is it, then?"

"An ape."

"An ape? 'Taint an ape. Don't I know a monkey when I see it?"

"No, if you say that is a monkey."

"I do know a monkey. I've seen lots of them in the street with the organs. I know a monkey better than you do, 'cause I always go out into the street to see them when they come by, and you don't."

"But, Tad, listen to me. An ape is a species of the monkey. It looks like a monkey, but it is not a monkey."

"It shouldn't look like a monkey, then. Here, Yib"—he always called me Yib—"isn't this a monkey and don't A-P-E spell monkey? Ma don't know anything about it"; and he thrust his book into my face in an earnest, excited manner.

I could no longer restrain myself, and burst out laughing. Tad looked very much offended, and I hastened to say: "I beg your pardon, Master Tad; I hope that you will excuse my want of politeness."

He bowed his head in a patronizing way, and returned to the original question: "Isn't this a monkey? Don't A-P-E spell monkey?"

"No, Tad; your mother is right. A-P-E spells ape."

"You don't know as much as Ma. Both of you don't know anything"; and Master Tad's eyes flashed with indignation.

Robert entered the room, and the question was referred to him. After many explanations, he succeeded in convincing Tad that A-P-E does not spell monkey, and the balance of the lesson was got over with less difficulty.

Whenever I think of this incident, I am tempted to laugh; and then it occurs to me that had Tad been a Negro boy, not the son of a president, and so difficult to instruct, he would have been called thick-skulled, and would have been held up as an example of the inferiority of race.

I know many full Negro boys, able to read and write, who are not older than Tad Lincoln was when he persisted that A-P-E spelt monkey. Do not imagine that I desire to reflect upon the intellect of little Tad. Not at all; he is a bright boy, a son that will do honor to the genius and greatness of his father; I only mean to say that some incidents are about as damaging to one side of the question as to the other. If a colored boy appears dull, so does a white boy sometimes; and if a whole race is judged by a single example of apparent dullness, another race should be judged by a similar example.

I returned to Washington, with Mrs. Lincoln's best wishes for my success in business. The journey was devoid of incident. After resting a few days, I called at the White House, and transacted some business for Mrs. Lincoln. I had no desire to enter the house, for everything about it bitterly reminded me of the past; and when I came out of the door, I hoped that I had crossed the threshold for the last time. I was asked by some of my friends if I had sent my business cards to Mr. Johnson's family, and my answer was that I had not, as I had no desire to work for the president's family. Mr. Johnson was no friend to Mr. Lincoln, and he had failed to treat Mrs. Lincoln, in the hour of her greatest sorrow, with even common courtesy.

Having promised to make a spring trousseau for Mrs. Senator Douglas as soon as I should return from Chicago, I called on her to meet the engagement. She appeared pleased to see me, and in greeting me, asked, with evident surprise: "Why, Keckley"—she always called me Keckley—"is this you? I did not know you were coming back. It was reported that you designed remaining with Mrs. Lincoln all summer."

"Mrs. Lincoln would have been glad to have kept me with her had she been able."

"Able! What do you mean by that?"

"Simply this: Already she is laboring under pecuniary embarrassment, and was only able to pay my expenses, and allow me nothing for my time."

"You surprise me. I thought she was left in good circumstances."

"So many think, it appears. Mrs. Lincoln, I assure you, is now practicing the closest economy. I must do something for myself, Mrs. Douglas, so I have come back to Washington to open my shop."

The next day I collected my assistants, and my business went on as usual. Orders came in more rapidly than I could fill them. One day, in the middle of the month of June, the girl who was attending the door came into the cutting room, where I was hard at work:

"Mrs. Keckley, there is a lady below who wants to see you."

"Who is she?"

"I don't know. I did not learn her name."

"Is her face familiar? Does she look like a regular customer?"

"No, she is a stranger. I don't think she was ever here before. She came in an open carriage, with a black woman for an attendant."

"It may be the wife of one of Johnson's new secretaries. Do go down, Mrs. Keckley," exclaimed my workgirls in a chorus. I went below, and on entering the parlor, a plainly dressed lady rose to her feet, and asked:

"Is this the dressmaker?"

"Yes, I am a dressmaker."

"Mrs. Keckley?"

"Yes."

"Mrs. Lincoln's former dressmaker, were you not?"

"Yes, I worked for Mrs. Lincoln."

"Are you very busy now?"

"Very, indeed."

"Can you do anything for me?"

"That depends upon what is to be done, and when it is to be done."

"Well, say one dress now, and several others a few weeks later."

"I can make one dress for you now, but no more. I cannot finish the one for you in less than three weeks."

"That will answer. I am Mrs. Patterson, the daughter of President Johnson. I expect my sister, Mrs. Stover, here in three weeks, and the dress is for her. We are both the same size, and you can fit the dress to me."

The terms were satisfactorily arranged, and after measuring Mrs. Patterson, she bade me good morning, entered her carriage, and drove away.

When I went upstairs into the workroom, the girls were anxious to learn who my visitor was.

"It was Mrs. Patterson, the daughter of President Johnson," I answered, in response to several questions.

"What! the daughter of our good Moses. Are you going to work for her?"

"I have taken her order."

"I fear that Johnson will prove a poor Moses, and I would not work for any of the family," remarked one of the girls. None of them appeared to like Mr. Lincoln's successor.

I finished the dress for Mrs. Patterson, and it gave satisfaction. I afterward learned that both Mrs. Patterson and Mrs. Stover were kind-hearted, unassuming women, making no pretensions to elegance. One day when I called at the White House, in relation to some work that I was doing for them, I found Mrs. Patterson busily at work with a sewing machine. The sight was a novel one to me for the White House, for as long as I remained with Mrs. Lincoln, I do not recollect ever having seen her with a needle in her hand. The last work done for the Johnsons by me were two dresses, one for each of the sisters. Mrs. Patterson subsequently wrote me a note, requesting me to cut and fit a dress for her; to which I replied that I never cut and fitted work to be made up outside of my work room. This brought our business relations to a very abrupt end.

The months passed, and my business prospered. I continually received letters from Mrs. Lincoln and as the anniversary of her husband's death approached, she wrote in a sadder strain. Before I left Chicago she had exacted the promise that should Congress make an appropriation for her benefit, I must join her in the West and go with her to visit the tomb of the president for the first time.

The appropriation was made one of the conditions of my visit, for without relief from Congress she would be unable to bear my expenses. The appropriation was not made; and so I was unable to join Mrs. Lincoln at the appointed time. She wrote me that her plan was to leave Chicago in the morning with Tad, reach Springfield at night, stop at one of the hotels, drive out to Oak Ridge the next day, and take the train for Chicago the same evening, thus avoiding a meeting with any of her old friends.

This plan, as she afterward wrote me, was carried out. When the second anniversary approached, President Johnson and party were "swinging round the circle," and as they were to visit Chicago, she was especially anxious to be away from the city when they should arrive; accordingly she hurried off to Springfield, and spent the time in weeping over the tomb where repose the hallowed ashes of her husband.

During all this time I was asked many questions about Mrs. Lincoln, some prompted by friendship, but a greater number by curiosity; but my brief answers, I fear, were not always accepted as the most satisfactory.

XIII

The Origin of the Rivalry Between Mr. Douglas and Mr. Lincoln

Mrs. Lincoln from her girlhood up had an ambition to become the wife of a president. When a little girl, as I was told by one of her sisters, she was disposed to be a little noisy at times, and was self-willed. One day she was romping about the room making more noise than the nerves of her grandmother could stand. The old lady looked over her spectacles, and said, in a commanding tone: "Sit down, Mary. Do be quiet. What on earth do you suppose will become of you if you go on this way?"

"Oh, I will be the wife of a president some day," carelessly answered the petted child.

Mrs. Lincoln, as Miss Mary Todd, was quite a belle in Springfield, Illinois, and from all accounts she was fond of flirting. She generally managed to keep a half-dozen gentlemen biting at the hook that she baited so temptingly for them. The world, if I mistake not, are not aware that the rivalry between Mr. Lincoln and Mr. Stephen A. Douglas commenced over the hand of Miss Mary Todd. The young lady was ambitious, and she smiled more sweetly upon Mr. Douglas and Mr. Lincoln than any of her other admirers, as they were regarded as rising men. She played her part so well that neither of the rivals for a long time could tell who would win the day. Douglas first proposed for her hand, and she discarded him. The young man urged his suit boldly:

"Mary, you do not know what you are refusing. You have always had an ambition to become the wife of a president of the United States. Pardon the egotism, but I fear that in refusing my hand tonight you have thrown away your best chance to ever rule in the White House."

"I do not understand you, Mr. Douglas."

"Then I will speak more plainly. You know, Mary, that I am ambitious like yourself, and something seems to whisper in my ear, 'You will be president some day.' Depend upon it, I shall make a stubborn fight to win the proud position."

"You have my best wishes, Mr. Douglas; still I cannot consent to be your wife. I shall become Mrs. President, or I am the victim of false prophets, but it will not be as Mrs. Douglas."

I have this little chapter in a romantic history from the lips of Mrs. Lincoln herself.

At one of the receptions at the White House, just shortly after the first inauguration, Mrs. Lincoln joined in the promenade with Senator Douglas. He was holding a bouquet that had been presented to her, and as they moved along, he said: "Mary, it reminds me of old times to have you lean upon my arm."

"You refer to the days of our youth. I must do you the credit, Mr. Douglas, to say that you were a gallant beau."

"Not only a beau, but a lover. Do you remember the night our flirtation was brought to an end?"

"Distinctly. You now see that I was right. I am Mrs. President, but not Mrs. Douglas."

"True, you have reached the goal before me, but I do not despair. Mrs. Douglas—a nobler woman does not live—if I am spared, may possibly succeed you as Mrs. President."

A few evenings after Mr. Douglas had been discarded, Mr. Lincoln made a formal proposal for the hand of Miss Todd, but it appears that the young lady was not willing to capitulate at once. She believed that she could send her lover adrift today and win him back tomorrow.

"You are bold, Mr. Lincoln."

"Love makes me bold."

"You honor me, pardon me, but I cannot consent to be your wife."

"Is this your final answer, Miss Todd?" and the suitor rose nervously to his feet.

"I do not often jest, Mr. Lincoln. Why should I reconsider tomorrow my decision of today."

"Excuse me. Your answer is sufficient. I was led to hope that I might become dearer to you than a friend, but the hope, it seems, has proved an idle one. I have the honor to say good night, Miss Todd," and pale, yet calm, Mr. Lincoln bowed himself out of the room.

He rushed to his office in a frantic state of mind. Dr. Henry, his most intimate friend, happened to come in, and he was most surprised to see that the young lawyer was walking the floor in a most agitated manner.

"What is the matter, Lincoln? You look desperate."

"Matter! I am sick of the world. It is a most heartless, deceitful world; I care not how soon I am out of it."

"You rave. What has happened? Have you been quarreling with your sweetheart?"

"Quarrel! I wish to God it was a quarrel, for then I could look forward to reconciliation; the girl has refused to become my wife, after leading me to believe that she loved me. She is a heartless coquette."

"Don't give up the conquest so easily. Cheer up, man, you may succeed yet. Perhaps she is only testing your love."

"No! I believe that she is going to marry Douglas. If she does, I will blow my brains out."

"Nonsense! That would not mend matters. Your brains were given to you for different use. Come, we will go to your room now. Go to bed and sleep on the question, and you will get up feeling stronger tomorrow"; and Dr. Henry took the arm of his friend Lincoln, led him home, and saw him safely in bed.

The next morning the doctor called at Mr. Lincoln's room, and found that his friend had passed a restless night. Excitement had brought on fever, which threatened to assume a violent form, as the cause of the excitement still remained. Several days passed, and Mr. Lincoln was confined to his bed. Dr. Henry at once determined to call on Miss Todd, and find out how desperate the case was. Miss Todd was glad to see him, and she was deeply distressed to learn that

Mr. Lincoln was ill. She wished to go to him at once, but the doctor reminded her that she was the cause of his illness. She frankly acknowledged her folly, saying that she only desired to test the sincerity of Mr. Lincoln's love, that he was the idol of her heart, and that she would become his wife.

The doctor returned with joyful news to his patient. The intelligence proved the best remedy for the disease. Mutual explanations followed, and, in a few months, Mr. Lincoln led Miss Todd to the altar in triumph.

I learned these facts from Dr. Henry and Mrs. Lincoln. I believe them to be facts, and as such have recorded them. They do not agree with Mr. Herndon's story,[1] that Mr. Lincoln never loved but one woman, and that woman was Ann Rutledge; but then Mr. Herndon's story must be looked upon as a pleasant piece of fiction. When it appeared, Mrs. Lincoln felt shocked that one who pretended to be the friend

[1]The antagonism between Mary Todd Lincoln and William H. Herndon, Abraham Lincoln's junior law partner in Springfield, Illinois, has been well documented. In 1866, Herndon delivered the fourth in a series of lectures on the president. It was reprinted as a broadside entitled *Abraham Lincoln. Miss Ann Rutledge. New Salem Pioneering, and the Poem.* He stated that Lincoln's only true love had been Ann Rutledge, the daughter of the New Salem boarding-house proprietor with whom Lincoln lived early in his career. Despite the fact that Ann Rutledge had been engaged to Lincoln's friend John McNamar when she died in 1835, the story continues to be debated to this day. In 1889, Herndon employed journalist Jesse Weik to ghostwrite *Herndon's Life of Lincoln.*

of her dead husband should deliberately seek to blacken his memory. Mr. Lincoln was far too honest a man to marry a woman that he did not love. He was a kind and an indulgent husband, and when he saw faults in his wife, he excused them as he would excuse the impulsive acts of a child. In fact, Mrs. Lincoln was never more pleased than when the president called her his child-wife.

Before closing this rambling chapter, I desire to refer to another incident. After the death of my son, Miss Mary Welsh, a dear friend and one of my old St. Louis patrons, called to see me, and on broaching the cause of my grief, she condoled with me. She knew that I had looked forward to the day when my son would be a support to me—knew that he was to become the prop and mainstay of my old age, and knowing this, she advised me to apply for a pension.

I disliked the idea very much, and told her so—told her that I did not want to make money out of his death. She explained away all of my objections—argued that Congress had made an appropriation for the specific purpose of giving a pension to every widow who should lose an only son in the war, and insisted that I should have my rights. She was so enthusiastic in the matter that she went to see Honorable Owen Lovejoy, then a member of the House from Illinois, and laid my case before him. Mr. Lovejoy was very kind, and said as I was entitled to the pension, I should have it, even if he had to bring the subject before Congress. I did not desire public agitation, and

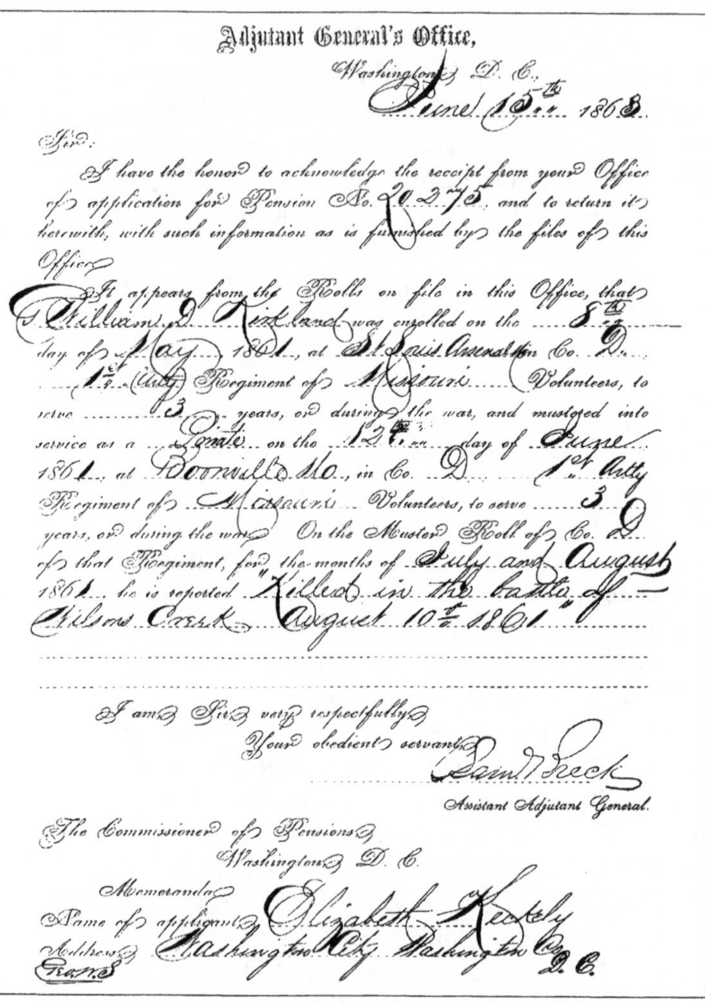

Adjutant General's Office,

Washington, D. C.

June 15th 1868.

Sir:

I have the honor to acknowledge the receipt from your Office of application for Pension No. 20275 and to return it herewith, with such information as is furnished by the files of this Office.

It appears from the Rolls on file in this Office, that G William D Kirkland was enrolled on the 8th day of May 1861, at St Louis Arsenal in Co. D 1st Arty Regiment of Missouri Volunteers, to serve 3 years, or during the war, and mustered into service as a Private on the 12th day of June 1861, at Boonville Mo, in Co. D 1st Arty Regiment of Missouri Volunteers, to serve 3 years, or during the war. On the Muster Roll of Co. D of that Regiment, for the months of July and August 1861, he is reported "Killed in the battle of Wilsons Creek August 10th 1861"

I am Sir very respectfully

Your obedient servant,

Saml Breck

Assistant Adjutant General.

The Commissioner of Pensions,

Washington, D. C.

Memoranda

Name of applicant Elizabeth Keckly

Address Washington City Washington Co. D. C.

Keckley's government pension papers

Courtesy Black Fashion Museum, Washington, D.C.

Mr. Lovejoy prepared my claim and laid it before the commissioners. In the meantime he left Washington, and Mr. Joseph Lovejoy, his brother, prosecuted the claim for me, and finally succeeded in securing me a pension of eight dollars per month. Mr. Joseph Lovejoy was inclined to the Democratic party, and he pressed my claim with great earnestness; he hoped that the claim would not be allowed, as he said the rejection of it would make capital for his party. Nevertheless the pension was granted, and I am nonetheless thankful to Mr. Joseph Lovejoy for his kindness to me, and interest in my welfare.

XIV

Old Friends

In order to introduce a pleasant chapter of my life, I must take a slight retrospective glance. Mrs. Anne Garland, the mistress from whom I purchased my freedom in St. Louis, had five daughters, all lovely, attractive girls. I used to take pride in dressing the two eldest, Miss Mary and Miss Carrie, for parties. Though the family labored under pecuniary embarrassment, I worked for these two young girls, and they were always able to present a good appearance in society. They were much admired, and both made the best matches of the season. Miss Mary married Dr. Pappan, and Miss Carrie, Dr. John Farrow. I loved them both tenderly, and they were warmly attached to me. Both are now dead, and when the death-film was gathering in the eyes, each called for me and asked to die in my arms. Miss Carrie did not long survive her sister, and I wept many tears over the deathbeds of the two lovely flowers that had blossomed so sweetly beneath my eyes. Each breathed her last in the arms that had sheltered them so often in the bright rosy period of life.

My mother took care of my son, and Miss Nannie Garland, the fourth daughter, when a wee thing, became my especial charge. She slept in my bed, and I watched over her as if she had been my own child. She called me Yiddie, and I could not have loved her more tenderly had she been the sister of my unfortunate boy. She was about twelve years old when I purchased my freedom, and resigned my charge to other hands. After Mr. Garland's death, the widow moved to Vicksburg, Mississippi, and I lost sight of the family for a few years. My mother accompanied them to Vicksburg, where she died. I made two visits to Vicksburg as a free woman, the object of my second visit being to look after the few effects left by my mother. As I did not visit my mother's grave at the time, the Garlands were much surprised, but I offered no explanation. The reason is not difficult to understand. My mother was buried in a public ground, and the marks of her grave, as I learned, were so obscure that the spot could not be readily designated. To look upon a grave, and not feel certain whose ashes repose beneath the sod, is painful, and the doubt that mystifies you weakens the force if not the purity of the love-offering from the heart. Memory preserved a sunny picture of my mother's face, and I did not wish to weave somber threads—threads suggestive of a deserted graveyard—into it, and thus impair its beauty. After spending a few weeks with the family, I returned to St. Louis and then came north. The war broke out, and I lost all trace of the Garlands. Often, during my residence in Washington, I recalled the past and wondered what had become of those who claimed my first duty and my first love. When I would mention their names and express interest in their welfare, my Northern friends would roll up their eyes in surprise.

"Why, Lizzie, how can you have a kind thought for those who inflicted a terrible wrong upon you by keeping you in bondage?" they would ask.

"You forget the past is dear to everyone, for to the past belongs that golden period, the days of childhood. The past is a mirror that reflects the chief incidents of my life. To surrender it is to surrender the greatest part of my existence—early impressions, friends, and the graves of my father, my mother, and my son. These people are associated with everything that memory holds dear, and so long as memory proves faithful, it is but natural that I should sigh to see them once more."

"But they have forgotten you. They are too selfish to give a single thought to you, now that you no longer are their slave."

"Perhaps so, but I cannot believe it. You do not know the Southern people as well as I do—how warm is the attachment between master and slave."

My Northern friends could not understand the feeling, therefore explanation was next to useless. They would listen with impatience, and remark at the close, with a shrug of the shoulders, "You have some strange notions, Lizzie."

In the fall of 1865, a lady called on me at my apartments in Washington. Her face looked familiar, but I could not place her. When I entered the room, she came towards me eagerly: "You are surprised to see me, I know. I am just from Lynchburg, and when I left Cousin Ann, I promised to call and see you if I came to Washington. I am here, you see, according to promise."

I was more bewildered than ever.

"Cousin Ann! pardon me—"

"Oh, I see you do not recognize me. I am Mrs. General Longstreet, but you knew me when a girl as Bettie Garland."

"Bettie Garland! and is this indeed you? I am so glad to see you. Where does Miss Ann live now?" I always called my last mistress, Miss Ann.

"Ah! I thought you could not forget old friends. Cousin Ann is living in Lynchburg. All the family are in Virginia. They moved to the old state during the war. Fannie is dead. Nannie has grown into a woman, and is married to General Meem. Hugh was killed in the war, and now only Spot, Maggie, and Nannie are left."

"Fannie, dead! And poor Hugh! You bring sad news as well as pleasant. And so my little pet is married—I can hardly believe it; she was only a child when I saw her last."

"Yes, Nannie is married to a noble man. General Meem belongs to one of the best families in Virginia. They are now living at Rude's Hill, up beyond Winchester, in the Shenandoah Valley. All of them want to see you very badly."

"I should be delighted to go to them. Miss Bettie, I can hardly realize that you are the wife of General

Longstreet; and just think, you are now sitting in the very chair and the very room where Mrs. Lincoln has often sat!"

She laughed: "The change is a great one, Lizzie; we little dream today what tomorrow will bring forth. Well, we must take a philosophical view of life. After fighting so very long against the Yankees, General Longstreet is now in Washington, suing for pardon, and we propose to live in peace with the United States again."

I had many questions to ask her about old friends, and the time passed rapidly. She greeted me with the frankness that she had always extended to me, and I was transported to days of the long-ago. Her stay in Washington was brief, as the general arranged his business, and they left the next day.

Mrs. Longstreet gave me the Garlands' address, and I wrote to them, expressing the hope that I would be able to see them before long.

In reply came letters full of tender sympathy and affection. In the winter of 1865, Miss Nannie wrote to me that she had the best husband in the world; that they designed going to housekeeping in the spring, and that they would be glad to have me make them a visit in July 1866. She sent me a pressing invitation. "You must come to me, dear Lizzie," she wrote. "We are now living at Rude's Hill. I am dying to see you. Ma, Maggie, Spot, and Minnie, sister Mary's child, are with me, and only you can make the circle complete. Come; I will not take no for an answer."

I was anxious to go myself, and when I received the urgent invitation, I concluded to go at once, and I wrote them to expect me in August.

On the tenth of August I left Washington for Virginia, taking the train for Harper's Ferry. The journey was attended with several disappointments. We arrived at Harper's Ferry in the night, and being asleep at the time, I was carried to the station beyond, where I had to wait and take the return train. After returning to Harper's Ferry, where I changed cars for Winchester, I missed the train, and was detained another day. From Winchester the only way to reach Rude's Hill was by a line of stages. We commenced the weary drive in the evening, and rode all night. A young gentleman in the stage said that he knew General Meem well, and that he would tell me when we reached the place. Relying upon him, I went to sleep, and it appears that the polite young gentleman followed my example. About four o'clock in the morning one of the passengers shook me, and asked:

"Aunty, don't you want to get out at Rude's Hill?"

I started up, rubbing my eyes. "Yes. Are we there?"

"More than there. We have passed it."

"Passed it!"

"Yes. It is six miles back. You should not sleep so soundly, Aunty."

"Why *did* you not tell me sooner? I am *so* anxious to be there."

"Fact is, I forgot it. Never mind. Get out at this village, and you can find conveyance back."

The village, New Market, was in a dilapidated condition; everything about it spoke plainly of the sad destruction of war. Getting out of the stage, I went into a house, by courtesy named a hotel, where I obtained a cup of coffee.

"Is there no conveyance from here to Rude's Hill?" I asked.

"Yes; the stage returns this evening," answered the landlord.

"This evening! I want to go as soon as possible. I should die if I had to stay all day in this lonely place."

A colored man behind the bar, seeing how earnest I was, came forward, and informed me that he would drive me over to General Meem's place in an hour. This was joyful news, and I urged him to get ready to start as soon as possible.

While standing in the door of the hotel, impatiently waiting for my colored friend to drive round with his little wagon, a fat old lady waddled across the street and greeted me.

"Ain't you Lizzie?"

"Yes," I answered, surprised that she should know my name.

"I thought so. They have been expecting you at Rude's Hill every day for two weeks, and they do little but talk about you. Mrs. Meem was in town yesterday, and she said that she expected you this week certain. They will be mighty glad to see you. Why, will you believe it! They actually have kept a light burning in the front window every night for ten nights, in order that you might not go by the place should you arrive in the night."

"Thank you. It is pleasant to know that I am expected. I fell asleep in the stage, and failed to see the light, so am here instead of at Rude's Hill."

Just then the colored man drove up with the wagon, and I got in with him, and was soon on the road to General Meem's country seat.

As we drove up to Rude's Hill, I observed a young man standing in the yard, and believing it to be Spot, whom I had not seen for eight years, I beckoned to him. With an exclamation of joy, he came running toward me. His movements attracted the attention of the family, and in a minute the door was crowded with anxious, inquiring faces. "It is Lizzie! It is Lizzie!" was the happy cry from all parties. In my eagerness to get to them, I stepped from the wagon to the top of the stile, intending to make a triumphant leap into the yard; but, alas! my exultation was brief. My hoop-skirt caught on one of the posts, and I fell sprawling into the yard. Spot reached me first and picked me up, only to put me into the arms of Miss Nannie, her sister Maggie, and Mrs. Garland. Could my friends of the North have seen that meeting, they would never have doubted again that the mistress had any affection for her former slave. I was carried to the house in triumph. In the parlor I was divested of my things, and placed in an easy-chair before a bright fire. The servants looked on in amazement.

"Lizzie, you are not changed a bit. You look as

young as when you left us in St. Louis, years ago," and Mrs. Meem, my foster child, kissed me again.

"Here, Lizzie, this is Minnie, Minnie Pappan, sister Mary's child. Hasn't she grown?" and Miss Maggie led a tall, queenly lady up to me.

"Minnie! poor dear Miss Mary's child! I can hardly believe it. She was only a baby when I saw her last. It makes me feel old to see how large she has grown. Miss Minnie, you are larger than your mother was—your dear mother whom I held in my arms when she died"; and I brushed a tear from each of my eyes.

"Have you had your breakfast, Lizzie?" asked Mrs. Garland.

"No, she has not," exclaimed her children in a chorus. "I will get her breakfast for her," and Nannie, Maggie, and Minnie started for the kitchen.

"It is not necessary that all should go," said Mrs. Garland. "Here is the cook, she will get breakfast ready."

But the three did not heed her. All rushed to the kitchen, and soon brought me a nice hot breakfast.

While I was eating, the cook remarked: "I declare, I nebber did see people carry on so. Wonder if I should go off and stay two or three years, if all ob you wud hug and kiss me so when I come back?"

After I had finished my breakfast, General Meem came in. He greeted me warmly. "Lizzie, I am very glad to see you. I feel that you are an old acquaintance, I have heard so much of you through my wife, her sister, and her mother. Welcome to Rude's Hill."

I was much pleased with his appearance, and closer acquaintance proved him to be a model gentleman.

Rude's Hill, during the war, was once occupied by General Stonewall Jackson for his headquarters, which gave more than ordinary interest to the place. The location was delightful, but the marks of war could be seen everywhere on the plantation. General Meem was engaged in planting, and he employed a large number of servants to assist him in his work. About a mile from Rude's Hill was Mount Airy, the elegant country seat of the general's brother. The two families visited each other a great deal, and as both entertained plenty of company, the autumn months passed pleasantly. I was comfortably quartered at Rude's Hill, and I was shown every attention. We sewed together, talking of old times, and every day either drove out, or rode on horseback. The room in which I sat in the daytime was the room that General Jackson always slept in, and people came from far and near to look at it. General Jackson was the ideal soldier of the Southern people, and they worshipped him as an idol. Every visitor would tear a splinter from the walls or windows of the room, to take away and treasure as a priceless relic.

It did not take me long to discover that I was an object of great curiosity in the neighborhood. My association with Mrs. Lincoln, and my attachment for the Garlands, whose slave I had once been, clothed me with romantic interest.

Colonel Harry Gilmore, well known as a partisan

leader in Maryland and Virginia during the war, was a frequent visitor at Mount Airy and Rude's Hill. One day I accompanied a party to a tournament, and General Meem laughed pleasantly over the change that had come to me in so short a time. "Why, Lizzie, you are riding with Colonel Gilmore. Just think of the change from Lincoln to Gilmore! It sounds like a dream. But then the change is an evidence of the peaceful feeling of this country; a change, I trust, that augurs brighter days for us all."

I had many long talks with Mrs. Garland, in one of which I asked what had become of the only sister of my mother, formerly maid to Mrs. G.'s mother.

"She is dead, Lizzie. Has been dead for some years. A maid in the old time meant something different from what we understand by a maid at the present time. Your aunt used to scrub the floor and milk a cow now and then, as well as attend to the orders of my mother. My mother was severe with her slaves in some respects, but then her heart was full of kindness. She had your aunt punished one day, and not liking her sorrowful look, she made two extravagant promises in order to effect a reconciliation, both of which were accepted. On condition that her maid would look cheerful, and be good and friendly with her, the mistress told her she might go to church the following Sunday, and that she would give her a silk dress to wear on the occasion.

"Now my mother had but one silk dress in the world, silk not being so plenty in those days as it is now, and yet she gave this dress to her maid to make friends with her. Two weeks afterward mother was sent for to spend the day at a neighbor's house, and on inspecting her wardrobe, discovered that she had no dress fit to wear in company. She had but one alternative, and that was to appeal to the generosity of your Aunt Charlotte. Charlotte was summoned, and enlightened in regard to the situation. Then the maid proffered to loan the silk dress to her mistress for the occasion; the mistress was only too glad to accept.

"She made her appearance at the social gathering, duly arrayed in the silk that her maid had worn to church on the preceding Sunday."

We laughed over the incident, when Mrs. Garland said: "Lizzie, during the entire war I used to think of you every day, and have longed to see you so much. When we heard you were with Mrs. Lincoln, the people used to tell me that I was foolish to think of ever seeing you again—that your head must be completely turned. But I knew your heart, and could not believe that you would forget us. I always argued that you would come and see us some day."

"You judged me rightly, Miss Ann. How could I forget you whom I had grown up with from infancy. Northern people used to tell me that you would forget me, but I told them I knew better, and hoped on."

"Ah! Love is too strong to be blown away like gossamer threads. The chain is strong enough to bind life even to the world beyond the grave. Do you always feel kindly toward me, Lizzie?"

"To tell you candidly, Miss Ann, I have but one unkind thought, and that is, that you did not give me the advantages of a good education. What I have learned has been the study of after years."

"You are right. I did not look at things then as I do now. I have always regretted that you were not educated when a girl. But you have not suffered much on this score, since you get along in the world better than we who enjoyed every educational advantage in childhood."

I remained five weeks at Rude's Hill, and they were five of the most delightful weeks of my life. I designed going direct to Richmond, but the cholera was reported to be raging in that city, so I took the train for Baltimore. In Baltimore I stopped with Mrs. Annette Jordan. Mrs. Garland had given me a letter to Mrs. Douglas Gordon, who introduced me to several Baltimore ladies, among others Mrs. Doctor Thomas, who said to me with tears in her eyes: "Lizzie, you deserve to meet with success for having been so kind to our friends in the days of the past. I wish there were more women in the world like you. I will always do what little I can to promote your welfare."

After remaining in Baltimore a few days, I came to the conclusion that I could do better in Washington; so I returned to the capital, and I then reopened my business.

In the spring of 1867, Miss Maggie Garland paid a visit to Baltimore. Before leaving Virginia, she said to some of her friends in Lynchburg that she designed going by Washington to see Lizzie. Her friends had ridiculed the idea, but she persisted:

"I love Lizzie next to Mother. She has been a mother to us all. Half the pleasure of my visit is that I will be able to see her."

She wrote me a letter, saying that she wanted to visit me, asking if it would be agreeable. I replied, "Yes, come by all means. I shall be so glad to see you."

She came and stayed at my rooms, and expressed surprise to find me so comfortably fixed.

I cannot do better than conclude this chapter with two letters from my dear young friends, the first from Mrs. General Meem, and the second from Miss Maggie Garland. These letters show the goodness of their hearts and the frankness of their natures. I trust that they will not object to the publicity that I give them:

Rude's Hill, 14 September 1867.

My Dear Lizzie: I am nearly ashamed of myself for neglecting to acknowledge the receipt of your letter, and the very acceptable box of patterns, some weeks ago; but you will pardon my remissness, I know, for you can imagine what a busy time I've had all summer, with a house full of company most of the time, and with very inefficient servants, and in some departments *none at all;* so I have had to be at times dining-room servant, housemaid, and the last and most difficult, dairymaid. But I have turned that department over to our gardener, who, though as green at the business as myself, seems willing to learn, and has been doing the milking all summer. These are a *few* of the reasons why I have not written to you before, for I hope you will always believe that you occupy a large place in my memory and affection, whether I write to you or not; and such a poor correspondent as yourself ought not to complain. Mother, Mag, Uncle John, and Spot are still with us; the former will pass the winter with me, but the others all talk of leaving before long. The approach of winter always scatters our guests, and we have to spend the long, dreary winters alone. But we are to have the railroad to Mt. Jackson by Christmas, perhaps sooner; and then, if we can raise the wind, we can spend a portion of the winter in the city, and I hope you will find time to come up and *spend the day* with me, as we will be near neighbors. I so seldom indulge in the pleasant task of writing letters that I scarcely know what will interest my correspondent, but I flatter myself that you will be glad to hear anything and everything about us all, so I'll begin with the children. Hugh has improved a great deal, and is acknowledged to be the smartest child and the finest looking in the state; he talks as plainly as I do, and just as understandingly as a child of ten years old; his nurse often says we need not set our hearts on that child, he is too smart ever to be raised; but I trust his *badness* will save him, for he is terribly spoilt, as such interesting children are bound to be. Miss Eliza, no longer called *Jane,* is getting to be a little "star girl," as her papa calls her; she is just learning to walk, and says a good many words quite plainly. You would never take her for the same little *cry-baby* of last summer, and she is a little beauty too—as white as the driven snow, with the most beautiful blue eyes, and long, dark lashes you ever saw. She will set *somebody* crazy if she grows up to be as lovely as she now promises to be. My dear good husband has been, like myself, run to death this summer; but it agrees with him, and I never saw him looking better. He has fallen off a little, a great improvement,

I think. He often speaks of you, and wonders if you were sufficiently pleased with your visit last summer to repeat it. I hope so, for we will always be glad to welcome you to Rude's Hill, whenever you have time to come; provided, of course, you have the wish also. Spot expects to hang out his shingle in St. Louis next winter. His health is greatly improved, though he is still very thin, and very, very much like dear father. Mag has promised to teach a little cousin of ours, who lives in Nelson County, until February, and will leave here in two weeks to commence her labors. I hate to see her leave, but she is bent on it, and our winters are so unattractive that I do not like to insist on her shutting herself up all winter with three old people. She will have very pleasant society at Cousin Buller's, and will perhaps spend the rest of the winter with Aunt Pris, if Uncle Armistead remains in Binghampton, New York, as he talks of doing. Do write to me before you get too busy with your fall and winter work; I am so anxious to hear all your plans, and about your stay in New York. By the by, I will have to direct this to Washington, as I do not know your New York address. I suppose your friends will forward it. If you are going to remain any length of time in New York, send me your address, and I will write again.

I have somehow made out a long letter, though there is not much in it, and I hope you will do the same before long. *All* send love.

Yours affectionately,
N.R.G. Meem.

My pen and ink are both so wretched that I fear you will find some difficulty in making out this scratch; but *put on your specks,* and what you can't read, just guess at. I enclose a very poor likeness of Hugh taken last spring; don't show it to anybody, for I assure you there is scarcely the faintest resemblance to him now in it.

N.R.G.M.

I give only a few extracts from the pleasant letter from Miss Maggie Garland. The reader will observe that she signs herself "Your child, Mag," an expression of love warmly appreciated by me:

Seddes, 17 December 1867.

SO MANY MONTHS have passed, my dear Lizzie, since I was cheered by a sight of your welcome handwriting, that I must find out what is the matter, and see if I can't persuade you to write me a few lines. Whatever comes, "weal or woe," you know I shall always love you, and I have no idea of letting you forget me; so just make up your mind to write me a nice long letter, and tell me what you are doing with yourself this cold weather. I am buried in the wilds of Amherst, and the cold, chilling blasts of December come whistling around, and tell us plainly that the reign of the snow-king has begun in good earnest. Since October I have been teaching for my cousin, Mr. Claiborne, and although I am very happy, and everyone is so kind to me, I shall not be sorry when the day comes when I shall shut up school-books forever. None of "Miss Ann's" children were cut out for "school-marms," were they, Yiddie? I am sure I was only made to ride in my carriage, and play on the piano. Don't you think so?. . . You must write me where you are so I can stop and see you on my way north; for you know, dear Lizzie, no one can take your place in my heart. I expect to spend the Christmas holidays in Lynchburg. It will be very gay there, and I will be glad enough to take a good dance. This is a short letter to send you after such a long silence, but 'tis too cold to write. Let me hear from you very soon.

Your child, *Mag.*
Please write, for I long to hear from you.

New Market Village, Virginia

Courtesy Virginia Historical Society

XV

The Secret History of Mrs. Lincoln's Wardrobe in New York

In March 1867, Mrs. Lincoln wrote to me from Chicago that, as her income was insufficient to meet her expenses, she would be obliged to give up her house in the city, and return to boarding. She said that she had struggled long enough to keep up appearances, and that the mask must be thrown aside. "I have not the means," she wrote, "to meet the expenses of even a first-class boardinghouse, and must sell out and secure cheap rooms at some place in the country. It will not be startling news to you, my dear Lizzie, to learn that I must sell a portion of my wardrobe to add to my resources, so as to enable me to live decently, for you remember what I told you in Washington, as well as what you understood before you left me here in Chicago. I cannot live on seventeen hundred dollars a year, and as I have many costly things which I shall never wear, I might as well turn them into money, and thus add to my income, and make my circumstances easier. It is humiliating to be placed in such a position, but as I am in the position, I must extricate myself as best I can. Now, Lizzie, I want to ask a favor of you. It is imperative that I should do something for my relief. I want you to meet me in New York, between the thirtieth of August and the fifth of September next, to assist me in disposing of a portion of my wardrobe."

I knew that Mrs. Lincoln's income was small, and also knew that she had many valuable dresses, which could be of no value to her, packed away in boxes and trunks. I was confident that she would never wear the dresses again, and thought that, since her need was urgent, it would be well enough to dispose of them quietly, and believed that New York was the best place to transact a delicate business of the kind. She was the wife of Abraham Lincoln, the man who had done so much for my race, and I could refuse nothing for her, calculated to advance her interests. I consented to render Mrs. Lincoln all the assistance in my power, and many letters passed between us in regard to the best way to proceed. It was finally arranged that I should meet her in New York about the middle of September. While thinking over this question, I remembered an incident of the White House. When we were packing up to leave Washington for Chicago, she said to me, one morning:

"Lizzie, I may see the day when I shall be obliged to sell a portion of my wardrobe. If Congress does not do something for me, then my dresses some day may have to go to bring food into my mouth, and the mouths of my children."

I also remembered of Mrs. L. having said to me at different times, in the years of 1863 and 1864, that her expensive dresses might prove of great assistance to her some day.

"In what way, Mrs. Lincoln? I do not understand," I ejaculated, the first time she made the remark to me.

"Very simple. Mr. Lincoln is so generous that he will not save anything from his salary, and I expect that we will leave the White House poorer than when we came into it; and should such be the case, I will have no further need for an expensive wardrobe, and it will be policy to sell it off."

I thought at the time that Mrs. Lincoln was borrowing trouble from the future, and little dreamed that the event which she so dimly foreshadowed would ever come to pass.

I closed my business about the tenth of September, and made every arrangement to leave Washington on the mission proposed. On the fifteenth of September I received a letter from Mrs. Lincoln, postmarked Chicago, saying that she should leave the city so as to reach New York on the night of the seventeenth, and directing me to precede her to the metropolis, and secure rooms for her at the St. Denis Hotel in the name of Mrs. Clarke, as her visit was to be *incog.*[1] The contents of the letter were startling to me. I had never heard of the St. Denis, and therefore presumed that it could not be a first-class house. And I could not understand why Mrs. Lincoln should travel, without protection, under an assumed name. I knew that it would be impossible for me to engage rooms at a strange hotel for a person whom the proprietors knew

[1]*Incog.:* Abbreviation for incognito, which means in disguise or under an assumed identity.

nothing about. I could not write to Mrs. Lincoln, since she would be on the road to New York before a letter could possibly reach Chicago. I could not telegraph her, for the business was of too delicate a character to be trusted to the wires that would whisper the secret to every curious operator along the line. In my embarrassment, I caught at a slender thread of hope, and tried to derive consolation from it. I knew Mrs. Lincoln to be indecisive about some things, and I hoped that she might change her mind in regard to the strange program proposed, and at the last moment dispatch me to this effect. The sixteenth and then the seventeenth of September passed, and no dispatch reached me, so on the eighteenth I made all haste to take the train for New York. After an anxious ride, I reached the city in the evening, and when I stood alone in the streets of the great metropolis, my heart sank within me. I was in an embarrassing situation, and scarcely knew how to act. I did not know where the St. Denis Hotel was, and was not certain that I should find Mrs. Lincoln there after I should go to it.

I walked up to Broadway, and got into a stage going uptown, with the intention of keeping a close lookout for the hotel in question. A kind-looking gentleman occupied the seat next to me, and I ventured to inquire of him:

"If you please, sir, can you tell me where the St. Denis Hotel is?"

"Yes; we ride past it in the stage. I will point it out to you when we come to it."

"Thank you, sir."

The stage rattled up the street, and after a while the gentleman looked out of the window and said:

"This is the St. Denis. Do you wish to get out here?"

"Thank you. Yes, sir."

He pulled the strap, and the next minute I was standing on the pavement. I pulled a bell at the ladies' entrance to the hotel, and a boy coming to the door, I asked:

"Is a lady by the name of Mrs. Clarke stopping here? She came last night, I believe."

"I do not know. I will ask at the office"; and I was left alone.

The boy came back and said:

"Yes, Mrs. Clarke is here. Do you want to see her?"

"Yes."

"Well, just walk round there. She is down here now."

I did not know where "round there" exactly was, but I concluded to go forward. I stopped, however, thinking that the lady might be in the parlor with some company; and pulling out a card, asked the boy to take it to her. She heard me talking, and came into the hall to see for herself.

"My dear Lizzie, I am so glad to see you," she exclaimed, coming forward and giving me her hand. "I have just received your note"—I had written her that I should join her on the eighteenth—"and have been trying to get a room for you. Your note has been here all day, but it was never delivered until tonight. Come in here, until I find out about your room"; and she led me into the office.

The clerk, like all modern hotel clerks, was exquisitely arrayed, highly perfumed, and too self-important to be obliging or even courteous.

"This is the woman I told you about. I want a good room for her," Mrs. Lincoln said to the clerk.

"We have no room for her, madam," was the pointed rejoinder.

"But she must have a room. She is a friend of mine, and I want a room for her adjoining mine."

"We have no room for her on your floor."

"That is strange, sir. I tell you that she is a friend of mine, and I am sure you could not give a room to a more worthy person."

"Friend of yours, or not, I tell you we have no room for her on your floor. I can find a place for her on the fifth floor."

"That, sir, I presume, will be a vast improvement on my room. Well, if she goes to the fifth floor, I shall go too, sir. What is good enough for her is good enough for me."

"Very well, madam. Shall I give you adjoining rooms, and send your baggage up?"

"Yes, and have it done in a hurry. Let the boy show us up. Come, Elizabeth," and Mrs. L. turned from the clerk with a haughty glance, and we commenced climbing the stairs. I thought we should never reach the top; and when we did reach the fifth story, what accommodations! little three-cornered rooms, scantily furnished. I never expected to see the widow of President Lincoln in such dingy, humble quarters.

"How provoking!" Mrs. Lincoln exclaimed, sitting down on a chair when we had reached the top, and panting from the effects of the climbing. "I declare, I never saw such unaccommodating people. Just to think of them sticking us away up here in the attic. I will give them a regular going over in the morning."

"But you forget. They do not know you. Mrs. Lincoln would be treated differently from Mrs. Clarke."

"True, I do forget. . . . Why did you not come to me yesterday, Lizzie? I was almost crazy when I reached here last night, and found you had not arrived. I sat down and wrote you a note—I felt so badly—imploring you to come to me immediately." This note was afterward sent to me from Washington:

St. Denis Hotel, Broadway, N.Y.
Wednesday, 17 September.

My Dear Lizzie: I arrived *here* last evening in utter despair *at not* finding you. I am frightened to death, being here alone. Come, I pray you, by *next* train. Inquire for

Mrs. Clarke,
Room 94, 5th or 6th Story.

House so crowded could not get another spot. I wrote you especially to meet me here last evening; it makes me wild to think of being here alone. Come by *next train* without fail.

Your friend,
Mrs. Lincoln.

I am booked Mrs. Clarke; inquire for *no other person. Come, come, come.* I will pay your expenses when you arrive here. I shall not leave here or change my room until you come.

Your friend, M. L.

Do not leave this house without seeing me.

Come!

I transcribe the letter literally.

In reply to Mrs. Lincoln's last question I explained what has already been explained to the reader, that I was in hope she would change her mind, and knew that it would be impossible to secure the rooms requested for a person unknown to the proprietors or attachés of the hotel.

The explanation seemed to satisfy her. Turning to me suddenly, she exclaimed:

"You have not had your dinner, Lizzie, and must be hungry. I nearly forgot about it in the joy of seeing you. You must go down to the table right away."

She pulled the bell-rope, and a servant appearing, she ordered him to give me my dinner. I followed him downstairs, and he led me into the dining hall, and seated me at a table in one corner of the room. I was giving my order, when the steward came forward and gruffly said:

"You are in the wrong room."

"I was brought here by the waiter," I replied.

"It makes no difference; I will find you another place where you can eat your dinner."

I got up from the table and followed him, and when outside of the door, said to him:

"It is very strange that you should permit me to be seated at the table in the dining room only for the sake of ordering me to leave it the next moment."

"Are you not Mrs. Clarke's servant?" was his most abrupt question.

"I am with Mrs. Clarke."

"It is all the same; servants are not allowed to eat in the large dining room. Here, this way; you must take your dinner in the servants' hall."

Hungry and humiliated as I was, I was willing to follow to any place to get my dinner, for I had been riding all day and had not tasted a mouthful since early morning.

On reaching the servants' hall we found the door of the room locked. The waiter left me standing in the passage while he went to inform the clerk of the fact.

In a few minutes the obsequious clerk came blustering down the hall: "Did you come out of the street or from Mrs. Clarke's room?"

"From Mrs. Clarke's room," I meekly answered.

My gentle words seemed to quiet him, and then he explained: "It is after the regular hour for dinner. The room is locked up. Annie has gone out with the key."

My pride would not let me stand longer in the hall. "Very well," I said. I began climbing the stairs. "I will tell Mrs. Clarke that I cannot get any dinner."

He looked after me, with a scowl on his face: "You need not put on airs! I understand the whole thing."

I said nothing, but continued to climb the stairs, thinking to myself: "Well, if you understand the whole thing, it is strange that you should put the widow of ex-President Abraham Lincoln in a three-cornered room in the attic of this miserable hotel."

When I reached Mrs. Lincoln's rooms, tears of humiliation and vexation were in my eyes.

"What is the matter, Lizzie?" she asked.

"I cannot get any dinner."

"Cannot get any dinner! What do you mean?" I then told her of all that had transpired below.

"The insolent, overbearing people!" she fiercely exclaimed. "Never mind, Lizzie, you shall have your dinner. Put on your bonnet and shawl."

"What for?"

"What for! Why, we will go out of the hotel, and get you something to eat where they know how to behave decently"; and Mrs. Lincoln already was tying the strings of her bonnet before the glass.

Her impulsiveness alarmed me.

"Surely, Mrs. Lincoln, you do not intend to go out on the street tonight?"

"Yes I do. Do you suppose I am going to have you starve, when we can find something to eat on every corner?"

"But you forget. You are here as Mrs. Clarke and not as Mrs. Lincoln. You came alone, and the people already suspect that everything is not right. If you go outside of the hotel tonight, they will accept the fact as evidence against you."

"Nonsense; what do you suppose I care for what these low-bred people think? Put on your things."

"No, Mrs. Lincoln, I shall not go outside of the hotel tonight, for I realize your situation, if you do not. Mrs. Lincoln has no reason to care what these people may say about her as Mrs. Lincoln, but she should be prudent, and give them no opportunity to say anything about her as Mrs. Clarke."

It was with difficulty I could convince her that she should act with caution. She was so frank and impulsive that she never once thought that her actions might be misconstrued. It did not occur to her that she might order dinner to be served in my room, so I went to bed without a mouthful to eat.

The next morning Mrs. Lincoln knocked at my door before six o'clock: "Come, Elizabeth, get up, I know you must be hungry. Dress yourself quickly and we will go out and get some breakfast. I was unable to sleep last night for thinking of you being forced to go to bed without anything to eat."

I dressed myself as quickly as I could, and together we went out and took breakfast at a restaurant on Broadway. I do not give the number, as I prefer leaving it to conjecture. Of one thing I am certain—the proprietor of the restaurant little dreamed who one of his guests was that morning.

After breakfast we walked up Broadway, and entering Union Square Park, took a seat on one of the benches under the trees, watched the children at play, and talked over the situation. Mrs. Lincoln told me:

"Lizzie, yesterday morning I called for the *Herald* at the breakfast table, and on looking over the list of diamond brokers advertised, I selected the firm of W. H. Brady & Co.,[2] 609 Broadway. After breakfast I walked down to the house and tried to sell them a lot of jewelry. I gave my name as Mrs. Clarke. I then first saw Mr. Judd, a member of the firm, a pleasant gentleman. We were unable to agree about the price. He went back into the office, where a stout gentleman was seated at the desk, but I could not hear what he said. [I know now what was said, and so shall the reader, in parentheses. Mr. Brady has since told me that he remarked to Mr. Judd that the woman must be crazy to ask such outrageous prices, and to get rid of her as soon as possible.] Soon after Mr. Judd came back to the counter, another gentleman, Mr. Keyes as I have since learned, a silent partner in the house, entered the store. He came to the counter, and in looking over my jewelry discovered my name inside of one of the rings. I had forgotten the ring, and when I saw him looking at the name so earnestly, I snatched the bauble from him and put it into my pocket. I hastily gathered up my jewelry and started out. They asked for my address, and I left my card, Mrs. Clarke, at the St. Denis Hotel. They are to call to see me this forenoon, when I shall enter into negotiations with them."

Scarcely had we returned to the hotel, when Mr. Keyes called, and Mrs. Clarke disclosed to him that

[2]W.H. Brady & Co. were commission brokers of indifferent reputation, whom Mary Lincoln apparently chose at random.

New York City, 1860s

Photograph by Mathew Brady

Mrs. Lincoln's wardrobe under examination at the offices of W.H. Brady, 1866

From Harper's Weekly, *1866; courtesy Lloyd Ostendorf Collection*

Jewelry and clothes from the sale: Point lace parasol cover and a cape made of the feathers of Japanese birds

From Frank Leslie's Illustrated Newspaper, *26 October 1867; courtesy University of Chicago Library*

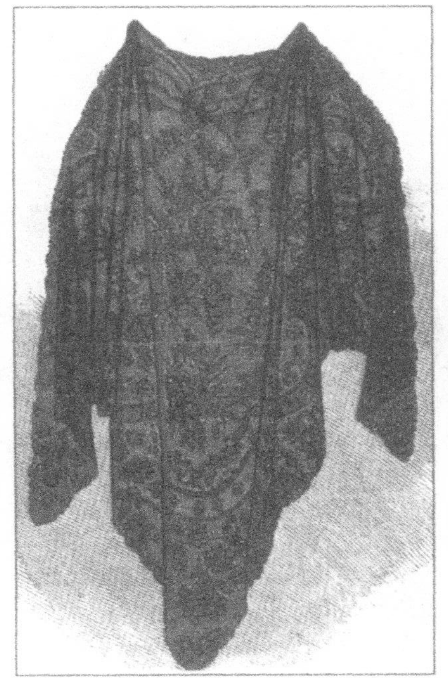

Jewelry and clothes from the sale: Black lace shawl and a fine camel-hair shawl

From Frank Leslie's Illustrated Newspaper, *26 October 1867; courtesy University of Chicago Library*

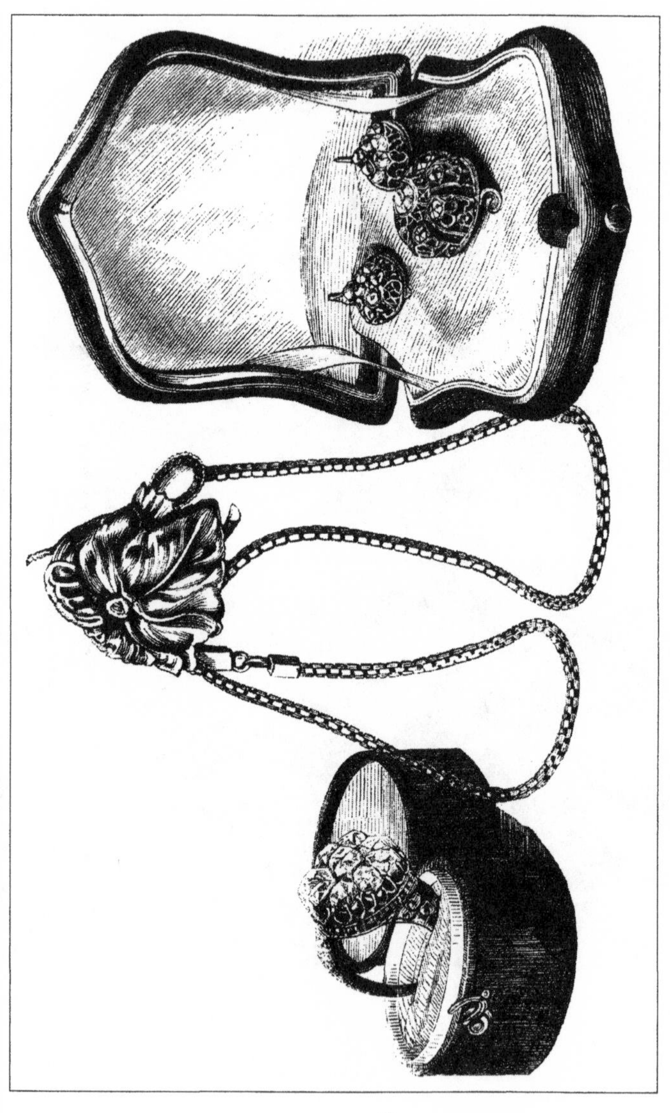

Jewelry and clothes from the sale: Cluster diamond ring, gold necklace, and diamond ear-drops and brooch

From Frank Leslie's Illustrated Newspaper, *26 October 1867; courtesy University of Chicago Library*

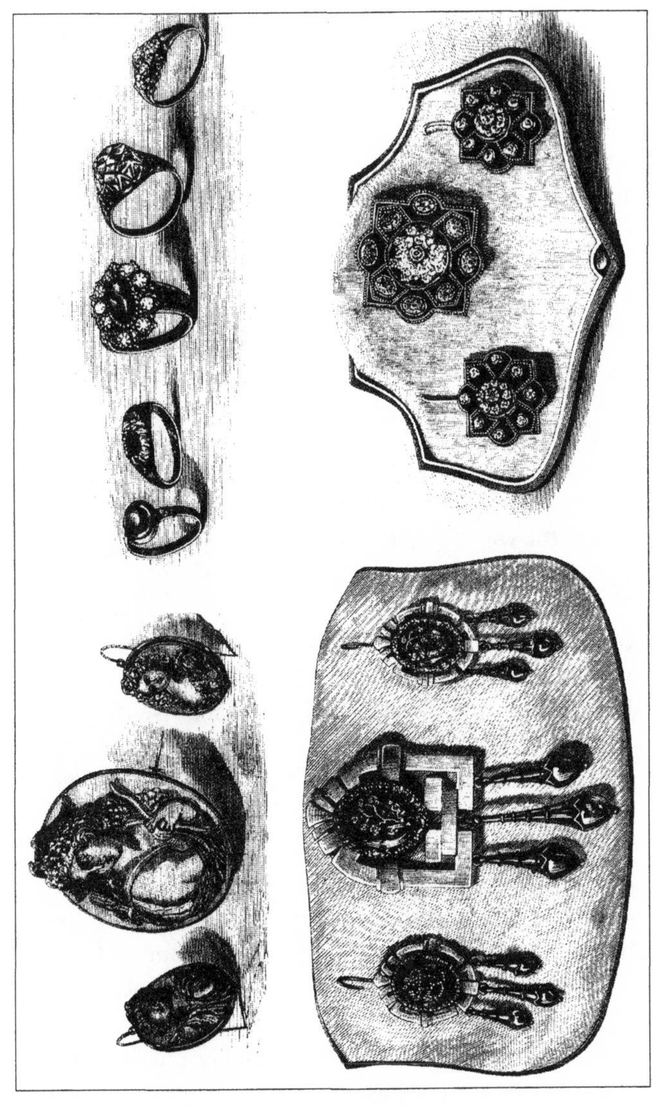

Jewelry and clothes from the sale: Rings, brooches, and earrings made with precious gems

From Frank Leslie's Illustrated Newspaper, *26 October 1867; courtesy University of Chicago Library*

she was Mrs. Lincoln. He was much elated to find his surmise correct. Mrs. L. exhibited to him a large number of shawls, dresses, and fine laces, and told him that she was compelled to sell them in order to live. He was an earnest Republican, was much affected by her story, and denounced the ingratitude of the government in the severest terms. She complained to him of the treatment she had received at the St. Denis, and he advised her to move to another hotel forthwith. She readily consented, and as she wanted to be in an out-of-the-way place where she would not be recognized by any of her old friends, he recommended the Earle Hotel in Canal Street.

On the way down to the hotel that morning she acceded to a suggestion made by me, and supported by Mr. Keyes, that she confide in the landlord, and give him her name without registering, so as to ensure the proper respect. Unfortunately, the Earle Hotel was full, and we had to select another place. We drove to the Union Place Hotel, where we secured rooms for Mrs. Clarke, Mrs. Lincoln changing her mind, deeming it would not be prudent to disclose her real name to anyone. After we had become settled in our new quarters, Messrs. Keyes and Brady called frequently on Mrs. Lincoln, and held long conferences with her. They advised her to pursue the course she did, and were sanguine of success.

Mrs. Lincoln was very anxious to dispose of her things and return to Chicago as quickly and quietly as possible; but they presented the case in a different light, and, I regret to say, she was guided by their counsel. "Pooh," said Mr. Brady, "place your affairs in our hands, and we will raise you at least one hundred thousand dollars in a few weeks. The people will not permit the widow of Abraham Lincoln to suffer; they will come to her rescue when they know she is in want."

The argument seemed plausible, and Mrs. Lincoln quietly acceded to the proposals of Keyes and Brady.

We remained quietly at the Union Place Hotel for a few days. On Sunday Mrs. Lincoln accepted the use of a private carriage and, accompanied by me, she drove out to Central Park. We did not enjoy the ride much, as the carriage was a close one, and we could not throw open the window for fear of being recognized by someone of the thousands in the park. Mrs. Lincoln wore a heavy veil so as to more effectually conceal her face. We came near being run into, and we had a great spasm of alarm, for an accident would have exposed us to public gaze, and of course the masquerade would have been at an end. On Tuesday I hunted up a number of dealers in second-hand clothing, and had them call at the hotel by appointment. Mrs. Lincoln soon discovered that they were hard people to drive a bargain with, so on Thursday we got into a close carriage, taking a bundle of dresses and shawls with us, and drove to a number of stores on Seventh Avenue, where an attempt was made to dispose of a portion of the wardrobe. The dealers wanted the goods for little or nothing, and we found it a hard matter to drive a bargain with them. Mrs. Lincoln met the dealers squarely, but all of her tact and shrewdness failed to accomplish much. I do not care to dwell upon this portion of my story. Let it answer to say that we returned to the hotel more disgusted than ever with the business in which we were engaged. There was much curiosity at the hotel in relation to us, as our movements were watched, and we were regarded with suspicion.

Our trunks in the main hall below were examined daily, and curiosity was more keenly excited when the argus-eyed reporters for the press traced Mrs. Lincoln's name on the cover of one of her trunks. The letters had been rubbed out, but the faint outlines remained, and these outlines only served to stimulate curiosity. Messrs. Keyes and Brady called often, and they made Mrs. Lincoln believe that, if she would write certain letters for them to show to prominent politicians, they could raise a large sum of money for her. They argued that the Republican party would never permit it to be said that the wife of Abraham Lincoln was in want; that the leaders of the party would make heavy advances rather than have it published to the world that Mrs. Lincoln's poverty compelled her to sell her wardrobe. Mrs. L.'s wants were urgent, as she had to borrow six hundred dollars from Keyes and Brady, and she was willing to adopt any scheme that promised to place a good bank account to her credit. At different times in her room at the Union Place Hotel she wrote the following letters:

Chicago, 18 September 1867
Mr. Brady, *Commission Broker, No. 609 Broadway, New York.*

I HAVE this day sent to you personal property, which I am compelled to part with, and which you will find of considerable value. The articles consist of four camels' hair shawls, one lace dress and shawl, a parasol cover, a diamond ring, two dress patterns, some furs, etc.

Please have them appraised, and confer by letter with me.

Very respectfully,
MRS. LINCOLN.

Chicago,———
Mr. Brady, *No. 609 Broadway, N.Y. City.*

. . . DEAR SIR: The articles I am sending you to dispose of were gifts of dear friends, which only urgent necessity compels me to part with, and I am especially anxious that they shall not be sacrificed.

The circumstances are peculiar, and painfully embarrassing; therefore, I hope you will endeavor to realize as much as possible for them. Hoping to hear from you, I remain, very respectfully,

MRS. A. LINCOLN.

25 September 1867.

W.H. BRADY, ESQ.: My great, great sorrow and loss have made me painfully sensitive, but as my feelings and pecuniary comforts were never regarded or even recognized in the midst of my overwhelming bereavement—*now* that I am pressed in a most startling manner for means of subsistence, I do not know why I should shrink from an opportunity of improving my trying position.

Being assured that all you do will be appropriately executed, and in a manner that will not startle me very greatly, and excite as little comment as possible, again I shall leave all in your hands.

I am passing through a very painful ordeal, which the country, in remembrance of my noble and devoted husband, should have spared me.

I remain, with great respect, very truly,

MRS. LINCOLN.

P.S. As you mention that my goods have been valued at over $24,000, I will be willing to make a reduction of $8,000, and relinquish them for $16,000. If this is not accomplished, I will continue to sell and advertise largely until every article is sold.

I must have means to live, at least in a medium comfortable state.

M. L.

The letters are dated Chicago and addressed to Mr. Brady, though every one of them was written in New York, for when Mrs. L. left the West for the East, she had settled upon no definite plan of action. Mr. Brady proposed to show the letters to certain politicians, and ask for money on a threat to publish them if his demands, as Mrs. Lincoln's agent, were not complied with. When she wrote the letters, I stood at Mrs. Lincoln's elbow, suggesting that they be couched in the mildest language possible. "Never mind, Lizzie," she said; "anything to raise the wind. One might as well be killed for a sheep as a lamb."

This latter expression was a favorite one of hers; she meaning by it, that if one must be punished for an act, such as theft for instance, that the punishment would be no more severe if a sheep were taken instead of a lamb.

Mr. Brady exhibited the letters quite freely, but the parties to whom they were shown refused to make any advances. Meanwhile our stay at the Union Place Hotel excited so much curiosity that a sudden movement was rendered expedient to avoid discovery. We sent the large trunks to 609 Broadway, packed the smaller ones, paid our bills at the hotel, and one morning we hastily departed for the country, where we remained three days. The movement was successful. The keen-eyed reporters for the papers were thrown off the scent; when we returned to the city, we took rooms at the Brandreth House, where Mrs. Lincoln registered as "Mrs. Morris." I had desired her to go to the Metropolitan Hotel, and confide in the proprietors, as the Messrs. Leland had always been very kind to her, treating her with distinguished courtesy whenever she was their guest; but this she refused to do. Several days passed, and Messrs. Brady and Keyes were forced to acknowledge that their scheme was a failure. The letters had been shown to various parties, but everyone declined to act. Aside from a few dresses sold at small prices to second-hand dealers, Mrs. Lincoln's wardrobe was still in her possession.

Her visit to New York had proved disastrous, and she was goaded into more desperate measures. Money she must have, and to obtain it she proposed to play a bolder game. She gave Mr. Brady permission to place her wardrobe on exhibition for sale, and authorized him to publish the letters in the *World.*

After coming to this determination, she packed the trunks to return to Chicago. I accompanied her to the depot, and told her good-bye, on the very morning that the letters appeared in the *World.* Mrs. Lincoln wrote me the incidents of the journey, and the letter describes the story more graphically than I could hope to do. I suppress many passages, as they are of too confidential a nature to be given to the public:

Chicago, 6 October.

My Dear Lizzie: My ink is like myself and my spirits failing, so I write you today with a pencil. I had a solitary ride to this place, as you may imagine, varied by one or two amusing incidents. I found, after you left me, I could not continue in the car in which you left me, owing to every seat's berth being engaged; so, being simple Mrs. Clarke, I had to eat "humble-pie" in a car less commodious. My thoughts were too much with my "dry goods and interests" at 609 Broadway to care much for my surroundings, as uncomfortable as they were. In front of me sat a middle-aged, gray-haired, respectable-looking gentleman, who, for the whole morning, had the page of the *World* before him, which contained my letters and business concerns. About four hours before arriving at Chicago, a consequential-looking man of formidable size, seated himself by him, and it appears they were entirely unknown to each other. The well-fed looking individual opened the conversation with the man who had read the *World* so attentively, and the conversation soon grew warm and earnest. The war and its devastation engaged them. The bluffy individual, doubtless a Republican who had pocketed his many thousands, spoke of the widows of the land, made so by the war. My reading man remarked to him:

"Are you aware that Mrs. Lincoln is in indigent circumstances, and has to sell her clothing and jewelry to gain means to make life more endurable?"

The well-conditioned man replied: "I do not blame her for selling her clothing, if she wishes it. I suppose *when sold,* she will convert the proceeds into five-twenties to enable her to have means to be buried."

The *World* man turned toward him with a searching glance, and replied, with the haughtiest manner: "That woman is not dead yet."

The discomfited individual looked down, never spoke another word, and in half an hour left his seat, and did not return.

I give you word for word as the conversation occurred. May it be found through the execution of my friends, Messrs. Brady and Keyes, that "that woman is not yet dead," and being alive, she speaketh and gaineth valuable hearers. Such is life! Those who have been injured, how gladly the injurer would consign them to mother earth and forgetfulness! Hoping I should not be recognized at Fort Wayne, I thought I would get out at dinner for a cup of tea. . . . will show you what a creature of *fate* I am, as miserable as it sometimes is. I went into the dining room alone, and was ushered up to the table, where, at its head, sat an elegant-looking gentleman—at his side a middle-aged lady.

My black veil was doubled over my face. I had taken my seat next to him—he at the head of the table, I at his left hand. I immediately felt a pair of eyes was gazing at me. I looked him full in the face, and the glance was earnestly returned. I sipped my water, and said: "Mr. S.,[3] is this indeed you?" His face was as pale as the tablecloth.

We entered into conversation, when I asked him how long since he had left Chicago. He replied, "Two weeks since." He said, "How strange you should be on the train and I not know it!"

As soon as I could escape from the table, I did so by saying, "I must secure a cup of tea for a lady friend with me who has a headache." I had scarcely returned to the car when he entered it with a cup of tea borne by his own aristocratic hands. I was a good deal annoyed by seeing him, and he was so agitated that he spilled half of the cup over my *elegantly gloved* hands. *He* looked very sad, and I fancied 609 Broadway occupied his thoughts. I apologized for the absent lady who wished the cup, by saying that "in my absence she had slipped out for it." His heart was in his eyes, notwithstanding my veiled face. Pity for me, I fear, has something to do with all this. I never saw his manner so gentle and sad. This was nearly evening, and I did not see him again. . . .

What evil spirit possessed me to go out and get that cup of tea? When he left me, *woman-like* I tossed the cup of tea out of the window, and tucked my head down and shed *bitter tears*. . . . At the depot my darling little Taddie was waiting for me, and his voice never sounded so sweet. . . . My

[3]Mr. S: This was probably Charles Sumner, a senator representing Massachusetts for more than twenty years and one of Mary Lincoln's confidants and supporters.

dear Lizzie, do visit Mr. Brady each morning at nine o'clock, and urge them all you can. I see by the papers Stewart has returned. Tomorrow I will send the invoice of goods, which please to not give up. How much I miss you, tongue cannot tell. Forget my fright and nervousness of the evening before. Of course you were as innocent as a child in all you did. I consider you my best living friend, and I am struggling to be enabled some day to repay you. Write me often, as you promised.

Always truly yours,
M. L.

It is not necessary for me to dwell upon the public history of Mrs. Lincoln's unfortunate venture. The question has been discussed in all the newspapers of the land, and these discussions are so recent that it would be useless to introduce them in these pages, even if I had an inclination to do so. The following, from the New York *Evening Express,* briefly tells the story:

The attraction for ladies, and the curious and speculative of the other sex in this city just now is the grand exposition of Lincoln dresses at the office of Mr. Brady, on Broadway, a few doors south of Houston Street. The publicity given to the articles on exhibition and for sale has excited the public curiosity, and hundreds of people, principally women with considerable leisure moments at disposal, daily throng the rooms of Mr. Brady, and give himself and his shop-woman more to do than either bargained for, when a lady, with face concealed with a veil, called and arranged for the sale of the superabundant clothing of a distinguished and titled, but nameless lady. Twenty-five dresses, folded or tossed about by frequent examinations, lie exposed upon a closed piano, and upon a lounge; shawls rich and rare are displayed upon the backs of chairs, but the more exacting obtain a better view and closer inspection by the lady attendant throwing them occasionally upon her shoulders, just to oblige, so that their appearance on promenade might be seen and admired. Furs, laces, and jewelry are in a glass case, but the "four thousand dollars in gold" point outfit is kept in a paste-board box, and only shown on special request.

The feeling of the majority of visitors is adverse to the course Mrs. Lincoln has thought proper to pursue, and the criticisms are as severe as the cavillings are persistent at the quality of some of the dresses. These latter are labeled at Mrs. Lincoln's own estimate, and prices range from twenty-five dollars to seventy-five dollars—about 50 percent less than cost. Some of them, if not worn long, have been worn much; they are jagged under the arms and at the bottom of the skirt, stains are on the lining, and other objections present themselves to those who oscillate between the dresses and dollars, "notwithstanding they have been worn by Madam Lincoln," as a lady who looked from behind a pair of gold spectacles remarked. Other dresses, however, have scarcely been worn —one, perhaps, while Mrs. Lincoln sat for her picture, and from one the basting threads had not yet been removed. The general testimony is that the wearing apparel is high priced, and some of the examiners say that the cost-figures must have been put on by the dress-makers; or, if such was not the case, that gold was 250 when they were purchased, and is now but 140—so that a dress for which one-hundred and fifty dollars was paid at the rate of high figures cannot be called cheap at half that sum, after it has been worn considerable, and perhaps passed out of fashion. The peculiarity of the dresses is that the most of them are cut low-necked—a taste which some ladies attribute to Mrs. Lincoln's appreciation of her own bust.

On Saturday last an offer was made for all the dresses. The figure named was less than the aggregate estimate placed on them. Mr. Brady, however, having no discretionary power, he declined to close the bargain, but notified Mrs. Lincoln by mail. Of course, as yet, no reply has been received. Mrs. L. desires that the auction should be deferred till the thirty-first of the present month, and efforts made to dispose of the articles at private sale up to then.

A Mrs. C——called on Mr. Brady this morning, and examined minutely each shawl. Before leaving the lady said that, at the time when there was a hesitancy about the president issuing the Emancipation Proclamation, she sent to Mrs. Lincoln an ashes-of-rose shawl, which was manufactured in China, forwarded to France, and thence to Mrs. C—— in New York. The shawl, the lady remarked, was a very handsome one, and should it come into the hands of Mr. Brady to be sold, would like to be made aware of the fact, so as to obtain possession again. Mr. Brady promised to acquaint the ashes-of-rose donor, if the prized article should be among the two trunks of goods now on the way from Chicago.

So many erroneous reports were circulated, that I made a correct statement to one of the editors of the New York *Evening News.* The article based upon the memoranda furnished by me appeared in the *News* of 12 October 1867. I reproduce a portion of it in this connection:

Mrs. Lincoln feels sorely aggrieved at many of the harsh criticisms that have been passed upon her for traveling incognito. She claims that she adopted this course from motives of delicacy, desiring to avoid publicity. While here, she spoke to but two former acquaintances, and these two gentlemen whom she met on Broadway. Hundreds passed her who had courted her good graces when she reigned supreme at the White House, but there was no recognition. It was not because she had changed much in personal appearance, but was merely owing to the heavy crepe veil that hid her features from view.

She seeks to defend her course while in this city—and with much force, too. Adverting to the fact that the empress of France frequently disposes of her cast-off wardrobe, and publicly too, without being subjected to any unkind remarks regarding its propriety, she claims the same immunity here as is accorded in Paris to Eugenie. As regards her obscurity while in this city, she says that foreigners of note and position frequently come to our shores, and under assumed names travel from point to point throughout our vast domain, to avoid recognition and the inconveniences resulting from being known, though it even be in the form of honors. For herself she regards quiet preferable to ostentatious show, which would have cost her much indirectly, if not directly; and this she felt herself unable to bear, according to the measure of her present state of finances.

In a recent letter to her bosom friend, Mrs. Elizabeth Keckley, Mrs. Lincoln pathetically remarks, "Elizabeth, if evil come from this, pray for my deliverance, as I did it for the best." This referred to her action in placing her personal effects before the public for sale, and to the harsh remarks that have been made thereon by some whom she had formerly regarded as her friends.

As to the articles which belonged to Mr. Lincoln, they can all be accounted for in a manner satisfactory even to an overcritical public. During the time Mr. Lincoln was in office, he was the recipient of several canes. After his death one was given to the Honorable Charles Sumner; another to Fred. Douglass; another to the Reverend H. H. Garnet of this city, and another to Mr. Wm. Slade, the present steward of the White House, who, in Mr. Lincoln's lifetime, was his messenger. This gentleman also received some of Mr. Lincoln's apparel, among which was his heavy gray shawl. Several other of the messengers employed about the White House came in for a share of the deceased president's effects.

The shepherd plaid shawl which Mr. Lincoln wore during the milder weather, and which was rendered somewhat memorable as forming part of his famous disguise, together with the Scotch cap, when he wended his way secretly to the Capitol to be inaugurated as president, was given to Dr. Abbot, of Canada, who had been one of his warmest friends. During the war this gentleman, as a surgeon in the United States army, was in Washington in charge of a hospital, and thus became acquainted with the head of the nation.

His watch, his penknife, his gold pencil, and his glasses are now in possession of his son, Robert. Nearly all else than these few things have passed out of the family, as Mrs. Lincoln did not wish to retain them. But all were freely given away, and not an article was parted with for money.

The Reverend Dr. Gurley of Washington was the spiritual adviser of the president and his family. They attended his church. When little "Willie" died, he officiated at the funeral. He was a most intimate friend of the family, and when Mr. Lincoln lay upon his deathbed, Dr. Gurley was by his side. He, as his clergyman, performed the funeral rites upon the body of the deceased president, when it lay cold in death at the city of Washington. He received the hat worn last by Mr. Lincoln, as we have before stated, and it is still retained by him.

The dress that was worn by Mrs. Lincoln on the night of the assassination was presented to Mrs. Wm. Slade.[4] It is a black silk with a little white stripe. Most of the other articles that adorned Mrs. Lincoln on that fatal night became the property of Mrs. Keckley. She has the most of them carefully stowed away, and intends keeping them during her life as mementos of a mournful event. The principal articles among these are the earrings, the bonnet, and the velvet cloak. The writer of this saw the latter on Thursday. It bears most palpable marks of the assassination, being completely bespattered with blood that has dried upon its surface, and which can never be removed.

A few words as regard the disposition and habits of Mrs. Lincoln. She is no longer the sprightly body she was when her very presence illumed the White House with gaiety. Now she is sad and sedate, seeking seclusion, and maintaining communication merely with her most intimate personal friends. The most of her time she devotes to instructive reading within the walls of her boudoir. Laying her book aside spasmodically, she places her hand upon her forehead, as if ruminating upon something momentous. Then her hand wanders amid her heavy tresses, while she ponders for but a few seconds—then, by a sudden start, she approaches her writing stand, seizes a pen, and indites

[4]Mary Lincoln knew Josephine Slade because she was not only the wife of William Slade and a friend of Elizabeth Keckley, but her three children (Katherine, Andrew, and Jessie) sometimes played with Tad both at their home and at the White House.

a few hasty lines to some trusty friend, upon the troubles that weigh so heavily upon her. Speedily it is sent to the post office; but, hardly has the mail departed from the city before she regrets her hasty letter, and would give much to recall it. But, too late, it is gone, and probably the secrets it contains are not confidentially kept by the party to whom it was addressed, and soon it furnishes inexhaustible material for gossip-loving people.

As some citizens have expressed themselves desirous of aiding Mrs. Lincoln, a subscription-book was opened at the office of her agent, Mr. Brady, No. 609 Broadway, this morning. There is no limitation as to the amount which may be given, though there was a proposition that a dollar should be contributed by each person who came forward to inspect the goods. Had each person who handled these articles given this sum, a handsome amount would already have been realized.

The colored people are moving in this matter. They intend to take up collections in their churches for the benefit of Mrs. Lincoln. They are enthusiastic, and a trifle from every African in this city would, in the aggregate, swell into an immense sum, which would be doubly acceptable to Mrs. Lincoln. It would satisfy her that the black people still have the memory of her deceased husband fresh in their minds.

The goods still remain exposed to sale, but it is now announced that they will be sold at public auction on the thirtieth of this month, unless they be disposed of before that at private sale.

It is stated in the article that the "colored people are moving in this matter." The colored people were surprised to hear of Mrs. Lincoln's poverty, and the news of her distress called forth strong sympathy from their warm, generous hearts. Reverend H. H. Garnet, of New York City, and Mr. Frederick Douglass, of Rochester, New York, proposed to lecture in behalf of the widow of the lamented president, and schemes were on foot to raise a large sum of money by contribution. The colored people recognized Abraham Lincoln as their great friend, and they were anxious to show their kind interest in the welfare of his family in some way more earnest and substantial than simple words. I wrote Mrs. Lincoln what we proposed to do, and she promptly replied, declining to receive aid from the colored people. I showed her letter to Mr. Garnet and Mr. Douglass and the whole project was at once abandoned. She afterward consented to receive contributions from my people, but as the services of Messrs. Douglass, Garnet, and others had been refused when first offered, they declined to take an active part in the scheme; so nothing was done. The following letters were written before Mrs. Lincoln declined to receive aid from the colored people:

183 Bleecker St.,
New York,
16 October 1867

W.H. Brady, Esq:

I have just received your favor, together with the circulars. I will do all that lies in my power, but I fear that will not be as much as you anticipate. I think, however, that a contribution from the colored people of New York will be worth something in a moral point of view, and likely that will be the most that will be accomplished in the undertaking. I am thoroughly with you in the work, although but little may be done.

I am truly yours,
HENRY HIGHLAND GARNET.

P. S. I think it would be well if you would drop a line to Mr. Frederick Douglass, at Rochester, New York.

H.H.G.

Rochester, 18 October 1867.

MY DEAR MRS. KECKLEY: You judge me rightly—I am willing to do what I can to place the widow of our martyr president in the affluent position which her relation to that good man and to the country entitles her to. But I doubt the wisdom of getting up a series of lectures for that purpose; that is just the last thing that should be done. Still, if the thing is done, it should be done on a grand scale. The best speakers in the country should be secured for the purpose. You should not place me at the head nor at the foot of the list, but sandwich me between, for thus out of the way, it would not give color to the idea. I am to speak in Newark on Wednesday evening next, and will endeavor to see you on the subject. Of course, if it would not be too much to ask, I would gladly see Mrs. Lincoln, if this could be done in a quiet way without the reporters getting hold of it, and using it in some way to the prejudice of that already much-abused lady. As I shall see you soon, there is less reason to write you at length.

I am, dear madam, with high respect,
Very truly yours,
FREDERICK DOUGLASS.

Pottsville, 29 October 1867.

MY DEAR MRS. KECKLEY: You know the drift of my views concerning the subscription for Mrs. Lincoln. Yet I wish to place them more distinctly before you, so that, if you have occasion to refer to me in connection with the matter, you can do so with accuracy and certainty.

It is due Mrs. Lincoln that she should be indemnified, as far as money can do so, for the loss of her beloved husband. Honor, gratitude, and a manly sympathy, all say yes to this. I am willing to go further than this, and say that Mrs. Lincoln herself should be the judge of the amount which shall be deemed sufficient, believing that she would not transcend reasonable limits. The obligation resting on the nation at large is great and increasing, but especially does it become colored men to recognize that obligation. It was the hand of Abraham Lincoln that broke the fetters of our enslaved people, and let them out of the house of bondage. When he was slain, our great benefactor fell, and left his wife and children to the care of those for whom he gave up all. Shame on the man or woman who, under such circumstances, would grudge a few paltry dollars, to smooth the pathway of such a widow! All this, and more, I feel and believe. But such is the condition of this question, owing to party feeling, and personal animosities now mixed up with it, that we are compelled to consider these in the effort we are making to obtain subscriptions.

Now, about the meeting in Cooper Institute; I hold that that meeting should only be held in concert with other movements. It is bad generalship to put into the field only a fraction of your army when you have no means to prevent their being cut to pieces. It is gallant to go forth single-handed, but is it wise? I want to see something more than the spiteful *Herald* behind me when I step forward in this cause at the Cooper Institute. Let Mr. Brady with his circulars, with his list of commanding names, let the *Herald* and *Tribune* give a united blast upon their bugles, let the city be placarded, and the doors of Cooper Institute be flung wide open, and the people, without regard to party, come up to the discharge of this national duty.

Don't let the cause be made ridiculous by failure at the outset. Mr. Garnet and I could bear any mortification of this kind; but the cause could not. And our cause must not be damaged by any such generalship, which would place us in the vanguard unsupported.

I shall be at home by Saturday; please write me and let me know how matters are proceeding. Show this letter to Messrs. Brady and Garnet.

I am, dear madam,
Very truly yours,
FREDERICK DOUGLASS.

Rochester, 30 October 1867.

MY DEAR MRS. KECKLEY: It is just possible that I may not take New York in my route homeward. In that case please write me directly at Rochester, and let me know fully how the subscription business is proceeding. The meeting here last night was a grand success. I speak again this evening, and perhaps at Reading tomorrow evening. My kind regards to all who think of me at 21, including Mrs. Lawrence.

Very truly yours,
FREDERICK DOUGLASS.

Rochester, 10 November 1867.

MY DEAR MRS. KECKLEY: I very easily read your handwriting. With practice you will not only write legibly but elegantly; so no more apologies for *bad* writing. Penmanship has always been one of my own deficiencies, and I know how to sympathize with you.

I am just home, and find your letter awaiting me. You should have received an earlier answer but for this absence. I am sorry it will be impossible for me to see you before I go to Washington. I am leaving home this week for Ohio, and shall go from Ohio to Washington. I shall be in New York a day or two after my visit to Washington, and will see you there. Any public demonstration in which it will be desirable for me to take part ought to come off the last of this month or the first of next. I thank you sincerely for the note containing a published letter of dear Mrs. Lincoln; both letters do credit to the excellent lady. I prize her beautiful letter to me very highly. It is the letter of a refined and spirited lady, let the world say what it will of her. I would write her a word of acknowledgment but for fear to burden her with correspondence.

I am glad that Mr. Garnet and yourself saw Mr. Greeley,[5] and that he takes the right view of the matter; but we want more than right views, and delay is death to the movement. What you now want is action and cooperation. If Mr. Brady does not for any reason find himself able to move the machinery, somebody else should be found to take his place; he made a good impression on me when I saw him, but I have not seen the promised simultaneous movement of

[5]Horace Greeley, editor of the New York *Tribune* and founder of *The New Yorker,* led a campaign to raise money for Mary Todd Lincoln.

which we spoke when together. This whole thing should be in the hands of some recognized solid man in New York. No man would be better than Mr. Greeley; no man in the state is more laughed at, and yet no man is more respected and trusted; a dollar placed in his hands would be as safe for the purpose as in a burglarproof safe, and what is better still, everybody believes this. This testimonial must be more than a Negro testimonial. It is a great national duty. Mr. Lincoln did everything for the black man, but he did it not for the black man's sake, but for the nation's sake. His life was given for the nation; but for being president, Mr. Lincoln would have been alive, and Mrs. Lincoln would have been a wife, and not a widow as now. Do all you can, dear Mrs. Keckley—nobody can do more than you in removing the mountains of prejudice toward that good lady, and opening the way of success in the plan.

I am, dear madam, very truly yours,
FREDERICK DOUGLASS.

Many persons called at 609 Broadway to examine Mrs. Lincoln's wardrobe, but as curiosity prompted each visit, but few articles were sold. Messrs. Brady and Keyes were not very energetic, and, as will be seen by the letters of Mrs. Lincoln, published in the Appendix, that lady ultimately lost all confidence in them. It was proposed to send circulars, stating Mrs. Lincoln's wants, and appealing to the generosity of the people for aid, broadcast over the country; but the scheme failed. Messrs. Brady and Keyes were unable to obtain the names of prominent men, whom the people had confidence in, for the circular, to give character and responsibility to the movement—so the whole thing was abandoned. With the Reverend Mr. Garnet, I called on Mr. Greeley, at the *Tribune,* in connection with this scheme. Mr. Greeley received us kindly, and listened patiently to our proposals—then said:

"I shall take pleasure in rendering you what assistance I can, but the movement must be engineered by responsible parties. Messrs. Brady & Keyes are not the men to be at the head of it. Nobody knows who they are, or what they are. Place the matter in the hands of those that the people know and have some confidence in; then there will be a chance of success."

We thanked Mr. Greeley for his advice, for we believed it to be good advice, and bowed ourselves out of his room. When Messrs. Brady & Keyes were informed of the result of our interview, they became very much excited, and denounced Mr. Greeley as "an old fool." This put an end to the circular movement. The enterprise was nipped in the bud, and with the bud withered Mrs. Lincoln's last hope for success. A portion of the wardrobe was then taken to Providence, to be exhibited, but without her consent. Mr. Brady remarked that the exhibition would bring in money, and as money must be raised, this was the last resort. He was of the impression that Mrs. Lincoln would approve of any movement, so it ended in success. This, at least, is a charitable view to take of the subject. Had the exhibition succeeded in Providence, it is my opinion that the agents of Brady and Keyes would now be traveling over the country, exposing Mrs. Lincoln's wardrobe to the view of the curious, at so much per head. As is well known, the city authorities refused to allow the exhibition to take place in Providence; therefore Mr. Brady returned to New York with the goods, and the traveling-show scheme, as well as the circular scheme, was abandoned.

Weeks lengthened into months, and at Mrs. Lincoln's urgent request I remained in New York to look after her interests. When she left the city, I engaged quiet lodgings with a private family, where I remained about two months, when I moved to 14 Carroll Place,[6] and became one of the regular boarders of the house. Mrs. Lincoln's venture proved so disastrous that she was unable to reward me for my services, and I was compelled to take in sewing to pay for my daily bread.

My New York expedition has made me richer in experience, but poorer in purse. During the entire winter I have worked early and late, and practiced the closest economy. Mrs. Lincoln's business demanded much of my time, and it was a constant source of trouble to me. When Mrs. L. left for the West, I expected to be able to return to Washington in one week from the day; but unforeseen difficulties arose, and I have been detained in the city for several months.

As I am writing the concluding pages of this book, I have succeeded in closing up Mrs. Lincoln's impru-

[6]Keckley first stayed with Mrs. Bell, a relative of the William Slade family, at 543 Broome Street. Amelia Lancaster, with whom she lived at 14 Carroll Place, was a hairdresser for fashionable New Yorkers.

dent business arrangement at 609 Broadway. The firm of Brady and Keyes is dissolved, and Mr. Keyes has adjusted the account. The story is told in a few words. On the fourth of March I received the following invoice from Mr. Keyes:

4 March '68.
Invoice of articles sent to Mrs. A. Lincoln:

1 Trunk.	1 Set furs.
1 Lace dress.	2 Paisley shawls.
1 do.[7] do. flounced.	2 Gold bracelets.
5 Lace shawls.	16 Dresses.
3 Camel hair shawls.	2 Opera cloaks.
1 Lace parasol cover.	1 Purple shawl.
1 do. handkerchief.	1 Feather cape.
1 Sable boa.	28 yds. silk.
1 White do.	

ARTICLES SOLD.

1 Diamond ring.	1 Red do.
3 Small do.	2 Dresses.
1 Set furs.	1 Child's shawl.
1 Camel hair shawl.	1 Lace Chantilly shawl.

The charges of the firm amounted to eight hundred dollars. Mrs. Lincoln sent me a check for this amount. I handed this check to Mr. Keyes, and he gave me the following receipt:

RECEIVED, New York, 4 March 1868, from Mrs. Abraham Lincoln, eight hundred and twenty dollars by draft on American National Bank, New York.

S. C. KEYES.

[7]do.: Abbreviation for "ditto."

I packed the articles invoiced, and expressed the trunks to Mrs. Lincoln at Chicago. I then demanded and received a receipt worded as follows:

RECEIVED, New York, March 4, 1868, from Mrs. Abraham Lincoln, eight hundred and twenty dollars in full of all demands of every kind up to date.

S. C. KEYES.

This closed up the business, and with it I close the imperfect story of my somewhat romantic life. I have experienced many ups and downs, but still am stout of heart. The labor of a lifetime has brought me nothing in a pecuniary way. I have worked hard, but fortune, fickle dame, has not smiled upon me. If poverty did not weigh me down as it does, I would not now be toiling by day with my needle, and writing by night, in the plain little room on the fourth floor of No. 14 Carroll Place. And yet I have learned to love the garret-like room. Here, with Mrs. Amelia Lancaster as my only companion, I have spent many pleasant hours, as well as sad ones, and every chair looks like an old friend. In memory I have traveled through the shadows and the sunshine of the past, and the bare walls are associated with the visions that have come to me from the long-ago. As I love the children of memory, so I love every article in this room, for each has become a part of memory itself. Though poor in worldly goods, I am rich in friendships, and friends are a recompense for all the woes of the darkest pages of life. For sweet friendship's sake, I can bear more burdens than I have borne.

The letters appended from Mrs. Lincoln to myself throw a flood of light upon the history of the "old clothes" speculation in New York.

APPENDIX

Chicago,
Sunday Morning,
6 October [1867].

My Dear Lizzie [Elizabeth Keckley]: I am writing this morning with a broken heart after a sleepless night of great mental suffering. R[obert] came up last evening like a maniac, and almost threatening his life, looking like death, because the letters of the *World* were published in yesterday's paper. I could not refrain from weeping when I saw him so miserable. But yet, my dear good Lizzie, was it not to protect myself and help others—and was not my motive and action of the purest kind? Pray for me that this cup of affliction may pass from me, or be sanctified to me. I weep whilst I am writing. . . . I pray for death this morning. Only my darling Taddie prevents my taking my life. I shall have to endure a round of newspaper abuse from the Republicans because I dared venture to relieve a few of my wants. Tell Mr. Brady and Keyes not to have a line of mine once more in print I am nearly losing my reason.

Your friend,
M[ary]. L[incoln].

Chicago, 8 October.

My Dear Lizzie: Bowed down with suffering and anguish, again I write you. As we might have expected, the Republicans are falsifying me, and doing *just* as they did when they prevented the Congressional appropriation. Mrs. ——— knows something about these same people. As her husband *is living* they dare not utter all they would desire to speak. You know yourself how innocently I have acted, and from the best and purest motives. They will *howl* on to prevent my disposing of my things. What a *vile, vile* set they are! The *Tribune* here, Mr. White's paper, wrote a very beautiful editorial yesterday in my behalf; yet knowing that I have been deprived of my rights by the party, I suppose I would be *mobbed* if I ventured out. What a world of anguish this is—and how I have been made to suffer! . . . You would not recognize me now. The glass shows me a pale, wretched, haggard face, and my dresses are like bags on me. And all because I was doing what I felt to be my duty. Our minister, Mr. S[wazey], called on me yesterday and said I had done perfectly right. Mrs. F[owler] says everyone speaks in the same way. The politicians, knowing they have deprived me of my just rights, would prefer to see me starve, rather than dispose of my things. They will prevent the sale of anything, so I have telegraphed for them. I hope you have received from B[rady] the letters I have consigned to his care. See to this. Show none of them. Write me every day.

M. L.

Chicago,
Wednesday,
9 October.

My Dear Lizzie: It appears as if the fiends had let loose, for the Republican papers are tearing me to pieces in this border ruffian West. If I had committed murder in every city in this *blessed Union,* I could not be more traduced. And you know how innocent I have been of the intention of doing wrong. A piece in the morning *Tribune,* signed "B," pretending to be a lady, says there is no doubt Mrs. L[incoln] *is* deranged—has been for years past, and will end her life in a lunatic asylum. They would doubtless like me to begin it *now.* Mr. Swazey, a very kind, sympathizing minister, has been with me this morning, and has now gone to see Mr. Medill, of the *Tribune,* to know if he sanctioned his paper publishing such an article.... Pray for me, dear Lizzie, for I am very miserable and broken-hearted. Since writing this, I have just received a letter from Mr. Keyes, begging and pleading with me to allow them to use my name for donations. I think I will consent....

Truly yours,
M. L.

Chicago,
Sunday,
13 October.

My Dear Lizzie: I am greatly disappointed, having only received one letter from you since we parted, which was dated the day after. Day after day I sent to Mrs. F[owler] for letters. After your promise of writing to me every other day, I can scarcely understand it. I hope tomorrow will bring me a letter from you. How much I miss you cannot be expressed. I hope you have arrived safely in Washington, and will tell me everything.... Was there ever such cruel newspaper abuse lavished upon an unoffending woman as has been showered upon my devoted head? The people of this ungrateful country are like the "dogs in the manger"; will neither do anything themselves, nor allow me to improve my own condition. What a government we have! All their abuse lavished upon me only lowers themselves in the estimation of all true-hearted people. The Springfield *Journal* had an editorial a few days since, with the important information that Mrs. Lincoln had been known to be *deranged* for years, and should be pitied for all her *strange acts.* I should have been *all right* if I had allowed *them* to take possession of the White House. In the comfortable stealings by contracts from the government, these low creatures are allowed to hurl their malicious wrath at me, with no one to defend me or protect me, if I should starve. These people injure themselves far more than they could do me, by their lies and villany. Their aim is to prevent my goods being sold, or anything being done for me. *In this,* I very much fear, they have succeeded. Write me, my dear friend, your candid opinion about everything. I wished to be made better off, quite as much to improve your condition as well as for myself. . . . Two weeks ago, dear Lizzie, we were in that *den* of discomfort and dirt. *Now* we are far asunder. Every other day, for the past week, I have had a chill, brought on by excitement and suffering of mind. In the midst of it I have moved into my winter quarters, and am now very comfortably situated. My parlor and bedroom are very sweetly furnished. I am lodged in a handsome house, a very kind, good, *quiet* family, and their meals are excellent. I consider myself fortunate in all this. I feel assured that the Republicans, who, to cover up their own perfidy and neglect, have used every villainous falsehood in their power to injure me—I fear they have *more* than succeeded, but if their day of reckoning does not come in this world, it *will surely* the next. . . .

Saturday—I have determined to shed no more tears over all their cruel falsehoods, yet, just now, I feel almost forsaken by God and man—except by the *latter* to be vilified. Write me all that Keyes and Brady think of the result. For myself, after *such* abuse, I *expect* nothing. Oh! That I could see you. Write me, dear Lizzie, if only a line; I cannot understand your silence. Hereafter direct your letters to Mrs. A. Lincoln, 460 West Washington Street, Chicago, Ill., care of D. Cole. Remember 460. I am always so anxious to hear from you, I am feeling so *friendless* in the world. I remain always your affectionate friend.

M. L.

Postscript to Letter of Oct. 24:
I cannot send this letter off without writing you two little incidents that have occurred within the past week. We may call it *justice* rendered for *evil words,* to say the least. There is a paper published in Chicago called the *Republican,* owned and published by Springfield men. Each morning since my return it has been thrown at my door, filled with abuse of myself. Four days ago a piece appeared in it, asking "What right had Mrs. L[incoln] to diamonds and laces?" Yesterday morning an article appeared in the same paper, announcing that the day previous, at the house of Mr. Joseph Bunn (the owner of the paper), in Springfield, Illinois—the house had been entered at 11 in the morning, by burglars, and had been robbed of *five* diamond rings, and a quantity of fine laces. This morning's paper announces the recovery of these articles. Mr. Bunn, who made his hundreds of thousands off our government, is ruining this paper, and denouncing the wife of the man from whom he obtained his means. I enclose you the article about the recovery of the goods. A few years ago he had a *small grocery* in S[pringfield]. These facts can be authenticated. Another case in point: The evening I left my house to come here, the young daughter of one of my neighbors in the same block, was in a house not a square

off, and in a childish manner was regretting that I could not retain my house. The man in the house said: "Why waste your tears and regrets on Mrs. Lincoln?" An hour afterward the husband and wife went out to make a call, doubtless to gossip about me; on their return they found their young boy had almost blinded himself with gunpowder. Who will say that the cry of the "widow and fatherless" is disregarded in *His sight!* If man is not merciful, God will be in his own time.

M. L.

Chicago,
29 October.

My Dear Lizzie: I received a very pleasant note from Mr. F[rederick] Douglass on yesterday. I will reply to it this morning, and enclose it to you to hand or send him immediately. In this morning's *Tribune* there was a little article *evidently* designed to make capital *against* me just now—that *three* of my brothers were in the Southern army during the war. If they had been friendly with me, they might have said they were *half* brothers of Mrs. L[incoln], whom she had not known since they were infants; and as she left Kentucky at an early age, her sympathies were entirely Republican—that her feelings were entirely with the North during the war, and always. I never failed to urge my husband to be an *extreme* Republican, and now, in the day of my trouble, you see how *this* very party is trying to work against me. Tell Mr. Douglass, and everyone, how deeply my feelings were enlisted in the cause of freedom. Why *harp* upon these *half* brothers, whom I never knew since they were infants, and scarcely then, for my early home was truly at a *boarding* school. Write to him all this, and talk it to everyone else. If we succeed, I will soon send you enough for a very large supply of trimming material for the winter.

Truly,
M. L.

Chicago,
2 November.

My Dear Lizzie: Your letter of last Wednesday is received, and I cannot refrain from expressing my surprise that before now K[eyes] and B[rady] did not go out in search of names, and have sent forth all those circulars. Their conduct is becoming mysterious. We have heard enough of *their talk*—it is time now they should be *acting*. Their delay, I fear, has ruined the business. The circulars should all have been out before the election. I cannot understand their slowness. As Mr. [Horace] Greeley's home is in New York, he could certainly have been found had he *been sought;* and there are plenty of other good men in New York, as well as himself I venture to say, that *before* the election not a circular will be sent out. I begin to think they are making a political business of *my clothes,* and not for *my* benefit either. Their delay in acting is becoming very suspicious. Their slow, bad management is *ruining* every prospect of success. I fear you are only losing your time in New York, and that I shall be left *in debt* for what I am owing the firm. I have written to K. and B., and they do nothing that I request. I want neither Mr. Douglass nor [Reverend Henry Highland] Garnet to lecture in my behalf. The conduct in New York is disgusting me with the whole business. I cannot understand what they have been about. Their delay has only given the enemies time to *gather* strength; what does it all mean? Of course give the lady at 609 [Broadway] permission to sell the dresses cheaper.... I am feeling wretchedly over the slowness and *do-nothing* style of B. & K. I believe in my heart I am being used as a tool for party purposes; and they do not design sending out a circular....

Your friend,
M. L.

Chicago,
9 November 1867.

My Dear Lizzie: .... Did you receive a letter a few days since, with one enclosed for F. Douglass? And also a printed letter of mine, which I wished him to read? Do write me every other day at least, I am so *nervous and miserable.* And Lizzie, dear, I fear we have not the least chance of success. *Do* remain in New York a little longer, and occupy yourself with the sewing of your friends. *Then* I shall be able to learn something about my business. In *your heart* you know there will be no success. *Why* do you not candidly express yourself to me? Write me, if only a few lines, and that very frequently. R[obert] called up on yesterday, with Judge Davis.[1] ... R[obert] goes with Judge D[avis] on Tuesday, to settle the estate, which will give us each about $25,000, with the income I told you of, $1,700 a year for each of us. You made a mistake about my house costing $2,700—it was $1,700.[2] The $22,000 Congress gave me I spent for house and furniture, which, owing to the small-

[1]Judge David Davis was a family friend from Springfield, Illinois, whom Robert Lincoln engaged as executor of his father's estate.

[2]Apparently a typographical error left off the final digits. Other sources indicate the house costs were seventeen thousand dollars and not the rumored twenty-seven thousand dollars.

ness of my income, I was obliged to leave. I mention about the division of the estate to you, dear Lizzie, because when it is done, the *papers* will harp upon it. You can explain everything in New York; please do so to everyone. Please see H[orace] G[reeley], if it should come out in the papers. I had hoped, if something was gained, to have immediately placed *you* in more pleasant circumstances. Do urge F[rederick] D[ouglass] to add his name to the circular; also get them to have [Henry Ward] Beecher's. There must not be an hour's delay in this. R. is very spiteful at present, and I think hurries up the division to *cross* my purposes. He mentioned yesterday that he was going to the Rocky Mountains as soon as Edgar Welles[3] joined him. He is very *deep*. . . . Write me, *do*, when you receive this. Your silence pains me.

Truly yours,
M. L.

Chicago,
9 November.

MY DEAR LIZZIE: I closed and sent off my letter before I had finished all I had to say. Do not hint to K[eyes] or B[rady], or anyone else, my doubts of them, *only watch them.* As to [Charles] S[umner], so many falsehoods are told in the papers that all the stuff about his wife and himself may be untrue.[4] I hope it may prove so. I received a let-

[3]Edgar Welles was the son of Mary Lincoln's long-time friend Mary Jane Welles. His father, Gideon, had been secretary of the navy when Abraham Lincoln was president.

[4]Charles Sumner had separated from his wife, the former Alice Mason Hooper, within a year of their marriage but did not divorce until 1873. Mrs. Lincoln often mentioned their marital problems in letters to their friends.

ter from Keyes this morning. I believe I wrote you that I had. How hard it is that I cannot see and talk with you in this time of great, *great* trouble. I feel as if I had not a friend in the world save yourself. . . . I sometimes wish myself out of this world of sorrow and care. I fear my fine articles at B[rady]'s are getting pulled to pieces and soiled. I do not wish you to leave N.Y. without having the finest articles packed up and returned to me. The *single* white camel's hair shawl and the two Paisleys I wish returned to me, if none of them are sold. Do you think there is the least chance of their being sold? I will give you a list of the articles I wish returned to me from Mr. Brady's before *you leave* New York for Washington.

1 Camel's hair shawl, double black centre.
1 Camel's hair shawl, double white centre.
1 Single white camel's hair shawl.
2 Paisley shawls—white.
1 Pair bracelets and diamond ring.
1 Fine lace handkerchief.
3 Black lace shawls.
2 Black llama shawls.
1 Dress, silk unmade, white and black.
1 White boa.
1 Russian sable boa.
1 Russian sable cape.
1 A. sable cape, cuffs and muff.
1 Chinchilla set.

The lace dress, flounce and shawl, if there is no possibility of their being sold. Also all other fine articles return me, save the dresses which, with prices lowered, *may be sold*. . . .

M. L.

Chicago,
15 November 1867.

My Dear Lizzie: Your last letter has been received, and believe me, I duly appreciate your great interest in my affairs. I hope the day *may* arrive when I can return your kindness in *more* than words. As you are aware of my beloved husband's great indulgence to me in pecuniary matters, thereby allowing me to indulge in bestowing favors on those whom I considered worthy of it, it is in this respect I feel chiefly the humiliation of my small circumscribed income. If Congress, or the nation, had given me the four years' salary, I should have been able to live as the widow of the great President Lincoln should, with sufficient means to give liberally to all benevolent objects, and at my death should have left at least half of it to the freedmen, for the liberty of whom his precious sacred life was sacrificed. The men who prevented *this* being done by their villanous unscrupulous falsehoods, are no friends of the colored race, and, as you well know, have led Johnson on in his wicked course.

"God is just," and the day of retribution will come to all such, if not in this world, in the great hereafter, to which those hoary-headed sinners are so rapidly hastening, with an innocent conscience. I did not feel it necessary to raise my weak woman's voice against the persecutions that have assailed me emanating from the tongues of such men as Weed & Co.[5] I have felt that their infamous false lives were

[5]Thurlow Weed, editor of the *Commerical Advertiser* and a highly influential New York Republican, was another of Mary Lincoln's personal enemies. Among his published attacks was an article that accused the first lady of numerous acts of financial extravagance and deception, including padding her reimbursement claims for a state dinner honoring Napoleon.

a sufficient vindication of my character. They have never forgiven me for standing between my pure and noble husband and themselves, when, for their own vile purposes, they would have led him into error. *All this* the country knows, and why should I dwell longer on it? In the blissful home where my worshipped husband dwells God is ever merciful, and it is the consolation of my broken heart that my darling husband is ever retaining the devoted love which he always so abundantly manifested for his wife and children in this life. I feel assured his watchful, loving eyes are always watching over us, and he is fully aware of the wrong and injustice permitted his family by a country he lost his life in protecting. I write earnestly, because I feel very deeply. It appears to me a very remarkable coincidence, that most of the good feeling regarding my straitened circumstances proceeds from the colored people, in whose cause my noble husband was so largely interested. Whether we are successful or not, Mr. F[rederick] Douglass and Mr. [Henry Highland] Garnet will always have my most grateful thanks. They are very noble men. If any *favorable* results should crown their efforts, you may well believe at my death, whatever sum it may be, will be bequeathed to the colored people, who are very near my heart. In yesterday's paper it was announced that Gov. Andrew's family were having $100,000 contributed to them.[6] Gov. A. was a good man, but what did *he* do compared to President Lincoln? Right and left the latter gave, when he had but little to bestow, and in consequence his family are now feeling it; yet for my life I would not recall a dollar he ever gave. Yet his favorite expression, when I have playfully

[6]Massachusetts Governor John A. Andrew had died 30 October 1867.

alluded to the "rainy day" that might be in store for *himself and his own* on several occasions, he has looked at me so earnestly and replied, "Cast your bread upon the waters." Although the petty sum of twenty-two thousand dollars was an insufficient return for Congress to make me, and allowanced to its meagerness by men who traduced and vilified the loved wife of the great man who *made them,* and from whom they amassed great fortunes—for *Weed, and Seward,*[7] *and R.[aymond]*[8] did this last. And yet, *all this* was permitted by an American people, who owed *their* remaining a nation to my husband! I have dwelt too long on this painful subject, but when I have been compelled from a pitiful income to make a boardinghouse of my home, as I now am doing, think you that it does not rankle in my heart?

Fortunately, with my husband's great, great love for me—the knowledge of this future for his petted and idolized wife was spared him, and yet I feel in my heart *he* knows it all. Mr. [Charles] Sumner, the intimate friend of better days, called to see me two or three weeks since—he who had been an habitué of the White House—both the rooms of the president and my own reception room, in either place he was always sure of a heartfelt welcome; my present situation must have struck a painful chord in his noble, sympathizing heart. And yet, when I endeavored to ameliorate my condition, the cry has been so fearful against me as to cause me to forget my own identity, and suppose I had plundered

[7]William H. Seward, Abraham Lincoln's rival for presidential nomination, had served as governor of New York, U.S. senator, and secretary of state.

[8]Henry J. Raymond, editor of the *New York Times* and author of *The Life and Public Services of Abraham Lincoln* (1865), had been elected to Congress from New York in 1865.

the nation, indeed, and committed murder. This, certainly, cannot be America, "the land of the *free,*" the "home of the *brave.*" The evening before Mr. Sumner's last call I had received Mr. Douglass's letter; I mentioned the circumstance to Mr. Sumner, who replied: "Mr. Frederick Douglass is a very noble, talented man, and I know of no one who writes a more beautiful letter." I am sending you a long letter, Lizzie, but I rely a great deal on your indulgence. My fear is that you will not be able to decipher the scrawl written so hastily.

I remain, truly yours,
MARY LINCOLN.

Chicago,
17 November.

MY DEAR LIZZIE: By the time you receive this note, you will doubtless find the papers raving over the large income which we are each said to have. Knowing exactly the amount we each will have, which I have already informed you, I was going to say, I have been shocked at the *fabulous* sum set down to each but I have learned not to be surprised at anything. Of course it is gotten up to defeat success. You will now see the necessity for those circulars being issued weeks since. I enclose you a scrap from yesterday's *Times* of C[hicago], marked No. 1; also No. 2, today's *Times.* The sum of $11,000 has been subtracted in twenty-four hours from the same paper. If it continues for a few days longer, it will soon be right. It is a secesh paper[9]—says Congress

[9]Secesh paper: "Secesh" is a slang term for secessionist. During the Civil War, it meant a Confederate or a Confederate sympathizer. The newspaper, then, is denounced as favoring the cause of the South and, by extension, being anti-Republican.

gave me $25,000 as a *present,* besides $20,000 of remaining salary. The $25,000 *you* know to be utterly false. You can show this note to B[rady] & K[eyes], also the scraps sent. Let no one see them but themselves, and then burn them. It is all just as I expected—that when the division took place, a "mountain would be made of a mole-hill." And I fear it will succeed in injuring the premeditated plans. If the *war rages,* the *Evening News* might simply say that the sum assigned each was false; that $75,000 was the sum the administrator, Judge Davis, filed his bonds for. But by all means *my authority* must not be given. And then the *Evening News* can descant on the $25,000 each, with income of $1,700 each, and Mrs. Lincoln's share, she not being able to touch any of her sons' portion. My *word* or *testimony* must not appear in the article; only the paper must speak *decidedly.* It must be managed very judiciously, and without a day's delay.

Yours truly,
M. L.

17 November—
(Private for yourself).

LIZZIE: Show the note enclosed with this to B[rady] & K[eyes]; do not let them retain it an instant after reading, nor the printed articles. I knew these falsehoods would be circulated when the estate was divided. What *has* been the cause of the delay about the circulars? I fear, between ourselves, we have reason to distrust those men. Whatever is raised by the colored people, I solemnly give my word at my death it shall *all,* every cent, be returned to them. And out of the sum, if it is $50,000, *you* shall have $5,000 at my death; and I cannot live long, suffering as I am now doing.

If $25,000 is raised by your people, you shall have the sum at my death; and in either event, the $25,000 raised, or $50,000, I will give you $300 a year, and the promised sum at my death. It will make your life easier. I have more faith in F[rederick] D[ouglass]'s and [Henry Highland] G[arnet]'s efforts, than in B[rady] & K[eyes], I assure you. This division has been trumped up just now through spite. . . . I have written to Judge Davis for an exact statement, which I will send to you when received. Write if anything is doing . . . .

Truly,
M. L.

Chicago,
21 November.

My Dear Lizzie: Your letter of Tuesday is just received. I have just written B[rady] a note of thanks for his kindness; also requesting the articles of which I gave you a list. Do see Keyes about it; K. will have it done. And will you *see* that they are forwarded to *me* before *you* leave New York? K. sent me a telegram on yesterday that eight names were on the circulars, and that they would be sent out *immediately*. What success do you think they will have? By all means assure K. & B. I have great confidence in them. These circulars must bring some money. Your letter made me quite sad. Talk to K. & B. of the *grateful feelings* I express toward them. Do pet up B., and see my things returned to me. Can you not, dear Lizzie, be employed in sewing for some of your lady friends in New York until December 1st? If I *ever* get any money you will be well remembered, be assured. R[obert] and a party of young men leave for the Rocky Mountains next Monday, to be absent three weeks.

If the circulars are sent out, of course the *blasts* will be blown over again. So R. is out of the way *at the time,* and if money comes in, I will not care. Write the hour you receive this. I hope they will send out 150,000 circulars. Urge K. & B. to do this.

Your friend,
M. L.

Saturday Morning,
23 November.

My Dear Lizzie: Although I am suffering with a fearful headache today, yet, as your note of Wednesday is received, I must write. I am grieved to find that you are so wretchedly lowspirited.... On Wednesday, the twentieth of November, K[eyes] sent me the telegram I send you. If he is not in earnest, what does it mean? What is the rate of expenses that B[rady] has gone to in my business, that he dares to withhold my immense amount of goods? Do you believe they *intend* sending out those circulars? Of course you will be well rewarded if we have any success, but as to $500 "now," I have it not for myself, or anyone else. Pray, what does B[rady] propose to charge for *his expenses.* I pray God there will be some success, although, dear Lizzie, entirely between ourselves, I fear I am in villainous hands. As to money, I haven't it for myself just now, even if nothing comes in. When I get my things back, if ever, from ——— , I will send you some of those dresses to dispose of at Washington for your own benefit. If we get something, *you* will find that *promises* and performance for *this* life will be forthcoming.... It is *mysterious* why B. NEVER writes, and K. *once,* perhaps, in three weeks. All this is very strange....

M. L.

Chicago,
Sunday,
24 November.

My Dear Lizzie: I wrote you on yesterday and am aware it was not a pleasant letter, although I wrote what I fear will turn out to be *truths.* It will be two weeks tomorrow since the legally attested consent from me was received by B[rady] & K[eyes], and yet *names* have not been obtained for it, when last heard from. . . . However, we will soon see for ourselves. If you and I are honest in our motives and intentions, it is no reason *all* the world is so. . . . If I should gain nothing pecuniarily by the loud cry that has been made over my affairs, it has been a losing game indeed. . . . And the laugh of the world will be against me if it turns out as I *now* think; there is no doubt it will be *all* failure. If they had issued those circulars when they should have done, before the election, then it would have been all right. Alas! Alas! what a mistake it has all been! I have thought seriously over the whole business, and know what I am about. I am grateful for the sympathy of Mr. F[rederick] Douglass and Mr. [Henry Highland] Garnet. I see that F. D. is advertised to lecture in Chicago some time this winter. Tell him, for me, he must call and see me; give him my number. If I had been able to retain a house, I should have offered him apartments when he came to C.; as it is, I have to content *myself* with lodgings. An ungrateful country this! I very much fear the malignity of Seward, Weed, and R[aymond] will operate in Congress the coming winter, and that I will be denounced *there,* with their infamous and villanous falsehoods. The father of wickedness and lies will get those men when they "pass away"; and such fiends as they are, always linger in this mortal sphere. The agitation of mind has very much impaired my health. . . . Why, why was not *I* taken when my darling husband was called from my side? I have been allowed no rest by those who, in my desolation, should have protected me. . . . How dearly I should love to see you this *very sad day*. Never, dear Lizzie, think of my great nervousness the night before we parted; I had been so harassed with my fears. . . .

Always yours,
M. L.

26 December.

My Dear Lizzie: Your letters just received. I have just written to K[eyes] to withdraw the C[ircular]. Go to him yourself the moment you receive this. The idea of Congress doing anything is ridiculous. How much____could effect *if he chose,* through others. Go to B. & K. the moment you receive this.

Yours,
M. L.

Chicago,
27 December.

Dear Lizzie: I wrote you a few lines on yesterday. I have twice written to Mr. K[eyes] to have the C[ircular] stopped. Go and see him on the subject. I believe any more newspaper attacks would *lay me low*. . . . As *influence* has passed away from me with my husband, my slightest act is misinterpreted. "*Time makes all things* right." I am positively suffering for a decent dress. I see Mr. A. and *some recent* visitors eyeing my clothing askance. . . . Do send my black merino[10] dress to me very soon; I must dress better in the future. I tremble at the bill that B[rady] & K[eyes] may send me, I am so ill prepared to meet any expense. All my articles not sold must be sent to me. I leave *this* place *early* in the spring; had you better not go with me and share my fortunes, for a year or more?... *Write.*

Yours, etc.,
M. L.

New York City,
1 January 1868.

Bishop Payne, D.D.[11] —Dear Sir: Allow me to donate certain valuable relics, to be exhibited for the benefit of Wilberforce University, where my son was educated and whose life was sacrificed for liberty. These sacred relics were presented to me by Mrs. Lincoln, after the assassination of our beloved president. Learning that you were struggling to get means to complete the college that was burned on the day our great emancipator was assassinated, prompted me to donate, in trust to J. P. Ball (agent for Wilberforce College) the identical cloak and bonnet worn by Mrs. Lincoln on that eventful night. On the cloak can be seen the life-blood of Abraham Lincoln. This cloak could not be purchased from me, though many have been the offers for it. I deemed it too *sacred* to sell, but donate it for the cause of educating the four millions of slaves liberated by our president, whose private character I revere. You well know that I had every

[10]Merino: Originally limited to the wool of a species of sheep from Spain, which was purportedly softer and finer than French cashmere. By this time it meant any luxurious wool or woolen blend fabric.

[11]Daniel A. Payne, minister, poet, and historian, was president of Wilberforce University.

chance to learn the true man, being constantly in the White House during his whole administration. I also donate the glove [I have since concluded to retain the glove as a precious souvenir of our beloved president] worn on his precious hand at the last inaugural reception. This glove bears the marks of thousands who shook his hand on that last and great occasion. This, and many other relics, I hope you will receive in the name of the Lincoln fund. I also donate the dress worn by Mrs. Lincoln at the last inaugural address of President Lincoln. Please receive these from—

Your sister in Christ,
E. KECKLEY.

Clifton House,
12 January.

MY DEAR LIZZIE: Your last letter was received a day or two since. I have moved my quarters to *this house,* so please direct all your letters here. Why did you *not* urge them not to take my goods to Providence? For heaven's sake see K[eyes] & B[rady] when you receive this, and have them immediately returned to me, *with their bill.* I am so miserable I feel like taking my own life. My darling boy, my Taddie *alone,* I *fully* believe, prevents the deed. Your letter announcing that my clothes were to be paraded in Europe—those I gave you—has almost turned me wild. R[obert] would go *raving distracted* if such a thing were done. If you have the least *regard* for *our reason,* pray write to the bishop that it *must* not be done. How little did I suppose you would do *such a thing;* you cannot imagine how much my overwhelming sorrows would be increased. May kind Heaven turn your heart, and have you write that *this* exhibition must not be attempted. R. would blast us all if you were to have this project carried out. Do remember us in our unmitigated anguish, and have those clothes, worn on those fearful occasions, recalled. . . I am positively dying with a broken heart, and the probability is that I shall be living, but a *very* short time. May we all meet in a better world, where *such grief* is unknown. Write me all about yourself. I should like you to have about four black widow's caps, just such as I had made in the fall in New York, sent to me. . . . Of course you would not suppose, if I had you come out here and work for me six weeks, I would not pay your expenses and pay you as you made *each* dress. The probability is that I shall need few more clothes; my rest, I am inclined to believe, is *near at hand.* Go to B. & K., and have my clothes sent me without further publicity. . . . I am feeling too weak to write more today. Why are you so silent? For the sake of *humanity,* if not *me* and my children, *do not* have those black clothes displayed in Europe. The thought has almost whitened every hair of my head. Write when you receive this.

Your friend,
M. L.

Clifton House,
15 January 1868.

My Dear Lizzie: You will think I am sending you a deluge of letters. I am so very sad today that I feel that I must write you. I went out last evening with Tad, on a little business, in a streetcar, heavily veiled, very imprudently having *my month's living* in my pocketbook—and, on return, found it gone. The loss I deserve for being so careless, but it comes very hard on poor me. Troubles and misfortunes are fast overwhelming me; may *the end* come soon. I lost $82, and quite a new pocketbook. I am very, very anxious about that bill B[rady] & K[eyes] may bring in. Do go, dear Lizzie, and implore them to be moderate, for I am in a very narrow place. Tell them, I pray you, of this last loss. As they have not been successful (BETWEEN OURSELVES) and only given me great sorrow and trouble, I think their demand should be very small. (Do not mention this to them.) *Do,* dear Lizzie, go to 609, and talk to them on this subject. Let my things be sent to me immediately, and *do* see to it that nothing is left behind. I can afford to lose nothing they have had placed in their hands. I am literally suffering for my black dress. Will you send it to me when you receive this? I am looking very shabby. I hope you have entirely recovered. *Write* when you receive this.

Very truly yours,
M. L.

Chicago,
7 February.

MR. BRADY: I hereby authorize Mrs. Keckley to request my bill from you; also my goods. An exact account must be given of everything, and all goods unsold returned to me. Pray hand Mrs. Keckley my bill, without fail, immediately.

Respectfully,
MRS. LINCOLN.

Saturday,
29 February.

DEAR LIZZIE: I am only able to sit up long enough to write you a line and enclose this check to Mr. K[eyes]. Give it to him when he gives you up my goods, and require from him an exact inventory of them. I will write you tomorrow. The hour you receive this go to him, get my goods, and do not *give him the check until* you get the goods, and be sure you get a receipt for the check from him. . . . In his account given ten days since, he said we had borrowed $807, now he writes for $820. Ask him what this means, and get him to deduct the $13. I cannot understand it. A letter received from K. this morning says if the check is not received the first of the week, my goods *will be sold;* so do delay not an hour to see him. . . . My diamond ring he writes has been sold; the goods sold have amounted to $824, and they appropriate all this for their expenses. A precious set, truly. My diamond ring itself cost more than that sum, and I charged them not to sell it under $700. Do get my things safely returned to me. . . .

Truly,
M. L.

SUGGESTIONS FOR FURTHER READING

Over the years, information about Elizabeth Keckley and *Behind the Scenes* has appeared in a variety of sources, ranging from scholarly articles and encyclopedia entries to newspaper articles debating the authenticity of her narrative and even Keckley's very existence. On this latter issue, a 1936 exchange of letters in the *Journal of Negro History* included testimonies by Arthur J. Landen, Carter G. Woodson, Carrie Syphax Watson, and the Reverend Francis J. Grimke. These letters along with Grimke's sermon preached at Keckley's funeral are collected in *The Works of Francis Grimke.* The two best sources of biographical information on Keckley are John E. Washington's *They Knew Lincoln* and Becky Rutberg's *Mary Lincoln's Dressmaker.*

The following list is a sample of articles and books that would reward scholars and general readers interested in knowing more about Keckley, ways of understanding the book *Behind the Scenes,* and the multiple versions in which her remarkable story has appeared and reappeared in the nearly nine score years since she was born.

Frances Smith Foster
September 2001

Alexander, Adele Logan. "White House Confidante of Mrs. Lincoln." *American Visions* (Feb.–Mar. 1995): 18-19.

Andrews, William L. "The Changing Moral Discourse of Nineteenth-Century African American Women's Autobiography: Harriet Jacobs and Elizabeth Keckley." in *De/Colonizing the Subject: The Politics of Gender in Women's Autobiography*. Ed.

Sidonie Smith and Julia Watson. Minneapolis: University of Minnesota Press, 1992. 225-241.

——. "Reunion in the Postbellum Slave Narrative: Frederick Douglass and Elizabeth Keckley." *Black American Literature Forum* 23 (Spring 1989): 5-16.

Benberry, Cuesta. *Always There: The African-American Presence in American Quilts.* Louisville: Kentucky Quilt Project, 1992. 40-42, 86.

Fleischner, Jennifer. "Objects of Mourning in Elizabeth Keckley's *Behind the Scenes.*" In *Mastering Slavery: Memory, Family, and Identity in Women's Slave Narratives.* New York: New York University Press, 1996. 93-132.

Foster, Frances Smith. "Autobiography after Emancipation: The Example of Elizabeth Keckley." In *Multicultural Autobiography: American Lives.* Ed. James Robert Payne. Knoxville: University of Tennessee Press, 1992. 32-63.

——. "Romance and Scandal in a Postbellum Slave Narrative." In *Written by Herself: Literary Production by African American Women, 1746-1892.* Bloomington: Indiana University Press, 1993. 115-130.

Russell, Thaddeus. "Keckley, Elizabeth." In *Encyclopedia of African American Culture and History.* Ed. Jack Saltzman, David Lloyd Smith, and Cornel West. New York: Macmillan, 1996. 1529-1530.

Rutberg, Becky. *Mary Lincoln's Dressmaker: Elizabeth Keckley's Remarkable Rise from Slave to White House Confidante.* New York: Walker and Company, 1995.

Scott, Neil. "One Woman's Rise from Slave to Lincoln's Confidante." *Washington Times,* Mar. 29, 1997, B3.

Turner, Justin G., and Linda Levitt Turner. *Mary Todd Lincoln:*

Her Life and Letters. New York: Alfred A. Knopf, 1972.

Valade, Roger M., III, ed. "Elizabeth Keckley." In *The Schomberg Center Guide to Black Literature from the Eighteenth Century to the Present.* Detroit: Gale Research, 1996. 243.

Washington, John E. "Elizabeth Keckley." *They Knew Lincoln.* New York: E. P. Dutton, 1942. 205-244.

Wefer, Marion. "Another Assassination, Another Widow, Another Embattled Book." *American Heritage* 18 (Aug. 1967): 79-88.